Hidden History

BOOKS BY DANIEL J. BOORSTIN
*
Hidden History
*
The Discoverers
*
The Americans: The Colonial Experience
The Americans: The National Experience
The Americans: The Democratic Experience
*
The Mysterious Science of the Law
The Lost World of Thomas Jefferson
The Genius of American Politics
America and the Image of Europe
The Image: A Guide to Pseudo-Events in America
The Decline of Radicalism
The Sociology of the Absurd
Democracy and Its Discontents
The Republic of Technology
The Exploring Spirit
*
For young readers:
The Landmark History of the American People
A History of the United States (with Brooks M. Kelley)

DANIEL J. BOORSTIN

Hidden History

Selected and Edited by

DANIEL J. BOORSTIN and RUTH F. BOORSTIN

Vintage Books

A DIVISION OF RANDOM HOUSE, INC.
NEW YORK

First Vintage Books Edition, April 1989

Copyright © 1987 by Daniel J. Boorstin

*All rights reserved under International and Pan-American
Copyright Conventions. Published in the United States by
Random House, Inc., New York. Originally published,
in hardcover, by Harper & Row, Publishers, Inc., in 1987.
Reprinted by arrangement with Harper & Row, Publishers, Inc.*

Library of Congress Cataloging-in-Publications Data

*Boorstin, Daniel J. (Daniel Joseph), 1914–
Hidden history/Daniel J. Boorstin; selected and edited by
Daniel J. Boorstin and Ruth F. Boorstin. — 1st Vintage Books ed.
    p. cm.
  Reprint. Originally published: New York: Harper & Row, © 1987.
  Includes index.
  ISBN 0-679-72223-8: $9.95
  1. United States — Civilization.   I. Boorstin, Ruth Frankel.
II. Title.
[E169.12.B659   1989]
973 — dc 19   88-40529   CIP*

Copyright acknowledgments appear on page 315.

Manufactured in the United States of America

10 9 8 7 6 5 4 3

TO THE LIBRARY OF CONGRESS

"Shining star and inspiration —
Worthy of a mighty nation—"
(and I do mean the L. o. C.)
            Ira Gershwin
                    June 3, 1966

Contents

PART IV: UNSUNG EXPERIMENTS

PART V: THE MOMENTUM OF TECHNOLOGY

A Personal Note to the Reader

A romantic philosopher once said that the Historian is the Prophet in Reverse. When we become historians, we are seduced by the prophet's temptations—to pretend to be wiser than we really are, and to underestimate the probability of the unexpected. But History should be our Cautionary Science. Our past is only a little less uncertain than our future, and, like the future, it is always changing, always revealing and concealing. We might better think of Prophecy as History in Reverse.

In these pages you share my historical adventures of the last forty years. I hope they will widen and deepen the perspectives opened in *The Americans* and *The Discoverers*. But none of the selections comes from those books. You will follow some paths that have especially piqued my curiosity. I call them Hidden History. Some are unfamiliar aspects of familiar events. Some are subjects which have seemed beneath the dignity of historians, or have not fitted academic catalogs. Some are samples of how historians have themselves obscured what they purport to show us. Some are reminders of the whimsies and the ravages of time. All will suggest how much still remains to be discovered about our past, and how uncertain is our grip on the future.

The approach in this book is not systematic but casual and serendipitous. Here are my vistas from two dozen different vantage points. I have kept the examples in each chapter which originally suggested its theme—even where more recent illustrations could easily be found—so the reader may share my first sense of discovery. And I have not tried to remove several references to the same striking features of our history as I have seen their variegated significance.

In "The Quest for History," I begin by describing the historian's forgotten battle with his mortality. The Law of the Survival of the Unread and other Biases of Survival give us hints of how time destroys essential clues to our whole past, and of the grand irony that misleads us by mere accidents of survival. How different was the personal Paul Revere from the historian's tempting figment! And the lonely Abigail, yearning behind the scenes, made it possible for the eloquent and talkative John Adams to cut a potent figure on the stage. Gibbon's *Decline and Fall of the Roman Empire* survives and speaks to us precisely because he did not offer us any skeleton key. Like other great amateurs who make our past live, he found his motive forces in our elusive human nature. Have we not been misled by the Historian's broad hindsight, which sweeps over the panorama of the world while living people are always myopic?

Then some cautionary tales against the temptations of ideology. While we Americans have been grandly successful in building decent democratic institutions, we have not built grand political theories. Do these facts explain each other? "A By-Product Nation," how have we been brought together and made experimental by "The Therapy of Distance"? By the good fortunes of a treasure-house continent, by a once-for-all, successful-at-the-first-try American Revolution? And we see Thomas Jefferson drawing on his American experience to dispel his nagging doubts about human equality.

The rhetoric which has emerged from our history has reshaped our thinking and talking about our wants, our leaders, and ourselves. Our democratic hope to sell—or give—everything to everybody has created the new vernacular of advertising. And this has transformed who our leaders are and how and when and where they reach us. We have even devised our own way of interpreting our past in historical monuments. We have become the most legislated, if also the freest, people on earth. But how have we been tempted to the dangerous rhetoric of unwritten law?

Some of our most distinctive and most successful American experiments have not held center-stage. Perhaps more distinctive than our Founding Fathers' Enlightenment faith in reason and in mankind was their Courage to Doubt. To doubt their own infallibility in religion, to doubt their own omniscience as Constitution makers. As a result, while other nations have turned out annual-model constitutions, we still live by the venerable outlines they sketched two centuries ago. And while other nations obstinately sharpen the contrast between the public and the private, our American kinds of communities have experimented with ways to serve culture, to uplift and educate, by some public-private hybrids. So our men and women of wealth—our Carnegies and Rosenwalds and Rockefellers—have advanced from Charity to Philanthropy, and tried to let the future make its own choices. In the first half of this century the miseries of the Old World have blessed us with the refreshing visions of the refugee-immigrants, making us a Laboratory of the Arts. Has not the Amateur Spirit been one of the secret virtues of democracy, which is government by amateurs? And what happens when time-honored ways of aristocrats and bureaucrats are displaced by the ever-risky question, "Why Not?"

Behind these scenes of experiment and enterprise, we glimpse "The Momentum of Technology." How different are the revolutions of science and technology from the celebrated revolutions of politics fought on the battlefield or on the barricades! Amid the surprising delights of our self-made world, the Momentum of Technology becomes ominous. "Pseudo-events"—experiences of our own contriving—begin to hide reality from us, to confuse our sense of reality, taking us headlong from the world of heroes to a world of celebrities, transforming us from travelers into tourists.

Finally, most unpredicted and unfathomable and seductive are the mysteries of the new Republic of Technology, where we now live. It is international. It has no constitution, knows no boundaries or passports, and was never created by treaty or charter. What are its laws, its frontiers, its opportunities, and its perils? And from the unheralded Machine Kingdom where we have entered, there can be no emigration.

PROLOGUE: The Fertile Verge

For the secret alchemy of creativity, the mystery which opens the Book of Genesis, we are not ever likely to find a formula. But of the several kinds of creativity, the least secret, the most public, the most discussable is *social* creativity. While this subject is much vaster and more amorphous than creativity in Mark Twain, William James, Ernest Hemingway, Jackson Pollock, or Aaron Copland, it is more open to our scrutiny.

American creativity, I will suggest, has flourished on what I call the Fertile Verge.

A verge is a place of encounter between something and something else. America was a land of verges—all sorts of verges, between kinds of landscape or seascape, between stages of civilization, between ways of thought and ways of life. During our first centuries we experienced more different kinds of verges, and more extensive and more vivid verges, than any other great modern nation. The long Atlantic coast, where early colonial settlements flourished, was, of course, a verge between land and sea. Every movement inward into the continent was a verge between the advanced European civilization and the stone-age culture of the American Indians, between people and wilderness. The earliest flourishing of a new American civilization was in New England and in Virginia, where people enjoyed the commerce of the sea.

As cities became sprinkled around the continent, each was a new verge between the ways of the city and those of the countryside. As immigrants poured in from Ireland, Germany, and Italy, from Africa and Asia, each group created new verges between their imported ways and the imported ways of their neighbors and the new-grown ways of the New World. Each immigrant himself lived the verge encounter between another nation's ways of thinking, feeling, speaking, and living and the American ways.

In ancient, more settled nations, uniformity was idealized. The national pride of Englishman, Frenchman, German, or Italian was a pride in the special genius of his own kind. "Outside" influences might spice the culture, might spark renaissances, might stir it to fulfill itself in new ways. But the promise of the nation in the long run lay in the fulfillment of this one particular genius. The organic image was then apt. For the French aimed at the "flowering" of a pure French spirit. Grandeur and vitality came somehow from within, from purity, from a refusal to fulfill any other people's destiny.

The American situation was different. The creativity, the hope, of the nation was in its verges, in its new mixtures and new confusions. At least until the middle of the twentieth century, the United States remained rich in verges. The expansion of empires from the fifteenth through the nineteenth century did provide European nations with their remote verges—far-off colonies in Africa or Asia or America or Oceania. But for our United States, the verges were within, and were the most fertile part of us.

The brilliant historian Frederick Jackson Turner did us a great service by reminding us of "The Significance of the Frontier in American History" (1893). He directed historians' attention away from the genealogy-ridden, overworked chronicles of the Atlantic seacoast to the novelties of westward-moving peoples. Describing the frontier as "the hither edge of free land," he surveyed the characteristic American ways of thinking and governing, strewn across the continent as that frontier line moved toward the Pacific.

Turner also did us a disservice. For he overcast the whole American experience with what he called the Frontier experience, the special character of only one of our stages. He gave a new vividness and a new name to the whole drama. But he obscured the fact that the encounter of European civilization with a wilderness—what he called "the outer edge of the wave—the meeting point between savagery and civilization"—was only the First Act. Turner took his clue, of course, from the Census of 1890, which reported that in the newly populated American West there was no longer a "frontier line." Therefore, he said, the frontier habitat had disappeared.

While Turner thought he was describing the archaeology of American life, he was actually describing its physiology. His example dazzled and delighted historians desperately seeking a theme. Yet the kind of encounter of which Turner described one example had myriad counterparts. The creative American encounter was a much less local phenomenon than any physical frontier with Old World connotation of fortified borderlands, or nineteenth-century imperial overtones of the contrast between civilization and savagery. At the outer edge of the free mind American creative energies were continually refreshed.

On these verges—gifts of our geography, our history, our demography—we find three characteristic ways of thinking and feeling. First, there is our exaggerated *self-awareness*. On the verge we notice more poignantly who we are, how we are thinking, what we are doing. Second, there is a special *openness to novelty and change*. When we encounter something different, we become aware that things can be different, our appetite is whetted for novelty and its charms. Third, there is a strong *community-consciousness*. In the face of the different and the unfamiliar, we, the similars, lean on one another. We seek to reassure one another as we organize our new communities and new forms of community. These three tendencies are all both opportunities and temptations. They are sometimes complementary, sometimes contradictory. Creativity in our United States has been a harvest of these hypertrophied American attitudes stirred on the Fertile Verge. Here are a few of the countless Fertile Verges dramatized in our nation's history.

Geographic Verges. The first English settlements in America called themselves plantations. We lose the flavor of their experience in the modern word "colony." Today we think of a colony as an outpost or a subordinated part of an empire.

The word "plantation" suggested something quite different. Francis Bacon's essay "Of Plantations" (1625) underlined the difference. "Planting of countries," he wrote, "is like planting of woods. For you must make account to lose almost twenty years' profit, and expect your recompense in the end. For the principal thing that hath been the destruction of most plantations hath been the base and hasty drawing of profit in the first years. It is true, speedy profit is not to be neglected, as far as it may stand with the good of the plantation, but no farther." A plantation, then, was a place of risk and of calculation. Its success required a sharpened self-awareness. You had to know what you were doing.

"If you plant where savages are," Bacon prescribed, "do not only entertain them with trifles and gingles [i.e. rattles], but use them justly and graciously, with sufficient guard nevertheless. And do not win their favour by helping them to invade their enemies. . . . Send oft of them over to the country that plants, that they may see a better condition than their own, and commend it when they return."

Two decades later, William Bradford called his classic chronicle a history *Of Plymouth Plantation* (1651) and his fellow planters were aware of a higher balance sheet. On the *Arbella,* John Winthrop made a familiar declaration of self-awareness for his community, who would be as a "City upon a Hill."

For the first time in modern history, large numbers of Europeans transplanted themselves to a place of mystery and emptiness. Of course, there were a few million of native Americans spread thinly. But it was the encounter with raw, uninhabited nature, with its unpredictable climate, its strange plants and animals, that sharpened their consciousness of where they were and what they were doing.

In the eighteenth century, American settlers came to be struck less by Divine Providence and more by the providential wealth and novelty of their new world. No longer could they follow the familiar routines of Old World agriculture. New crops—Indian corn (maize), tobacco, cotton, and others equally strange—offered new challenges, with a new need to become informed, to notice how and when to plant.

Natural History, as it was then called, flourished here. In 1743 Benjamin Franklin alerted his fellow Americans and enlisted their energies in what was to become the American Philosophical Society. He described as the special arena of their interests what might now be called the whole American "environment," which for quite other reasons still arrests our attention. The concerns shared by Franklin's group, announced in his circular letter, were all sorts of items "new-discovered" (plants, herbs, trees, roots; fossils, mines, minerals, quarries), "new methods," "new mechanical inventions," "new arts," and "new improvements" of every kind. Americans of lively mind became naturalists. Europeans eager to enlarge their catalogs of nature, disciples and ambassadors of Linnaeus, surveyed the strange American scene and explored the exotic American landscape. Peter Kalm and others came from Sweden, William Bartram set out from Philadelphia, and Haiti-born John James Audubon came, via France, to Kentucky and the fecund Mississippi Valley.

Not that Americans needed reminding, but the great European naturalists of the age still kept telling them that America was different. A delightful allegory of this inevitable American self-awareness was enacted one evening just outside Paris at the end of the American Revolution. For the American Peace Mission Benjamin Franklin was giving a dinner party at Passy, where half of those invited were French, the other half Americans. Among the French was the Abbé Raynal, a sprightly Jesuit-trained historian. Raynal steered the conversation to his theory, popular in France at the time, that all species of animals, including man, tended to degenerate and become smaller in the inhospitable American climate. Franklin, seeing how the guests were seated at the table (all the Americans on one side, and all the French on the other), proposed that they test the theory then and there. "Let both parties rise," he said, "and we will see on which side nature has degenerated." The Americans, including Franklin, who was not a tall man, towered over their French opposites—and it happened that the smallest of all was Raynal himself.

Even among our helpful French allies, Americans could not fail to be aware of countless still undiscovered consequences of being American. The City upon a Hill nourished cities in the wilderness. City-founding required an especially lively and informed awareness of what you were doing. In the Old World you were born into your city or onto the anciently settled countryside. Here, from the beginning, you had to help mark off where you and your children would be living. The colonial period was replete with town plans, still visible on the street maps of Savannah and Philadelphia, among many others. "Main Street" was a significant Americanism long before Sinclair Lewis gave it a sour connotation. Main Streets, so-called, bore witness all across the continent that *our* towns and cities were planned by self-aware Americans. The very first paid job undertaken by the Father of our Country, George Washington, was his assignment, at the age of sixteen, to work as assistant surveyor of a new town to be called Alexandria, just a few miles up the river from Mount Vernon.

When we think back on the situation of British North America at the time of the early settlements, it is quite conceivable that the cartographic ignorance and the vastness of the continent, its heart of darkness, the mountain ranges along both ocean coastlines, and the courses of the great rivers—all these might have impelled Americans to huddle along the seaboard. They might have clustered together in the first clearings to solidify, fortify, and populate areas already familiar. That was the settlement pattern of Africa, Australia, and elsewhere. It is not what happened here. Instead, the vastness, the mystery, the variety, the mountain and river and desert obstacles themselves became enticements. The center of population of the United States would be not far from midcontinent. Going West, where increasing numbers of Americans risked their lives and fortunes, meant willingness to face the unknown, to go out to the verge. The United States, then, became a civilization of more miscellaneous verges than we can count: river towns and prairie villages, mining camps and missions. Vitality of agriculture, commerce, industry, language, education, and folklore sparked where one place or people touched another.

American civilization grew by getting people out to the edges and by getting people and messages back and forth across the verges. This yen for the verges gave a newly dominating significance to technologies of transportation. American railroads, within only a few decades of their invention, were bringing thousands from Europe and the eastern United States out to the edge of the unknown. Much to the astonishment of Old World railroad experts, American railroads developed with no deliberate speed and reached beyond the reasonable needs of existing settlements.

In England, for example, railroads were solidly built, to run from London to Birmingham or Manchester or Edinburgh. In the United States, by contrast, the railroads seemed to run "from Nowhere-in-Particular to Nowhere-at-All." They went out to the verges and beyond. They were built hastily, sometimes flimsily—not so much to serve a population as to attract it, not so much to keep the wheels of old industries turning as to find new materials for new industries. And also to create new settlements to consume the products.

When the centers of growth were on the verges—in the Clevelands and Chicagos and Kansas Citys and Omahas and Denvers and Tulsas—the way to keep the whole nation vital was to keep it in touch with the outskirts. By the midnineteenth century, the United States had catapulted into primacy with the greatest railroad mileage in the world.

The same parable could be told of the American automobile,

which also quickly outran the highways and the reasonable needs of existing settlements. By 1970 Americans were spending billions to send a few of their number as far into space as they could reach.

The desire to keep in touch and the momentum of technology gave a boost to communications. Once again Americans were tempted to exceed their existing needs. Thoreau, retreating to his New England pond when others were adventuring out to more distant verges, missed the point. "We are in great haste," Thoreau complained (in *Walden* in 1854) in one of his most-quoted jeremiads, "to construct a magnetic telegraph from Maine to Texas; but Maine and Texas, it may be, have nothing important to communicate." Thoreau's fellow Americans confidently assumed that two such different distant places as Maine and Texas would sooner or later have something to say to each other. Might not the telegraph encourage them to find out what that was? Every later advance in the technology of communication—the telephone, the radio, and now television—has flourished here before Americans knew what they should say over it. These too grew on the Fertile Verge of emptiness.

Political Verges. Self-awareness breeds self-government and self-government breeds self-awareness. On board the *Mayflower*, even before arriving here, the Pilgrim Fathers noticed that if they were to have a government on landing, they would have to create it for themselves. The Mayflower Compact was dated November 11, 1620, and signed by forty-one passengers—all the heads of families, adult bachelors, and hired menservants. It was a declaration that they all intended to live under a rule of law and that they would shape a government for their special needs. Of course there had been so-called church compacts or church covenants often before, when a group of men and women decided to set up a new church. But now the *Mayflower* passengers extended their covenant to create a full civil government.

History and geography again and again sharpened Americans' awareness of the role that people played in shaping their own political institutions. The success of the American Revolution provided a vacuum which had to be filled by a new frame of government. The federal tradition, nurtured in the old "British" colonial system, required a nice awareness of the nuances of jurisdiction. Hypersensitized by the Revolution, Americans remained alert to the distinction between a constitution and mere legislation.

This drama of political self-awareness was reenacted all across the continent. Old empires had made the government of colonies simple problems of bureaucracy, of extending the jurisdiction of some colonial office. But the spread of self-governing states into the American West was quite another matter. It required constitutional conventions and the making of new constitutions. Even in their transient communities of westward-moving wagon trains, Americans remained aware of the responsibilities of self-government. En route they took the trouble to frame constitutions for the government of their company during the transcontinental trek.

The multiplication of self-governing States, each with its bicameral legislature, multiplied legislation. Every law was a community's recognition of a problem, another sharpener of self-awareness. The United States was to proliferate legislatures and legislators, laws and legal decisions, without precedent in modern history.

Our nation had been born in the politics of verges. "These united [sic] States" came into being from the difficulty of defining the bounds between the authority of the government in London and the authority of the governments in each of the colonies. The verges between state governments and the national government, the main battleground in the Constitutional Convention of 1787, have remained foggy into our own time. There grew the great political and constitutional issues over which the nation fought the bloodiest war of the nineteenth century. On the verges between state and nation, the issues of interstate commerce, civil rights, revenue sharing, offshore oil, education, welfare, and taxing power dominated the nation's political, legislative, and judicial life into the twentieth century.

While these verges have been battlegrounds, they have also been arenas of experiment and of progress. Each State legislature, as Justice Oliver Wendell Holmes was fond of reminding us, was a laboratory. In the limbo between State and national powers appeared some of the most ingenious and controversial entities, including the Federal Reserve Board, the Federal Trade Commission, the Federal Communications Commission, the Federal Aviation Administration, and countless others.

Explicit and repeated public declarations of the extent and the boundaries of their government reinforced the American obsession with limiting government (rooted in bitter colonial experience) and had unexpected by-products. The public conscience of private citizens flourished on the verge. There appeared a characteristic American frontier for private and voluntary institutions and for mixed public and private institutions—in areas which in the Old World had been sharply defined by law and tradition and preempted by the state. This included higher education. (I spent twenty-five years on the faculty of the great University of Chicago, whose stationery said "Founded by John D. Rockefeller.") And museums. (There in Chicago my family and I enjoyed the Museum of Natural History, a benefaction of Marshall Field.) And libraries. (I exploited the research treasures of the library endowed by a certain Walter J. Newberry.) These are examples of private, voluntary beneficence without close counterpart in Western Europe.

Technological Verges. As early as the mideighteenth century American technological verges bore fruit and stimulated the appetite for novelties. The so-called Kentucky rifle, earlier known here as the Pennsylvania rifle, was a good example. When Germans and German Swiss settled in western Pennsylvania, the German rifle, which had developed for Alpine uses, was still clumsy, heavy, and short-barreled. But here in America, hunting, Indian fighting, and skirmishes in the backwoods encouraged improvements. The Pennsylvania rifle became longer and more slender, with a smaller bore and using a ball weighing only about half the weight of that used in the German model. It was quicker to fire, became quicker to load, had less recoil, and offered more range and accuracy. By the time of the American Revolution this weapon, still practically unknown in England and found only among a few hunters in the mountain fastnesses of Europe, had become common in our backwoods. Americans became the best marksmen in the world. Revolutionary commanders encouraged troops to dress in the fringed buckskin of the backwoods to frighten their red-coated enemies. All this was possible because here on the edge, the Fertile Verge between expert and layman, German and Swiss gunsmiths could break traditional patterns.

And then American factories appeared in the wilderness. Just as with the rifle, the basic inventions and mechanized technology of the textile factory had been developed abroad, this time in England. But new things happened when they were brought here to the verge. After an adventurous young Englishman, Samuel Slater, managed to memorize the main features of the Arkwright cotton-spinning machinery and smuggled the secrets out of England to New England, a new era opened. Factories sprang up in the backwoods—on the New England rivers, in Waltham and Lowell—against a strange background of virgin countryside and tree-covered New England hills. Even Charles Dickens, who knew the English milltowns and who was not famous for his sympathy to anything American, could not restrain his enthusiasm in 1842 for these factories on the verges.

The most important American technological innovation of the early nineteenth century—the so-called System of Interchangeable Parts, which became known as the American System—also was a by-product of the verge. The scarcity of gunsmiths offered the opportunity, which Eli Whitney seized.

Cultural Verges. This most familiar of American verges is expressed in countless clichés—a Nation of Nations, the Melting Pot, the Mixing Bowl, etc., etc. But the clichés must not dull us to the extraordinary nature of what happened here. In our unexpected mix of peoples, people discovered things about themselves and about others which they could not have known or noticed in their more homogeneous places of origin.

Of course there was nothing new in the mere juxtaposition of peoples of different histories and languages and traditions. What was novel here was not the to-be-expected ethnic islands but the everywhere-verges. A special American creativity would be found not *within* the enclaves but on the borders between them. Here the borders were omnipresent and with a few exceptions were more open than they had been anywhere else. Unpredictable cultural verges appeared on the prairies, in mining camps, in cities, in churches and schools. Everyone shared the jurisdiction of the same government. The Balanced Ticket proved that all were expected to take part.

Perhaps the least appreciated by-product of American self-awareness on the verges of our national life is our American language. Of the widespread modern languages no other has more effectively allowed a whole people, literati included, to be continually alerted to colloquial enrichment. For the French language the authoritative dictionary is that edited and revised by the Académie Française, an elite group of forty "immortals" who certify words by the usage of the best authors. What happens at the meetings of this legislature for the French language? One of the members, François Mauriac, explained quite simply, "We watch ourselves grow old."

The *Oxford English Dictionary,* the counterpart of the dictionary of the Académie for the English language, is a monument of gargantuan scholarship. It too holds up as the mirror of linguistic propriety the published writings of the best authors.

But the spoken language is where the action is. And for our American language there is no single authoritative legislative source. H. L. Mencken's classic *American Language* is essentially an adventure story of what happened to respectable, virginal English when she encountered so many uncouth peoples in various places. The several standard unabridged dictionaries of our American language—Merriam-Webster, Random House—and the most widely used desk-dictionaries—American Heritage, New World, and others—are also distinctively different from those in French or English. Our American dictionaries hold up the mirror to our daily, ever-changing, colloquial usage. Others have tried to confine their sources to respectable literary matter. Our American lexicographers welcome the testimony of all speakers—gossips, athletes, reporters, businessmen, labor leaders, country-music singers, and all comers. Broken English is our true national dialect. When a New England Brahmin, proud of his *Mayflower* ancestry, objects to someone *kibitzing,* I hear what happens on the Fertile Verges of language.

Our dictionaries keep us promptly aware of how our fellow Americans are speaking, so we can understand them and ("hopefully," "at this point in time"!) imitate them. In our language, thanks to our lack of prestigious domineering academies and to the enterprise and alertness and docility of our own dictionary makers and our writers, we are unlike the members of Mauriac's French Academy. *"We* watch ourselves grow *young."*

Generational Verges. American circumstances created new verges between youth and age, between the generations. Self-government, as Thomas Jefferson again and again insisted, meant the sovereignty of the present generation. "We may consider each generation as a distinct nation," Jefferson wrote, "with a right, by the will of its majority, to bind themselves, but none to bind the succeeding generation, more than the inhabitants of another country." But every community includes relics of earlier generations, as well as scions of the next. Still, Jefferson expressed a characteristic American concern. Few other countries have been so preoccupied with the youthfulness of youth.

Immigration itself, for most of American history, deepened the sense of difference between the older and the younger generation, between parents and their children. While in long-settled countries the universal process was the parent instructing and acculturating the child, among millions of newly arrived immigrants in the United States the process was reversed. Parents spoke only German, Italian, Spanish, Polish, Yiddish, or Japanese. Their children, learning colloquial American English in the public schools, at home became instructors in the American language and in American ways.

Mary Antin's *Promised Land* (1912) is a classic account of how a little immigrant Jewish girl from Russia became an American and then taught her father how to speak and behave like an American. She reports her father's sentiments when he took her for her first day in the New York City public school:

> If education, culture, the higher life were shining things to be worshipped from afar, he had still a means left whereby he could draw one step nearer to them. He could send his children to school to learn all those things that he knew by fame to be desirable. The common school, at least, perhaps high school; for one or two, perhaps even college! His children should be students, should fill his house with books and intellectual company; and thus he would walk by proxy in the Elysian Fields of liberal learning.

Parents enjoyed their children's rapid rise. But the increasing gap between parent and child often produced heartaches. Today's American enthusiasm for youth may have roots in the peculiar American immigrant experience of children seeming wiser, or at least more acculturated, than their parents. All this, of course, was reinforced by speedy technological progress which bred admiration, or at least tolerance, for new models of everything, including new-model Americans.

In our own time, we see some perils in the traditional verges. The self-awareness, the City upon a Hill syndrome, threatens to become mere self-consciousness, conceit, or even self-flagellation. Old cultural verges threaten to become islands of ethnic or racial or pseudo-racial chauvinism. The appetite for novelty threatens to become the disease of Presentism, obsession with the recent and the present, when we displace history by social studies, classics by best-sellers, heroes by celebrities. Community consciousness, the concern of the *Mayflower* passengers for all their fellows, may become an obsession with the shifting currents of public opinion. The symptoms are demagoguery in politics, timid conformity in private life, and imitativeness in our businessmen, technicians, writers, artists, and architects.

The Fertile Verges of the next epoch of American life are bound to be somewhat different. American successes of the last two centuries have created unprecedented new verges. Perhaps these lie along the rim of creative dissatisfaction. Some living witnesses are our American institutions for teaching and learning, our American advertising industry, and our thriving enterprises of research and development.

Our institutions tell us that the Fertile Verges of our time are still on the outer bounds of the free mind. There is always more ignorance than knowledge, and on that boundary, which no Census can ever report closed, we find the verge which we must keep open, and which will always be fertile. We must be reminded not only of what we know, what we can do, but of what we do not know, what impossibilities still remain to be accomplished, or at least tried. Our task is to remain aware of these verges and to keep the borders open to a competitive world of new ideas, new products, new arts, new institutions. The frontier metaphor will no longer serve us. Surely we are not the last New World. The creativity of our nation will depend on our finding and exploring the verges between our new world and the next.

Hidden History

...like gazing at a Flemish tapestry
with the wrong side out: even though
the figures are visible, they are full
of threads that obscure the view and
are not bright and smooth as when seen
from the other side.

—CERVANTES, *Don Quixote*

PART I

THE QUEST FOR HISTORY

In the country of bridges
The bridge is more real
Than the shores it doth unsever.

FERNANDO PESSOA

CHAPTER 1

"A Wrestler with the Angel"

THE HISTORIAN is both discoverer and creator. To the uniqueness of his role we have a clue in the very word "history," which means both the course of the past and the legible account of the past. The historian is always trying to reduce, or remove, that ambiguity. If he is successful, he leads his readers to take—or mistake—his account for what was really there.

The historian sets himself a dangerous, even an impossible, task. In the phrase of the great Dutch historian, J. H. Huizinga, he is "A Wrestler with the Angel." It is the angel of death who makes his work necessary yet destined never to be definitive. If man were not mortal, we would not be deprived of the living testimony of the actors, and so required to give new form to the receding infinity. From my own experience I will describe the historian's quest. I will suggest both the universal obstacles to recovery of the past, and some special resources, opportunities, and temptations for the historian in our own time. And finally, I will recall some qualities of historians whose works of discovery and creation I have found most satisfying and most durable.

The Limits of Discovery: The Bias of Survival

The historian can rediscover the past only by the relics it has left for the present. Historians of all ages have worked under these limitations. Their mission requires that they make the most of whatever they can find. They try to convince us that the relics they have

3

examined and interpreted in their narrative are a reliable sample of the experience that men really had. But how reliable are the remains of the past as clues to what was really there?

My own experience as a historian has brought me vivid reminders of how partial is the remaining evidence of the whole human past, how casual and how accidental is the survival of its relics. One of my first shocks came, while exploring the American Experience in colonial times, in my effort to recapture the meaning of religion to the settlers of early New England. Their basic vehicle of religious instruction was the *New England Primer*. This, the chief text of compulsory education in early Massachusetts, carried a full rhymed alphabet—from "Adam" ("In Adams Fall we sinned all") to "Zaccheus" ("Zaccheus, he, did climb the tree, his Lord to see")—along with moral aphorisms, fragments of the Old Testament, and the text of prayers, including the familiar "Now I lay me down to sleep. . . ." This influential work, which first appeared about 1690, became the best-selling New England schoolbook, and had sold some 3 million copies within the next century. Benjamin Franklin, who knew a commercial opportunity when he saw one, made a tidy profit publishing his own secularized version.

For the flavor of New England religion, I went in search of original copies of the *Primer,* but they were hard to find. By contrast I found it easy to consult the heavy tomes of Puritan theology, the lengthy sermons and treatises, like those of Thomas Shepard, finally collected into three volumes in 1853. These volumes, kept in the rare-book rooms of university libraries, were often in mint condition, sometimes even with uncut pages. Modern scholars pore over such works in plush bibliophilic comfort to discover what the early Puritans were "really thinking" about religion.

This experience set me thinking about the limits of historical discovery. I had a similar experience when I came to the early nineteenth century, trying to learn about American heroes of the age and what people thought of them. I turned at once to the popular "Crockett Almanacs." These were pamphlets of wide appeal published in the name of Davy Crockett (1786–1836), the man of little education and little respect for book learning, who said the rules of spelling were "contrary to nature." Crockett died a martyr's death at the Alamo in the fight for Texas independence in 1836. Besides recipes, and useful everyday hints for health and crops, they recounted Crockett's astonishing feats wrestling men and alligators, along with legends of other frontier prodigies like Mike Fink, Daniel Boone, and Kit Carson. The earliest of these almanacs in 1835 offered an "autobiography," which Crockett supposedly wrote soon before his death.

Between 1835 and 1856 some fifty such almanacs poured out of Nashville, New York, Boston, Philadelphia, and elsewhere by the ten thousands, in the name of Davy Crockett or his "heirs." Embellished by crude woodcuts on cheap paper, these almanacs were carried in saddlebags, slipped into hip pockets, handed about Western inns and bars, and around campfires as Americans moved west. The appetite for them seemed inexhaustible. But in late twentieth century they have become rare and costly collectors' items.

A dramatic contrast for the historian of American hero worship was the monumental official life of George Washington, authorized by his nephew Bushrod Washington and written by Chief Justice John Marshall. The work came to five volumes, sold by subscription at the then considerable price of $3.00 a volume. Even the flamboyant Parson Weems, who put his best efforts into it, could not make it sell. And when the first volume of the much-touted project reached subscribers in 1804 it quickly established itself as the publishing catastrophe of the age. John Adams charitably characterized this as not a book at all but rather "a Mausoleum, 100 feet square at the base and 200 feet high." History justified Adams' description because the volumes survived, as unread as they were unreadable. And even now complete sets in mint condition are not hard to come by, sometimes in secondhand furniture stores. Today, of course, it is much more convenient, and more tempting for the scholar, to mine the elegant bound volumes of Marshall, than to handle the ragged half-legible fragments of Davy Crockett. These two episodes of my own research led me to a rather troubling hypothesis.

The Law of the Survival of the Unread. If there is a natural and perhaps inevitable tendency toward the destruction and disappearance of the documents most widely used, this poses a discomfiting problem for the historian. For he inevitably relies heavily on the surviving printed matter. Is the historian, then, the victim of a diabolical solipsism? Is there an inverse relation between the probability of a document surviving and its value as evidence of the daily life of the age from which it survives?

To this troublesome "law" of historical evidence there are, as we shall see, countless exceptions. But the exceptions themselves are also reminders of the casual and accidental causes of preservation, survival, and accessibility. These only confirm our doubts that there is any necessary positive correlation between probabilities of survival and importance as clues of past thought and ways of life. Survival is chancy, whimsical, and unpredictable. Yet it is not impossible to list some of the Biases of Survival. These themselves do not tell us anything substantial about the human past. But they do provide us some helpful cautions. They may save us from jumping to wrong conclusions. They remind us of how the very accidents of survival may skew our vision of the past, exaggerating certain kinds of human activity, concealing or dissolving others. The limits of historical discovery come from the physical qualities of objects as much as from the human activities which they suggest. They apply not only to documents and printed matter but to all kinds of relics.

Survival of the Durable, and That Which is Not Removed or Displaced. While this has the sound of tautology, its consequences are not always noticed—the tendency toward emphasis on the monumental, on experience recorded in writing or in books. Since religions are a deliberate effort to transcend the transience of the individual human life, monuments of religion are often more durable than other monuments. Tombs, burial objects, mummies, temples, churches, and pyramids tend to skew our view of the past. They give a prominence to religion in the relics of the past which it may not actually have had in the lives people lived. A contrast with monumental houses of religion are the simple dwellings of the people who did (or did not) worship there. Chartres Cathedral survives in its solid thirteenth-century glory, but the mud and wattle and wood houses of the citizens of Chartres surrounding it have been many times replaced.

In the United States this bias obscures some of the peculiar achievements of a mobile and technologically progressive civilization. One of the most characteristic architectural innovations in the United States is the balloon frame house. This American invention, which appeared in Chicago about 1833, was notable not for the durability of its product, but for its ease and speed of construction and removal. Houses built by nailing together light timbers (instead of by the mortise-and-tenon of heavy beams) were put up quickly by people without the carpenter's skill. Such houses were taken down, and their frames transported by wagon or riverboat to the next stopping place in the transient, booming West. In Omaha in 1856 General William Larimer lived in a balloon house that had been framed in Pittsburgh and shipped out by steamboat. Then, when Omaha grew beyond his taste, he took down his house and moved it to another site. While the country mansions of the Dutch patroons of New York and plantation mansions of Virginia and Maryland survive, where are the balloon frames? This momentous American invention, whose twentieth-century products surround us today, has hardly entered the historical record.

Incidentally, we have lost two of the most vivid dimensions of past experience—color and odor. For us "classical architecture" means the chaste elegance of weathered marble. But in fact when the Parthenon was completed in Athens' great age, it was a garish polychrome, more resembling the extravagance of a twentieth-century World's Fair than our cliché of Greek elegance. And as we admire the venerable yellow patina of Amiens, Canterbury, or Chartres Cathedrals, we again forget the original vision. As Le Corbusier reminds us, "The cathedrals were white because they were new. The freshly cut stone of France was dazzling in its whiteness as the Pyramids of Egypt had gleamed with polished granite."

In the ages before running water and modern plumbing, the characteristic odors of bodies and places intruded in daily experience. The perfumes, today a dispensable luxury, were then a common necessity for pleasant conversation. It is not only automobiles that corrupt the atmosphere by their excrement. We easily forget that smog is the price of the freedom of our streets from manure, and from the flies and diseases it brought. The American industry in deodorants thrives, but where are the odors of the past?

Survival of the Collected and the Protected: What Goes in Government Files. We emphasize political history and government in the life of the past partly because governments keep records, while families and other informal groups seldom do. Yet informal groups—for example the anonymous wagon trains into which Americans organized themselves to go west or cross the continent—were among the most remarkable and most characteristic of American communities. Much of the peculiarly American experience, which has had this voluntary, spontaneous character, has eluded historians. The foundings of colleges and universities in England and Europe are recorded in the government chartering of corporations, in the orders of central ministries of education or ancient religious foundations. But in the United States the efforts of local boosters to form colleges to attract settlers, the volunteer enthusiasms of ministers and their congregations, and the haphazard philanthropy of wealthy citizens leave few official records. A democratic society like ours, a community of voluntary mobile communities, leaves a random record of its past.

Survival of Objects Which Are Not Used or Which Have a High Intrinsic Value. It is not only in printed matter that rarity and scarcity induce survival. Illuminated manuscripts, the treasures of palaces and monasteries, survive, while pamphlets, leaflets, and broadsides which made revolutions and reformations disappear. Sometimes they were incriminating, almost always they were crudely printed on paper of poor quality, easily disintegrated by the weather to which they were exposed. Nowhere is this bias more evident than in the numismatic relics of the distant past. The hoards (from the Old English word, "to cover or conceal") of coins which survived the raids of bandits and conquerors were, naturally enough, collections of the most valuable coins and other precious objects. No one troubled to bury the everyday coins of small denomination and base metals, which therefore are unlikely to survive for our examination today. European palaces, churches, and now their museums, display the jeweled and filigreed clocks and watches of early modern times. But the special timekeeping triumph of nineteenth-century America was the inexpensive household clock and then the "dollar watch," the wonder of European visitors. These dollar watches were not made for ease of repair and seemed not worth repairing. They seldom find their way into museums. Similarly, the elegantly engraved muskets with which European princes and their hunting companions enjoyed their leisure can be admired in many European museums of the arts. But the plain Kentucky Rifle, which was the early westward-moving pioneer's weapon of defense and staff of life, was not preserved as an object of beauty.

Survival of the Academically Classifiable and the Dignified. Teachers teach the subjects in which they have been instructed. The trivium (grammar, logic, and rhetoric) and quadrivium (arithmetic, geometry, astronomy, and music), which composed the Seven Liberal Arts of the medieval universities, were an exhaustive catalogue of what students were expected to learn, and what these students, when they became professors, were expected to teach. Geography for example had no place in the medieval scheme. We must piece together their notions of the earth, its shapes and its dimensions, from works of theology, along with the ephemeral maps, portolans, and planispheres used by navigators, traders, pirates, and empire builders. In the early ages of exploration, when geographic knowledge was one of the most valuable kinds of merchandise, the cartographic secrets of shorter, safer passages to the remote treasure troves of pepper, spice, and precious gems were classified information. Now they are hidden from us, as they once were from imperial and commercial competitors. In the field of literature, this academic conservatism has perpetuated the study of familiar classics but left much of what many people read stigmatized as "subliterature," beneath the interest of serious students.

Survival of Printed and Other Materials Surrounding Controversies. What has passed for the study of the history of religion in America should more accurately be described as the history of religious controversies. The silent or spoken prayers of the devout leave few records behind. But the disputations of theologians, the acrimony of the religious academies, and the resolutions of church councils pour out print. Then it is these disputes that command the interest and the ingenuity of religious historians, while the passions of the heart and the yearnings of the God-struck spirit, however constant and universal, remain private and invisible. Similarly, if we go in quest of the daily eating and drinking habits of early Americans, it is not easy to find records. At the same time the organized polemics of vegetarians and food faddists leave a readable detritus. We know little about what and how much earlier Americans drank. Yet the history of the temperance movement and the prohibition of alcoholic beverages has left an abundant literature to arrest the attention of historians. The currents of daily life which flow smoothly, as Tolstoy noted, leave a meager record. It is the eddies, whirlpools, and cross-currents that attract notice. The daily sexual habits of those who conform to the prevalent mores are seldom recorded for future historians and have rarely been chronicled. The history of sexual conduct has tended to become a record of deviants, of contraception and abortion, of polygamy and homosexuality. In the United States we have had few adequate histories of family life and marriage, but abundant monographs on the history of divorce and the movements for women's rights. The history of law enforcement and obedience to law eludes us while our shelves are filled with detective stories and the chronicles of crime.

Survival of the Self-Serving: the Psychopathology of Diarists and Letter Writers. Historians in professional training are urged to seek records by participants in events, preferably those made at the time or soon after. So there is a natural tendency to rely on diaries and letters. The thoughts, feelings, and affairs of the family and neighbors of Sir John Fastolf (c. 1378–1459) live on in a thousand so-called Paston Letters which happened to survive and so seem to record the fifteenth century for us. The quirks and quiddities of the obsessive diarist Samuel Pepys (1633–1703) loom in the foreground of the social history of England in the seventeenth century. In America we inevitably lean heavily on the diaries and letters of William Byrd (1674–1744), a witty but atypical planter-politician, and on the memoirs of the articulate plantation tutor, Philip Vickers Fithian. And we make much of the copious nineteenth-century diary written in the barely legible minuscule hand of the observant New Yorker George Templeton Strong, or the gargantuan "confessions" of the eccentric Arthur Inman. Of course intimate feelings interest the historian. But does not our hunger for the recorded word exaggerate the unusual point of view of those who happened to be diarists and letter writers? Are we victims, willingly or not, of a Casanova syndrome, which puts us at the mercy of the most articulate self-servers and boasters of the past? To correct our vision we still need an ample study of the psychopathology of diarists and perhaps of letter writers too. We are also at the mercy, and eagerly put ourselves at the mercy, of egotists. Perhaps autobiographies are a record only of those who thought too well of themselves, from Benvenuto Cellini, Casanova, and Benjamin Franklin to the self-serving political memoirists of our age.

How will the rise of the telephone and the decline of letter writing and the postal service "correct" or newly distort our recorded past? When President Thomas Jefferson wanted to instruct his Secretary of State, James Madison, he would commonly write him a note, which remains for us. But when President Lyndon Johnson wanted to instruct Secretary of State Dean Rusk, he would more often have used the telephone. Consequently when historians find a memorandum from President Johnson to Secretary Rusk, they will wonder whether the record was made, not to guide action but to convey a desired impression to future historians. President Nixon's notorious effort to use the new electronic technology to provide a taped chronicle of his work in the Oval Office reveals the new biases, opportunities, and risks—and reminds us of how much we lack of the earlier historical record. Meanwhile the flood of press releases and pseudo-events, expressly created to be reported, further dilutes and confuses the record.

Survival of the Victorious Point of View: The Success Bias. The history of inventions which we read today seems to have become the story of successful inventors. Eli Whitney, Isaac Merritt Singer, Henry Ford, Thomas A. Edison, and other lucky ones leave a vivid record. But the countless anonymous experimenters, the frustrated tinkerers who nearly made it, disappear. How many of their efforts ought to be part of the story? Occasionally, as in the lengthy litigations over who was the "first inventor" of the sewing machine, of the mechanical reaper, of barbed wire, of the telephone, of the automobile, and of the phonograph, we glimpse at least a few of the competitors for the money, the spotlight, and the glory. An unsung, but surely not unpaid, service of the legal profession has been to provide documentary evidence of the struggles of the also-rans and the near-successful.

American history as a whole presents a spectacle of this bias. A dominant theme in the writing of American history has been the filling of the continent, the consolidating of a great nation. But the desire to secede, to move *away* from the larger political community might have become the leitmotif. Just as the Puritans came to America as seceders from Britain, so the westward movers in the nineteenth century were seceders from the heavily settled, increasingly urban Atlantic coastal nation. If the South had won the Civil War, if the Bear Flag Republic of 1846 had survived, if the Republic of Texas had remained independent, the earlier American settlers too would have continued to shine not as nation builders but as courageous seceders. During the Viet Nam War an unwilling American draftee, impressed by this aspect of American history, responded to his draft notice by informing the President that, in a great American tradition, instead of going into the United States Army, he would secede and become a nation all by himself.

A delightful irony in the earliest historical record arises from the difference between the survival powers of organic and of inorganic materials. For while organic material (what we now call biodegrada-ble) is quick to disintegrate, inorganic materials survive, and so our evidences of prehistory come mainly from flint and stone imple-ments. The bodies of people who used them were not apt to survive if they were not embalmed or, like the rare surviving hunter of the Stone Age, chemically preserved by nature in the bogs of Denmark. "It is a paradox," Grahame Clark reminds us, "that the best chance of organic material surviving in the ordinary way is that it should be destroyed by fire, but such remains, in being converted into carbon, acquire enormously enhanced powers of resistance." In the search for details of Early Iron Age culture in Jutland, it was found that houses abandoned to the processes of natural decay disappeared. Yet those destroyed by fire remained clearly defined by their charred stumps, by traces of carbonized roofing material found lying on the floor, and traces of wattle impressed on burnt daub. Charred wooden utensils also left archaeologically useful fragments. The bizarre moral is that while the houses of the victors vanished without a trace, gradually conquered by insects and weather and time, an Early Iron Age village had a better chance of earning a place in "history" if it was invaded and burned to the ground.

Survival of the Epiphenomenal. Often people write books and read them because they cannot personally experience what is de-scribed. We often remain uncertain whether writers were recording their experience or escaping it. In my own efforts to describe Ameri-can manners and household customs I have been tantalized by this ambiguity. Emily Post's *Etiquette*, first published in 1922, and fre-quently revised thereafter, was so popular that her name became a synonym for proper behavior. Her books, like the New England Primers, were used up, so that now a complete set is not readily available. Emily Post described proper behavior: the kind of silver to be set, the tablecover and glassware to be used, the role of servants. The style of private entertaining she prescribed during the Great Depression in the lean 1930s still resembled what Scott Fitzgerald depicted in the luxuriant age of the Great Gatsby (1925). And her books remained the popularly accepted guides. Was this because people expected to follow her economically obsolete impractical ad-vice or because they enjoyed fantasizing about how they never could, or could no longer, afford to entertain? The answers to these inward, private questions may be beyond the historian's ken.

Knowledge Survives and Accumulates, but Ignorance Disappears. A medieval folktale reports that a young alchemist was once told that, if he recited a certain formula, he could transform lead into silver and copper into gold. The only condition was that while reciting his formula, he must never be thinking of a white elephant. He learned the formula and tried reciting it. Unfortunately he could never make it work—for all the while he was earnestly trying not to think of a white elephant. The problem of latter-day historians is much like that of the young alchemist. For our minds are furnished with all the accumulated knowledge and experience of the ages since the period of the past we are trying to recapture. The modern globe of the earth is so firmly fixed in our vision that we find it hard to imagine the three-continent planet with a surface only one-seventh water, on which Columbus thought he was sailing. As we try to relive the experience of Americans hastening across the continent in the early nineteenth century, we see them traversing the fertile Great Plains, destined to be the granary of a great nation. But they thought they were crossing what on their maps was the Great American Desert. Some even sought camels to help their passage. How can we recapture their ignorance? Yet if we do not, we cannot really share their fears and their courage.

If this incomplete list of the biases of survival seems random and disorderly, it is because any neat and orderly catalog would be misleading. Every reader can add his own items to the list. The preservative and disintegrating processes of time are vagrant. The randomness of our list suggests both the unpredictable effects of the toll of time and the bizarre miscellany which is our inheritance from our past.

It is the sheerest folly to believe that we, Wrestlers with the Angel, can ever know the extent or the boundaries of our ignorance. Or that we can conquer the biases of survival by some new technology. We transfer inflammable, self-destructive nitrate motion picture films of the years before 1950 to acetate film and so avoid the immediate catastrophes of combustion. But how long will the acetate film survive? We have less than a century of use to guide us. We avoid the fragility of early phonograph discs by transferring them to sturdy plastic; we avoid the needle's wear by compact discs touched only by the laser's beam. But how long will these survive?

We should be chastened in our hope to master the whole real past by the ironic comprehensiveness of the oldest surviving records of civilization. We know more about some aspects of daily life in the ancient Babylon of 3000 B.C. than we do about daily life in parts of Europe or America a hundred years ago. By a happy accident, ancient Babylonians wrote not on paper or on wood, but on the clay which they found underfoot. "A little brick of clay," Edward Chiera reminds us, "if in pure condition and well kneaded may lie buried in the moist ground for thousands of years and not only retain its shape but harden again, when dried, to the same consistency as before. If it is covered with writing, as is generally the case with Babylonian tablets, one can take the small unbaked tablet and brush it vigorously with a good stiff brush without the slightest fear of damaging its surface. . . . If the salt encrustations should be too many and render decipherment impossible, then all one has to do is bake the tablet thoroughly. After baking, it can be immersed in water, subjected to acids, or even boiled, and it will be as fine and clean as on the day it was first made and written upon." Our grand dividend—the copious relics of this set of coincidences—is thousands of clay tablets recording everything from codes of laws and religious texts to teachers' copybooks, the notes of schoolchildren, the records of war booty, recipes, scientific works, diaries, and receipts for the sale of slaves and cattle. The messages we receive from that remote past were neither intended for us, nor chosen by us, but are the casual relics of climate, geography, and human activity. They, too, remind us of the whimsical dimensions of our knowledge and the mysterious limits of our powers of discovery.

The last two centuries in the West have seen a vast increase of the historian's resources and a multiplication of his physical and conceptual instruments of discovery. The modern social sciences have tried to overcome the limitations of the evidence, to extrapolate from the facts, to fill in gaps, and speculate productively about what is not or cannot be known. These additions to the historians' equipment have been a product and a by-product of two overwhelming enthusiasms of the modern West. The first is an enthusiasm for social reform. The second is an enthusiasm for science, and its application to society. The passion for reform was rooted in a growing belief that men had the right and should have the power to govern themselves, that inherited inequalities and privileges were unjust, that it was the scholar's and the ruler's duty to reduce human suffering. The passion for science was rooted in a similarly growing belief that there were no phenomena in nature, man, or society that could not be grasped, interpreted, predicted, and perhaps controlled, by human reason, if enlightened by facts and guided by science. These enthusiasms, nourished in the European Renaissance and in the Age of Exploration and Discovery, grew together. Social sciences and social reform were Siamese twins.

Of course, both movements had deep roots in classical antiquity, in the writings of Plato and Aristotle, in medieval science and theology, in Thomas Aquinas and Roger Bacon, as well as in the early modern writings of Machiavelli, Hobbes, Locke, and Rousseau. Although the expression "social sciences" did not enter the recorded English language until 1846 (as a translation of Comte), the social sciences had begun to find their separate identities by the later seventeenth century. An ample account of the rise of the social sciences would be nothing less than a survey of modern European history. In their origins and their applications, in the dogmas which grew out of them and the crusades for or against their dogmas, were the seeds of revolution, reformation, and reaction, of legislation and jurisprudence, of a wide assortment of political movements, and a fallout of countless pundits, agitators, saboteurs, dictators, celebrities, and national heroes.

By the midnineteenth century the English language had added a whole new vocabulary, a modern taxonomy of facts and theories about society, drawn from economics, political science, jurisprudence, anthropology, sociology, psychology, social psychology, statistics, and social and economic geography. The genealogy of these disciplines shows how each tried to declare its independence, and then its dominance over social thought. This is a tangled tale, another parable of how man's efforts to learn tempt him to arrogant belief that he knows more than he really does. Social scientists sought skeleton keys to human experience. Each of their dominant theories dramatized the hopes and frustrations of efforts to encapsulate and dogmatize human experience.

Of course, all these new "sciences" rested, or pretended to rest, on the solid data of "history." The accumulated facts about the past became the basis for newly discovered laws presumed to govern the present and offer confident predictions of the future. One of the most influential prophets of the new social science, Jean Jacques Rousseau (1712–1778), opened his potent treatise on the Social Contract with a single outrageous generalization about the whole human past and present: "Man is born free, and everywhere he is in chains." I will not recount the familiar story of the rise of each of the separate social sciences. Some of the biases of interpretation shared by these social sciences have affected the work of the historian. New knowledge and new disciplines have spawned new temptations.

Futuristic. The social sciences tend to study and interpret the past with an aim to changing the future. The founding fathers of the social sciences were prophets of progress. Condorcet (1743–1794) made important contributions to the theory of probability, and his most influential work was *A Sketch for a Historical Picture of the Progress of the Human Mind* (1795). After his historical survey of human development through its nine stages down to the French Revolution, he projected the future tenth epoch which would bring the final perfection of mankind. Adam Smith's *Wealth of Nations* (1776), the pioneer work of modern economics, offered many policy suggestions. He ended his views of the past with a prophetic look at the future.

> The rulers of Great Britain have, for more than a century past, amused the people with the imagination that they possessed a great empire on the west side of the Atlantic. This empire, however, has hitherto existed in imagination only. It has hitherto been, not an empire but the project of an empire; not a gold mine, but the project of a gold mine. . . . It is surely now time that our rulers should either realize this golden dream . . . or that they should awake from it themselves, and endeavour to awaken the people. . . . If any of the provinces of the British empire cannot be made to contribute towards the support of the whole empire, it is surely time that Great Britain should free herself from the expense of defending those provinces in time of war, and of supporting any part of their civil or military establishments in time of peace, and endeavour to accommodate her future views and designs to the real mediocrity of her circumstances.

Normative. The social sciences tend to seek laws or norms of experience, past, present, and future. Having founded knowledge in experience, English philosophers treated history as no more than "philosophy teaching by example." David Hume, in his *Enquiries Concerning Human Understanding* (1777), generalized from experience that "a miracle can never be proved, so as to be the foundation of a system of religion." His "Natural History of Religion" described the "normal" or natural course of the events surrounding all religions. In the same empiric tradition which dominated much of thinking about society in the English-speaking world, Jeremy Bentham provided one of the most extreme, most dogmatic, and most influential statements of the normative social sciences. His *Principles of Morals and Legislation* (1780; 1823) began from the "principle of utility" and described how the measurement of pleasures and pains and their allotment as incentives and punishments could be used to produce the greatest happiness of the society. His dogmas led to the reform of prisons and the rewriting of criminal laws around the world. He might have considered his greatest triumph the English Reform Bill of 1832.

John Stuart Mill's classic *Utilitarianism* (1863) gave his version of the "happiness principle," and elaborated its applications in government, while his *Principles of Political Economy* (1848) provided a handbook for modern liberal politicians. Even law, once thought to be the most characteristic of a society's institutions, was encapsulated in catchy generalizations. One of the most influential was Sir Henry Maine's assimilation (*Ancient Law,* 1861) of the institutions of ancient Rome, contemporary India, and Anglo-Saxon England into the convenient rule that society progresses from custom to law (using, in turn, fictions, equity, and legislation), and "from status to contract."

Quantitative. The social sciences tend to become quantitative, to reduce experience to numbers. In 1791 Sir John Sinclair had introduced the word "statistics" into the English language with the first of the twenty-one volumes of his *Statistical Account of Scotland.* We know of no public national census in the West before the eighteenth century, when the counting of people and resources became an institution. The connection between social reform, representative institutions, and a numerical approach to society was dramatized in the Constitution of the United States, which required a regular counting of the population every ten years to insure a proportionate voice in the Congress for every free citizen.

The Belgian pioneer of statistical science, Adolphe Quételet (1796–1874), took for his slogan Laplace's exhortation, "Let us apply to the political and moral sciences the method founded on observation and mathematics that has served us so well in the natural sciences." "We can judge of the perfection toward which a science has come by the facility, more or less great, with which it may be approached by calculation."

To provide grist for the statistical mills of the social scientists, the "questionnaire" was developed. (The word first appears in print in English in 1901.) It became the basis of Lewis Henry Morgan's (1818–1881) pioneer anthropology—his studies in kinship, sponsored by the Smithsonian Institution, which made common generalizations about the customs of American Indians and the peoples of Asia. Morgan's *Ancient Society* (1877) tracing "the Lines of Human Progress, from Savagery through Barbarism into Civilization" became a basis for the explosive generalizations, prophecies, and revolutionary dogmas of Karl Marx and Friedrich Engels.

The questionnaire was a forerunner, too, of a still newer device for quantifying social facts—the public opinion poll. Market research, seeking out customers for American industry, elaborated a new science of opinion polling. In the early twentieth century "public opinion" entered the American vocabulary, and by the 1930s Elmo Roper, Archibald M. Crossley, and George Gallup and their competitors were producing a new social science and the thriving new enterprise of "opinion polling." With it came a refined science of voting (psephology) and a growing tendency for Americans to think of elections and predict outcomes in percentages. These tendencies were of course compounded and dramatized by the fantastic new capacities of the computer to calculate rapidly and extrapolate indefinitely.

Fragmented. The social sciences tend to become professionalized. One result is an ever sharper definition of boundaries among the social science specialties. The early age of the modern sciences had been marked by Royal Societies, National Academies, and in the United States by the American Philosophical Society, where scholars pooled miscellaneous observations and personal speculations. The new age of professionalization created a host of specialized associations, each of which focused on its own proper province and defended its right to professional separatism and its prerogatives of employment against all trespassers. In the gregarious United States, long marked by insecurity about its humanistic culture, and by enthusiasms for voluntary organization, these new professions flourished and multiplied.

A rising American standard of living, improved means of transportation, and the growing interests of city boosters, Chambers of Commerce, travel agents, and hotel owners accelerated the trend to national and regional meetings. The chronology of the founding of these organizations attests the specialization and the fragmentation of the study of society: the American Statistical Association (1839), American Ethnological Society (1842), American Social Science Association (1865), American Library Association (1876), American Historical Association (1884), American Economic Association (1885), American Psychological Association (1892), American Anthropological Association (1902), American Political Science Association (1903), American Sociological Society (later Association; 1905), American Society for Applied Anthropology (1941). This short list gives only a hint of the proliferation of the separate professions interested in the human past. Each organization published its own periodicals and monographs, sponsored lectures and symposia, and gave prizes for the best work in the field. Even if each did not actually issue a professional code of ethics, they all aimed at explicit standards of professional competence in their specialty. Organizations have multiplied and divided into countless subspecialties.

The rise of the social sciences, dramatized in these and other learned associations, has of course produced a vast and growing resource of facts, concepts, and hypotheses, along with a growing community of experts to assist the historian in his effort to discover the past. Scholarly professionals have recognized the need to bring together their findings and pool their resources in such organizations as the American Council of Learned Societies (1919), which federated forty-three national scholarly groups, and has sponsored such publications as the *Dictionary of American Biography* (1928–   ) and the *Dictionary of Scientific Biography* (1970–1980). "Behavioral Sciences" became the name in the late 1950s for a new enthusiasm and a renewed effort to consolidate the study of mankind and make it still more scientific. Meanwhile, the multiplication of American colleges and universities increased the widening flood of knowledge about the human past, in channels not even imagined a century ago. The raw materials for the American historian in the late twentieth century are rich, diverse, and authentic beyond the wildest dreams of his predecessors.

Yet the historian's purpose today remains not much different from that of his earliest and greatest forebears. "These are the researches of Herodotus of Halicarnassus, which he publishes in the hope of thereby preserving from decay the remembrance of what men have done, and of preventing the great and wonderful acts of the Greeks and the barbarians from losing their due meed of glory; and withal to put on record what were their grounds of feud." "My conclusions," wrote Thucydides, "have cost me some labour from the want of coincidence between accounts of the same occurrences by different eye-witnesses, arising sometimes from imperfect memory, sometimes from undue partiality for one side or the other. The absence of romance in my history will, I fear, detract somewhat from its interest; but if it be judged useful by those inquirers who desire an exact knowledge of the past as an aid to the interpretation of the future, which in the course of human things must resemble if it does not reflect it, I shall be content. In fine, I have written my work, not as an essay which is to win the applause of the moment, but as a possession for all time."

When we think of survival, as Herodotus and Thucydides surely did, we must note the striking fact that works of the classic ancient historians are still read with pleasure by a vast audience for whom the physics of Aristotle, the botany of Theophrastus, the *Almagest* and *Geography* of Ptolemy, and the medical treatises of Galen have scant appeal. While the works of science and technology correct and displace their predecessors, the works of historians stay with us.

Perhaps the explanation is not so difficult. For the historian there is an uncanny continuing identity between his subject matter and his audience. Nowhere is this stated more eloquently than in the familiar words of Pericles' Funeral Oration (431 B.C.), as reported by Thucydides himself:

> Fix your eyes on the greatness of Athens as you have it before you day by day, fall in love with her, and when you feel her great, remember that this greatness was won by men with courage, with knowledge of their duty, and with a sense of honor in action. . . . So they gave their bodies to the commonwealth and received, each for his own memory, praise that will never die, and with it the grandest of all sepulchers, not that in which their mortal bones are laid, but a home in the minds of men, where their glory remains fresh to stir to speech or action as the occasion comes by. For the whole earth is the sepulcher of famous men; and their story is not graven only on stone over their native earth, but lives on far away, without visible symbol, woven into the stuff of other men's lives. For you now it remains to rival what they have done and, knowing the secret of happiness to be freedom and the secret of freedom a brave heart, not idly to stand aside from the enemy's onset.

In a word, historians are always writing about us. Not because they extrapolate "laws" of social science. But because they write for people about people, than whom nothing is more interesting or more inscrutable.

New temptations for the twentieth-century historian are the by-product of his new resources and his new instruments of discovery. Biases of the social sciences can seduce the historian into attitudes at odds with his role as a literary artist. We are unwilling victims of the Biases of Survival, grateful for whatever the past happens to leave us. But to the enthusiasms, dogmas, and academic fashions of the social sciences we have become willing victims. We embrace their emphases in the hope of sharing the scientific kudos of the social scientists.

While the modern social sciences are inevitably futuristic, the historian must remain oriented to the past. He is primarily a narrator. His suspense comes from the wonder of the past itself. The romantic philosopher's description of the historian as "the prophet in reverse" is true only when the historian shares the prophet's sense of mystery, as he too reaches into the unknown. While social sciences are normative, looking for rules and laws, the historian must sacrifice none of the idiosyncrasy of the past. His unique mission is to discover the uniqueness of people and places and moments. He dare not sacrifice this to his contemporaries' will to master the present and future. Similarly, the quantitative hopes of the social sciences, their appetite for the fungible, for whatever can be counted and classified, is alien to the historian's search for nuance, flow, and the elusiveness of experience.

Finally, the modern making of history into one of the most respectable, most fragmented, and most self-conscious of the social sciences has its perils. Organized professional historians become the target of every group with political or reformist objectives, urging positions on foreign policy, championing movements for minorities, for women or the handicapped. However morally desirable, these positions reinforce the social science biases. Yet, at the same time, the profession itself becomes the main, sometimes the only, audience for its publications. Inevitably the language of history tends to become the jargon of historians speaking to one another. The profession becomes preoccupied with its own "classic controversies" on which members write articles and monographs, or deliver polemics.

Still, we must remain wary of generalizing about the historian-creator. His hallmark is his originality. While the discoverer focuses our vision anew on something already out there, the creator, of whom the historian is a peculiar breed, makes the object for us to see. He does it with words, and so is inhibited, guided, and fulfilled by language. But his limitations are at least as restricting as the hardness of the sculptor's marble. Like other writers who seek a voluntary audience—like the poet and the novelist—he must give delight. His accents must give pleasure. If his periods are not Gibbonian, he must have his own way with words. This we find from Parkman, Prescott, and Henry Adams to Samuel Eliot Morison, in all historians who live. He shares this qualification with other men of letters. But in addition he labors under two other necessities.

Credibility. His work must be true according to the prevalent standards of truth in his age, but his standards of truth must transcend the ephemeral or fashionable demands of academic or political or religious or racial dogma. Though scholars have learned much about ancient Rome since Gibbon wrote, and the schools of Marx, Pareto, and Freud have had their day, Gibbon still tells a credible tale. This is partly, of course, from his good luck in having been born away from the tyranny of orthodoxy or totalitarianism. But it is also from his courage to resist the tyranny of passing opinion, of political sycophancy, of religious orthodoxy, and to create an original vision.

Suspense and Surprise. This is the most paradoxical and the most demanding of the arts of the historian. While the poet and the novelist can hold off the reader's knowledge of how it all turned out, and entice him by the promise of telling, where the historian labors we already know the last chapter. His greatest challenge, while conforming to the facts as best determined in his age, is to provide his reader with a new access of surprise at how and why and when and who. The successful historian at his best demands and secures a willing suspension of knowledge. He asks the reader to pretend that he does not already know, so that the historian can add suspense to the true course of events. He can do this by his more vivid portrait in detail, by his network of surprising connections, and his array of unexpected consequences. The great historian, the historian-creator, adds a new drama to everything we thought we already knew. Everybody knew that the Roman Empire declined and fell. Gibbon made his readers feel that they had not really known.

The historian-creator refuses to be defeated by the biases of survival. For he chooses, defines, and shapes his subject to provide a reasonably truthful account from miscellaneous remains. Of course he must use the social sciences, but he must transcend the dogmas and theories. Like other literary artists, creators in the world of the word, and unlike the advancing social scientist, he is not engaged merely in correcting and revising his predecessors. He adds to our inheritance. At his best he is not accumulating knowledge which becomes obsolete, but creating a work with a life of its own. While Adam Smith survives in the reflected light of Ricardo and Marx and Keynes, Gibbon shines with a light all his own. The truth which the historian in any age finds in the past becomes part of our literary treasure. Inevitably the historian is torn between his efforts to create anew what he sees was really there, and the urgent shifting demands of the living audience. His motto could be Tertullian's rule of faith, *Credo quia impossible,* I believe because it is impossible. At his best he remains a Wrestler with the Angel.

CHAPTER 2

The Transforming of Paul Revere

W HEN A PAUL REVERE enters the history books, strange things
happen to him. He suddenly becomes the conscious agent of worldwide events. He is forced onto a stage which he never knew and
which exists only in retrospect. Historians tempt us to see him as the
harbinger of events that reverberated through the courts of Europe,
that shaped empires and the destiny of Kings, that would provide a
republic enduring for centuries. But we must try to rediscover him
as an energetic, enterprising, public-spirited, anxious, hopeful, and
provincial Bostonian.

To enter Paul Revere's own world in space and in time, we must
exercise what I have called "a willing suspension of knowledge." We
must try to forget what *we* now know was happening during those
years in London or Paris, and what was to follow in the next century.
We then can come down from our twentieth-century vantage point,
abandon the macrocosm for the microcosm, and find a new intimacy
and vividness in the past.

Paul Revere's own eyes were focused on Boston and its environs.
What happened even in Philadelphia or in New York entered his
experience only when it seemed to help or hinder his locally urgent
causes. The population of Boston as a whole, much less of New England, the thirteen colonies, or the British Empire, hardly entered
his consciousness. Demography, "medical knowledge," or "public
health" meant nothing compared to the yearly menace of smallpox
to his own family. Death had a vividness which statistics could only
conceal. Paul, born in 1735, the third of twelve children, was unusu-

ally lucky in that only two of his brothers or sisters died in infancy. Of Paul Revere's own sixteen children—eight by his first wife and eight by his second—five died in infancy. His grandchildren were the same age as his own younger children.

When news arrived in Boston that George Washington had died, Revere, as a prominent Mason, helped organize the town's funeral ceremony, which became a procession of the Masonic Lodge with all the ritual and regalia of Masonry. They mourned Washington more conspicuously as a fellow lodge member than as the Father of his Country. Plainly the death of the great Washington affected Revere far less than that of one of his own infant sons (which made him resolve at age fifty-one that he would have no more children, a resolution he did not keep), or the death of his beloved wife when he was seventy-eight, or of his eldest son when he was eighty-three.

Other episodes in Paul Revere's life help us recapture his own perspective on his "country" and what it meant to be a colonial Briton. As a twenty-one-year-old second lieutenant, he fought courageously with the British provincial forces against the French-held forts in lower Canada. It was no grandiose political theory or Rights of Man dogma that made him support the American cause. We see Sam Adams sensationalizing the threat of the newly enforced British taxes and trade regulations to the craftsmen of Boston. And we can see, too, how real was that burden and that threat.

Guy Fawkes' Day (in Boston known as Pope's Day) had long been celebrated by boisterous parades when town roughnecks, led by an eponymous "Joyce Jr.," spread terror among respectable citizens. As agitation against England gained momentum, these same roughnecks exploited the political opportunity. From where Paul Revere stood, the war for independence had much the aspect of a civil war. Yet, except for the much touted Boston Massacre there were remarkably few war casualties within the civilian population of Boston. The struggle did split families and caused deep pain among old friends. When General Howe's troops occupied Boston, they cleared the pew out of Old South Church to make a riding ring for the favorite mounted British regiment, saving only one pew for a pigsty. Then, when Howe evacuated Boston, he gave the city's Tories ten days to pack up and join him. Many of the town's wealthiest merchants and most respectable citizens "preferred the innovations of England to those of Sam Adams." In their haste they had to make the painful decisions that have afflicted refugees in every generation. To take the sheets or the family portraits? Warm underwear or the scarlet robes of a judge of the King's Court? What to do with the old dog? Few ever saw Boston again.

Besides helping to organize the town's "mechanics," Paul Revere served the coming Revolution mainly in the prosaic role of courier on horseback. We are reminded that for him this task became routine. In the winter of 1773, he carried news of the Boston Tea Party to the Committee of Correspondence (about 350 miles, covered at about sixty-three miles a day) in Philadelphia; the following year he rode to Philadelphia and back four times. He also brought news of the Boston Port Bill to fellow Sons of Liberty in New York City (a twelve-day round trip). To Boston's experienced and hardy courier, the celebrated trip to Lexington on "the eighteenth of April, in Seventy-five" was just another assignment. And on that legendary ride, one of his most important tasks was to rescue from Buckman's Tavern in Lexington John Hancock's trunk, which held treasonable documents and probably also Hancock's dandyish wardrobe.

Paul Revere's own time dimensions, like his spatial vision, were those of the clock and the rising sun, rather than the decades or centuries. Of course the outcome of the local struggle was far from certain, which made his personal situation riskier than it seems in retrospect. What was happening at that moment on the streets and in the shops and homes of Boston and the neighborhood loomed largest for him. When the Depression, which came with Britain's enforcement of the restrictions on colonial trade, made Boston customers scarce for Revere's silver cups, he branched out, using his skills and his tools to make copperplate prints and false teeth. Wartime inflation and threats of famine encouraged even a solid mechanic like Revere to invest his money in privateering. Challenging new assignments were his opportunity to print the first issue of Continental money, to set up a mill for gunpowder, and to make an official seal, still in use, for the state of Massachusetts.

Local sensations and scandals overshadowed the broad stream of history. How appalling that the eminently respectable Dr. Benjamin Church (Harvard, 1754; chief physician of the American army hospital in Cambridge), who had joined the inner Revolutionary councils along with John Adams and Joseph Warren, should be caught red-handed sending coded letters to the enemy! Though he was convicted in a court-martial, they somehow never could catch the scoundrel.

The notorious Deborah Sampson Gannett, who hardly lives in our textbooks, incited the tsk-tsk-tsk-ing of Boston gossips and the knowing winks of barflies. At twenty Deborah had run away from home disguised as a boy, and then enlisted in the Continental army. Especially tall for a girl in her time (5 feet 7 1/2 inches), with her lithe figure she was said to be "fleet as a gazell, bounding through swamps many rods ahead of her companions." As "Robert Shurtleff" she proved a "faithful and gallant soldier and at the same time preserved the virtue and chastity of her sex unsuspected and unblemished." Her unshaven "smock face" roused no suspicions because so many others in the army were still too young to shave. She was so modest, the story went, that when wounded, she had pried out the bullet herself rather than risk a physician's examination. When her sex was finally discovered, General Knox gave her an honorable discharge. Paul Revere took a special interest in her case. After the war when her earnings from her published adventures and from occasional lectures would not support her, he tried to persuade Congress to grant her a pension. "I think her case much more deserving than hundreds to whom Congress has been generous."

Paul Revere's own reputation in the Boston neighborhood was far from unblemished. There was enough doubt about his conduct at the ill-fated expedition at Penobscot in 1779 to lead to his being relieved of his command under suspicion of "unsoldierly conduct and cowardice," and then to his house arrest. It was three years before he had the satisfaction of acquittal by a court-martial. Bostonians were not quick to forget.

The progress of Revere's own long careers as "mechanic" and businessman dramatizes the opportunities of life in a colonial capital. If he had been living in London, guild restrictions would have prevented him from trying his hand so casually at so many different crafts. Today he remains best known for his elegant silver pieces, like the bowls that still bear his seal or the teapot that he holds in John Singleton Copley's portrait. But he was not above teaching himself copperplate engraving, and then producing second-rate frontispieces for singing books and works of history, or crude pictures of the Boston Massacre. When there was a need for dentists, and a scarcity of customers for silver pieces, he learned the art of fixing false teeth from a Mr. John Baker who had practiced that craft in Boston for a year and a half. Though Revere was prudent enough to confine his claims to cleaning teeth and setting "foreteeth," his advertisement in *The Boston Gazette and Country Journal* on July 30, 1770, was less modest: "He has fixed some Hundred of Teeth and he can fix them as well as any Surgeon-Dentist who ever came from London, he fixes them in such a Manner that they are not only an Ornament, but of real use in Speaking and Eating."

The eighty-three years of Paul Revere's life brought him from an era of colonial craftsmen into the early modern industrial New England. He was alert to the new local opportunities in the new age. Outside Lexington he found an old powder-mill property that was blessed with abundant waterpower. With $25,000 of his own money and a loan of $10,000 from the United States Government, he set up there a mill for rolling sheet copper, and devised an improved machine for the process. His foundry then provided the bolts, spikes, and copper accessories for the *Constitution* ("Old Ironsides"). "The carpenters gave nine cheers," setting out after the Algerian pirates that ship's log reported on June 26, 1803, "which was answered by the seamen and calkers, because they had in fourteen days completed coppering the ship with copper made in the United States." Working closely with Robert Fulton, he had a stake in the hidden future, for he used his process to roll copper plates for the boilers of Fulton's steamship.

In the great bells he cast for churches and town halls, this success as a versatile Boston "mechanic" still resounds. Revere had picked up the techniques from a French engineer who happened to stop at the Abington Inn. Revere then went after the needed copper and tin, dug a great pit for the molten mass, and proudly inscribed his product for the Second Church: "The first bell cast in Boston 1792 by P. Revere." Not discouraged when some said the bell sounded "panny, harsh and shrill," he went on to an additional prosperous career as bell founder, witnessed by the 2,437-pound bell (his largest) which in late twentieth century still hung in the stone tower of King's Chapel in his home town. Despite complaints that Revere had "no ear & perhaps knows nothing of the laws of sound and his excess of copper to ensure the strength of his bells depreciates their value," all could admire him as a most "enterprising mechanic." At his death in 1818 he left an estate valued at some $30,000, a fortune in those days.

CHAPTER 3

The Adamses: A Family in the Public Service

F ROM THE FORTUNES of the Adams family we can learn much that lies hidden in the lives of its separate members. The achievements of the individual Adamses are dazzling in their brilliance, gripping in their drama. But the family history moves in the long deep currents of American civilization. For four generations Adamses played leading roles in the decisive battles of national life: the American Revolution, the movement against slavery, the Civil War, the railroad conquest of the continent. If we can understand what the Adamses did for America, and what America did to the Adamses, we will witness not merely the fortunes of a family but the panoramic transformation of a nation.

As democracy in America progressed, the capacity of the Adamses for national leadership declined. An egalitarian nation, motley with recent immigrants, no longer acquiescent to genteel New England leadership, left the Adamses behind. And with them, their Calvinistic morality, their belief in the battle of Virtue against Vice, their independence of popular whim, their noblesse oblige. By the late nineteenth century, John Adams' talented but bitter descendants used all the apparatus of classical learning and modern physics to document their frustration, to justify their pessimism, to prove that what was wrong was not just with the Adams clan or with America, but with the forces at work in the universe.

At the same time that America abandoned the Adamses, the Adamses abandoned America. "I believe," John Adams wrote to Jefferson in 1819, "no effort in favour of Virtue is lost." But his great-grandson Henry Adams wrote to John Hay from Paris in 1900 that he cared "not one French sour grape how soon or how late this damned humanity breaks its neck." What had become of the patriotism and morality that had made John an enthusiast for the Revolution, and John Quincy a passionate opponent of slavery?

The Adams saga shows us how ill-adapted to this New World civilization were the ancient institutions for accumulating distinction, for accelerating and increasing the motives of noblesse. The Family, like many other of the most potent Old World institutions, was cumulative, while the civilization of the United States in every generation remained a miracle of renewal. America was an annual-model civilization—obsessively reaching for the latest and newest. Just as others had learned that the Best might be the enemy of the Good, so Americans learned that the Good might be the enemy of the New. And was not the willingness to experiment the grand modern virtue? Among the Adamses we see how a nation which they tried to purify of demagoguery and populism became alien to the arrogance of moral absolutes.

The proper attitude to public office, John Quincy Adams observed in December 1808, should be "that which philosophers teach us should guide our views of death—never to be desired, never to be feared." Adams uttered this stoic maxim after he resigned his office as United States Senator from Massachusetts. By voting against the party line of the Federalists who had elected him, he had aroused the ire of his former supporters. "As to holding my seat in the Senate of the United States without exercising the most perfect freedom of agency, under the sole and exclusive control of my own sense of right, that is out of the question." Independence of partisan rule and of public opinion was an admirable—and thankless—Adams tradition.

In one generation after another, the Adams passion for public service was not quite matched by indifference to public office. On a few crucial occasions, Adamses had the strength to follow John Quincy Adams' maxim. More often than not they suffered the human addiction to power and prestige. By their obstinate refusal to speak for anybody but themselves, they brought discontent and frustration to themselves, their wives and children.

During the nineteenth century the nation elaborated beyond all precedent the means to articulate public opinion and to publicize the common view. Whole new industries developed to inform leaders of the whimsies of current opinion and new institutions arose for bringing them to heel. Would there remain a place for Adamses? For men whose idiosyncrasy, obstinacy, and character compelled them to tell the people what the people did not already know and did not want to hear?

In the early years of the Republic, the Adams temperament—Adams integrity, Adams indifference to public whim—found a ready role in American political life. The changing careers of the Adamses would dramatize the transformation of American political life and leadership. By the early twentieth century, Adamses became refugees from statesmanship into the world of letters.

John Adams, the family's Founding Father, has become a national hero, but he was never a popular hero. If the American electoral process then had been as democratic as it later became, it is doubtful if John Adams ever would have been elected to anything. For he owed his electoral successes to the confidence of a few of his fellow-leaders. He was elected as a delegate from Massachusetts to the First Continental Congress in 1774 by the vote of the 129-member legislature of the colony. He was elected to two terms as Vice-President not by popular acclaim but by the votes of the Electoral College, when that small body was still functioning as the Founding Fathers intended. When Adams was elected President in 1796, the electorate was still much restricted, and political parties had only begun to dominate the Electoral College by their instructions. By 1800, when national parties had the Electoral College firmly in control, Adams was not reelected. Adams' refusal to be a party man—even for the Federalist Party which his political philosophy had helped to found—ended his career in national office. "I have never sacrificed my judgment," he insisted, "to kings, ministers, nor people, and I never will." His political adversaries had to recognize his independence. "He is vain, irritable," Jefferson noted as early as 1787, "and a bad calculator of the force and probable effect of the motives which govern men. This is all the ill which can possibly be said of him. He is as disinterested as the Being who made him."

The career of John's son, John Quincy Adams, showed a similar pattern. So obstinate and dyspeptic a character as John Quincy could hardly have attained high elective office if the gift had not still been in hands of a small number of knowledgeable colleagues. He described himself in his diary as "a man of reserved, cold, austere, and forbidding manners: my political adversaries say, a gloomy misanthropist, and my personal enemies, an unsocial savage. With a knowledge of the actual defect in my character, I have not the pliability to reform it." He was elected to the United States Senate in 1803, not by the whole electorate of Massachusetts, but by the State legislature. And when this Adams was elected President in 1824, it was not by the national suffrage but by the House of Representatives, who had the power in that year to elect a President because none of the four candidates had received a majority of votes in the Electoral College. In 1828, John Quincy Adams, like his father before him, was not reelected; and his defeat by Andrew Jackson signaled the rise of populistic democracy. John Quincy Adams' second career—his seventeen years in the House of Representatives as a champion of the right of petition and of antislavery—was made possible by the confidence of his friends and neighbors in the farming district of Plymouth, which sent him to Washington with 1,817 votes of a district total of 2,565.

John Quincy Adams' son, Charles Francis Adams, was once elected to the House of Representatives, but after that no Adams was elected to an office in the national government. Charles Francis' brilliant and subtle diplomacy as United States Minister in London was crucial in keeping peace with Great Britain during the Civil War, in preventing Britain from siding with the South, and so in helping the North to victory. In a letter to his son, Charles Francis Adams, Jr., the elder Charles Francis summed up the family's political credo, and explained why, as partisanship and public opinion became more powerful on the national political scene, Adamses would be less conspicuous there. First among the qualifications of a statesman, he said, was "the mastery of the whole theory of morals which makes the foundation of all human society. The great and everlasting question of the right and wrong of every act whether of individual men or of collective bodies."

> In my opinion no man who has lived in America had so thoroughly constructed a foundation for his public life as your grandfather [John Quincy Adams]. His action was always deducible from certain maxims deeply graven on his mind. This it was that made him fail so much as a party-man. No person can be a thorough partisan for a long period without sacrifice of his moral identity. The skill consists in knowing exactly where to draw the line.

In the next generation, the achievements of the family were to be of another order. How and where "to draw the line"?

The Adams passion for public service did not die, but it became difficult—or impossible—for Adamses to satisfy that passion by election to office. Of Charles Francis Adams' four sons, only John Quincy Adams II sought the favor of a large electorate. He was several times elected to the Massachusetts state legislature, and once received the nomination for Vice President on a splinter-party ticket, but he repeatedly failed in his bid to be elected governor. Charles Francis, Jr., was among the first to sense that "application of steam to locomotion" was "the most tremendous and far-reaching engine of social revolution which has either blessed or cursed the earth." "I fixed on the railroad system," he said, "as the most developing force and largest field of the day, and determined to attach myself to it." But as for politics, he remained "convinced that I have no aptitude, I lack magnetism frightfully, & have no facility of doing the right thing at the right time. I am frightfully deficient in tact; I never can remember faces or names, and so I am by nature disqualified. I never could be a popular man." "I never could overcome my pre-natal manner, and learn to say gracious things in a gracious way." This Adams had to find his path into the bustling railroad world through the genteel pages of the *North American Review.* He created a niche for himself in the public service by persuading the Massachusetts legislature to set up the first State Railroad Commission, and then he secured appointment to it by the governor. His work made it a model for the regulatory commissions which became a fixture of twentieth-century America.

The Adamses kept their instinct for the sources of power. Charles Francis, Jr.'s vision of the new Industrial Leviathan was matched by his brother Henry's vision of the new power of opinion embodied in the newspaper press. With his usual unconvincing self-deprecation Henry recalled his thoughts on his own career, when he was a young man in his mid-twenties:

One profession alone seemed possible—the Press. In 1860 he would have said that he was born to be an editor, like at least a thousand other young graduates from American colleges who entered the world every year enjoying the same conviction; but in 1866 the situation was altered; the possession of money had become doubly needful for success, and double energy was essential to get money. America had more than doubled her scale. Yet the press was still the last resource of the educated poor who could not be artists and would not be tutors. Any man who was fit for nothing else could write an editorial or a criticism. The enormous mass of misinformation accumulated in ten years of nomad life could always be worked off on a helpless public, in diluted doses, if one could but secure a table in the corner of a newspaper office. The press was an inferior pulpit; an anonymous schoolmaster; a cheap boarding-school; but it was still the nearest approach to a career for the literary survivor of a wrecked education. For the press, then, Henry Adams decided to fit himself, and since he could not go home to get practical training, he set to work to do what he could in London.

Returning to the United States after seven years abroad, Henry kept this focus for his ambition. "For large work," Henry observed, "he could count on the *North American Review,* but this was scarcely a press." The circulation of the *Review* then was about 300! Yet, Henry noted, "for fifty years the *North American Review* had been the stage coach which carried literary Bostonians to such distinction as they had achieved." Well aware of these limitations, Henry Adams knew that "what he needed was a New York daily, and no New York daily needed him." So, with characteristic indirection, he decided to go to Washington where, by writing occasional columns for "the Free-trade Holy Land of the [New York] *Evening Post* under William Cullen Bryant," he hoped to work his way up to a regular position on that height of potent heights—a New York daily.

It was by default then that Henry Adams later turned to history. And through lack of other more contemporary outlets, Henry Adams became one of the great American historians of the century. To him, historical writing was a convenient vehicle for expressing his affected indifference to passing fads and to the tyranny of public opinion. His most important work was a nine-volume history of the sixteen years of the administrations of Presidents Jefferson and Madison. "The author is a peculiar man," Charles Scribner, the publisher, wrote to a business associate in London, explaining why he had not tried to secure the publication of those volumes in England, "and [he] don't care whether his book sells or not." Henry Adams' most widely read works, those on which his popular fame would rest—*Mont-St.-Michel and Chartres* and *The Education of Henry Adams*—he had privately printed. The *Mont-St.-Michel* (which Henry himself had had printed in 100 copies) was nearly posthumous for it was published under the auspices of the American Institute of Architects after the author had suffered the incapacitating stroke in 1912 which ended his writing career. The *Education* was posthumously published by the Massachusetts Historical Society.

Each of the Adamses, in his own fashion, preserved a posture of superiority to the verdict of the marketplace. But from the first generation of famous Adamses that posture was largely a pose. John Adams himself had fervently hoped for the honor of the Presidency. "I am weary of the game," he wrote to Abigail at the prospect of being elected to follow George Washington, "yet I don't know how I could live out of it. I don't love slight, neglect, contempt, disgrace, nor insult, more than others." Both John and John Quincy were deeply wounded by the nation's refusal to return either of them to a second term as President. John Quincy Adams never restrained his rage against "the skunks of party slander."

Toward the end of the nineteenth century, the same Adamses who pretended to set themselves above the vulgar opinion were yearning for best-sellerdom. Retreat from the White House and Congress, from State Street to the historian's study did not relieve them of their concern for what "everybody" thought of them. When Charles Francis Adams, Jr., turned from managing railroads to writing the colonial history of New England, he constantly wondered how many were listening. "If I could have heard that 20,000 copies of the 'Three Episodes' [of Massachusetts History] had been sold, my dearest ambition would have been satisfied; but I didn't hear it, and I never shall hear it." Henry Adams was anything but indifferent to the favorable reviews that the New York press gave to his *History*. How pleasant, he observed, to have "solid butter laid on with a trowel"! But how much more pleasant if the buying public had actually bought his books in large numbers. He compared himself to Gibbon and Macaulay, and resented the fact that the public did not do the same. In his *Education*, perhaps to conceal the depth of his resentment, he skipped over his work on that *History* (along with his marriage of thirteen years).

The Adams tradition of public service was not built without cost. Different members of the family, according to their sex, their age, and their natural temperament, were all called upon to pay a price. The least celebrated Adamses were, of course, the women. And if we ever doubted that women are the Forgotten Men of history, the Adams epic should remind us. While the men of the Adams family were performing their heroic deeds in public, the Adams women were doing a private work which required characters no less stoic and courageous.

The only female Adams who has had anything like her due from historians is John's wife, Abigail (1744–1818). Still, despite the fact that she was one of the brightest, most public-minded, and most sacrificing of the family, she has been treated as little more than a mirror for her husband and the age. The entry for her in the concise edition of the authoritative *Dictionary of American Biography* sums her up in the single phrase: "Wrote distinguished letters containing vivid pictures of the times." Her personal contribution, and her essential part in the careers of her husband John and her eldest son John Quincy, have not yet had the spotlight.

"Our history," Charles Francis Adams complained in his Memoir of his grandmother Abigail in 1875, "is for the most part wrapped up in the forms of office." And in explaining the sacrifices of Abigail he clearly revealed the institutions which confined her and hid her from view. "In every instance of domestic convulsions, and when the pruning hook is deserted for the sword and musket, the sacrifice of feelings made by the female sex is unmixed with a hope of worldly compensation. With them there is no ambition to gratify, no fame to be gained by the simple negative virtue of privations suffered in silence. There is no action to drown in its noise and bustle a full sense of the pain that must inevitably attend it. The lot of women, in times of trouble, is to be a passive spectator of events which she can scarcely hope to make subservient to her own fame, or indeed to control in any way."

Abigail Adams' accomplishments are doubly remarkable because in her youth, as she observed, "it was fashionable to ridicule female learning." "My early education," she recalled in 1817, "did not partake of the abundant opportunities which the present days offer, and which even our common country schools now afford. *I never was sent to any school.* I was always sick. Female education, in the best families, went no further than writing and arithmetic; in some few and rare instances, music and dancing." The custom of the age condemned her to the private heroics of loneliness and long separations from those she loved. In the midst of her husband's years of absence (1779–1784) on a diplomatic mission to France and England for the new nation, she wrote (December 23, 1782):

I look back to the early days of our acquaintance and friendship, as to the days of love and innocence, and with an indescribable pleasure I have seen near a score of years roll over our heads, with an affection heightened and improved by time; nor have the dreary years of absence in the smallest degree effaced from my mind the image of the dear, untitled man to whom I gave my heart. I cannot sometimes refrain considering the honors with which he is invested as badges of my unhappiness. . . . Yet a cruel world too often injures my feelings by wondering how a person possessed of domestic attachments can sacrifice them by absenting herself *for years*.

"If you had known," said a person to me the other day, "that Mr. Adams would have remained so long abroad, would you have consented that he should have gone?" I recollected myself a moment and then spoke the real dictates of my heart: "If I had known, sir, that Mr. Adams could have effected what he has done, I would not only have submitted to the absence I have endured, painful as it has been, but I would not have opposed it, even though three years more should be added to the number (which Heaven avert!). I feel a pleasure in being able to sacrifice my selfish passions to the general good, and in imitating the example which has taught me to consider myself and family but as the small dust of the balance, when compared with the great community."

During those lonely years she had heavy and diverse responsibilities: to direct the family farm, to record prices current and rates of exchange and make up the invoices to keep the farm afloat, to report political facts, to be mother and father to the children at home, and to instruct her absent eldest son in his morals and his duties.

She showed more than domestic fortitude. Later, when she rejoined her husband as the first woman in a diplomatic mission from the United States to Great Britain, she endured the snubs of Queen Charlotte and the court, and helped the ministry of the United States, despite strictest economy, cut a respected figure in London.

Even John Adams' Presidency did not end the times of separation. While Adams was serving as President in the capital at Philadelphia, Abigail—partly because of her illness, partly because of the high cost of everything—remained for long periods at Quincy. In a letter to her in February 1797, he explained the tribulations of the Presidency:

I hope you will not communicate to anybody the hints I give you about our prospects, but they appear every day worse and worse. House rent at twenty-seven hundred dollars a year, fifteen hundred dollars for a carriage, one thousand for one pair of horses, all the glasses, ornaments, kitchen furniture, the best chairs, settees, plateaus, etc., all to purchase, all the china, delf or wedgwood, glass and crockery of every sort to purchase, and not a farthing probably will the House of Representatives allow, although the Senate have voted a small addition. All the linen besides. I shall not pretend to keep more than one pair of horses for a carriage, and one for a saddle. Secretaries, servants, wood, charities which are demanded as rights, and the million dittoes present such a prospect as is enough to disgust anyone. Yet not one word must we say.

On November 1, 1800, when he became the first resident of the White House, he asked "heaven to bestow the best of blessings on this house, and on all that shall hereafter inhabit it. May none but honest and wise men ever rule under this roof!" Abigail, hastening down from Quincy to join him, lost her way on the muddy paths from Baltimore to the swamps then called Washington. They spent only an unhappy few months there, watching the nation refuse John Adams his expected accolade of a second term, and incidentally preparing the residence for occupancy by a bitter enemy.

From about the time of her husband's election to the Presidency, Abigail suffered an intermittent fever from which she never fully recovered. From 1801 until her death in 1818, she stayed at Quincy. Despite a series of family tragedies—a daughter lost in infancy, a son who died in 1800, the death of her only remaining daughter in 1813—she remained "a mortal enemy to anything but a cheerful countenance and a merry heart, which, Solomon tells us, does good like a medicine."

The other female Adamses, who lacked Abigail's epistolary eloquence, were left unsung, and almost unnoticed in history. Mrs. John Quincy Adams (Louisa Johnson Adams), born to an English mother and a Maryland father who was then the United States Consul in London, had lived her youth in France. On a meager budget, in extravagant St. Petersburg, she managed to maintain the dignity of a United States ministry, and, while Napoleon was approaching Paris, she conveyed her son Charles Francis across Europe to their new assignment in London. But she remains a shadowy figure, now best remembered through Henry Adams' characterization. "Louisa was charming, like a Romney portrait, but among her many charms that of being a New England woman was not one. The defect was serious. Her future mother-in-law, Abigail, . . . was troubled by the fear that

Louisa might not be made of stuff stern enough, or brought up in conditions severe enough, to suit a New England climate, or to make an efficient wife for her paragon son, and Abigail was right on that point, as on most others where sound judgment was involved. . . ." Henry as a boy saw her in her seventies "thoroughly weary of being beaten about a stormy world. To the boy she seemed singularly peaceful, a vision of silver gray, presiding over her old President and her Queen Anne mahogany; an exotic, like her Sèvres china; an object of deference to everyone, and of great affection to her son Charles; but hardly more Bostonian than she had been fifty years before, on her wedding-day, in the shadow of the Tower of London."

As for Henry's mother, Mrs. Charles Francis Adams (née Abigail Brown Brooks), he mentions her only twice in his *Education.* Once, to note that she was one of the seven surviving children who shared the bequest of "what was supposed to be the largest estate in Boston, about two million dollars," and again, with some flippancy, to observe that while his father was the United States Minister "her success and popularity in England exceeded that of her husband" and that she "averred that every woman who lived a certain time in England came to look and dress like an Englishwoman, no matter how she struggled." On the subject of this devoted and long-suffering mother, Charles Francis, Jr., is hardly more articulate than his brother. The only account of her in Charles Francis, Jr.'s own *Autobiography* recalls how she "at once fell into tears and deep agitation" when word was received in 1861 that her husband had been named Minister to Great Britain. "My mother, in some respects remarkably calculated for social life, took a constitutional and sincere pleasure in the forecast of evil. She delighted in the dark side of anticipation; she did not really think so; but liked to think, and say, she thought so. She indulged in the luxury of woe!"

From his *Education* Henry entirely omitted his own wife, Marion Hooper, perhaps because he felt her death so deeply, and held himself partly responsible. He did commission a memorial to her by Saint-Gaudens, which still stands in Rock Creek Park in Washington, but he would not talk about her after she died, and was known to leave the room when her name was mentioned. Henry's attitude toward women remains a dark conundrum which conceals the women we would like to learn about through him. In *Mont-St.-Michel and Chartres* he asserted with theological dogmatism the superiority of "Woman." At the same time he pontificated to his friend, Mrs. Winthrop Chanler, "American woman is a failure, she has held nothing together, neither State nor Church, nor Society nor Family. . . . On the whole I think she is a worse failure than the American man who is surely failure enough." Since his view of women—he preferred to call them "Woman"—was so extravagantly theological and sociological, it is small wonder that he had problems with individuals. His relations to his wife, with whom for many years he held one of the most successful salons ever known in Washington, were shrouded in posthumous gloom. His romantic attachment, after his wife's death, to Elizabeth Cameron, the attractive young wife of Senator James Donald Cameron, is puzzling and impenetrable. He revealed a traditional Adams problem when he told Elizabeth Cameron that "women are naturally neither daughters, sisters, lovers, nor wives, but mothers."

Perhaps the most tortured of Adams wives was Brooks's wife, "Daisy" Davis, the sister of Mrs. Henry Cabot Lodge, whom he married within a month after he met her. When he proposed, he warned her that he was "an eccentric almost to the point of madness" and that if she married him "she must do it on her own responsibility and at her own risk." This warning was one of the few understatements that the unstable Brooks ever uttered. She spent her life as nurse, scapegoat, travel agent, guide, and psychotherapist to the most frustrated of an easily frustrated clan.

If the democratic politician needs the capacity to make friends, the Adamses were staggeringly unqualified. While the Adamses had a talent for intimacy with a chosen few, they also possessed a remarkable talent for making enemies. Partly, it was a matter of temperament. "The Adamses have a genius," James Russell Lowell explained, "for saying even a gracious thing in an ungracious way!" "If it were not that I was under the perpetual stimulus of family pride," observed Charles Francis Adams at the age of twenty-seven, "I would never mix."

But, in a sense, too, it was a matter of principle. For them, the other side of personal independence was a contempt both for elegant opinion and for "vulgar opinion." Virtue, it seemed, must have a certain gruffness. "I cannot help suspecting," John Adams noted in Paris before the French Revolution, "that the more elegance, the less virtue, in all times and countries." Yet, at the same time, a democracy with no check on the whim of the populace was "the most ignoble, unjust, and detestable form of government." The Adamses' view of the world and of their own role in the public service thus made them peculiarly adept at casting others in the role of "enemies."

Personal independence meant being wary of dependence on *any*one's good opinion. "You recommend me to attend the town-meetings and make speeches; to meet with caucuses and join political clubs," the young John Quincy Adams wrote his father in April 1794, "But I am afraid of all these things. They might make me a better politician, and give me an earlier chance of appearing as a public man; but that would throw me completely in the power of the people, and all my future life would be one of dependence. I had rather continue some time longer in obscurity, and make some provision for fortune, before I sally out in quest of fame or of public honors." Perhaps it was this fear of dependence along with a dyspeptic caution that led him to another "principle," which he had learned from a boyhood crush on an actress whom he had seen performing in the Bois de Boulogne when he lived in Paris with his father and Benjamin Franklin—"that lesson of never forming an acquaintance with an actress to which I have since invariably adhered, and which I would lay as an injunction on all my sons."

When his son Charles Francis was first elected to the Massachusetts legislature in 1840, John Quincy warned him against the "opposition and defeats and slanders and treacheries, and above all fickleness of public favor." And this same Charles Francis warned *his* son Charles Francis, Jr., from London in November 1861 against the demagogues who "become the mere sport of fortune. Today they shine because they have caught at a good opportunity. Tomorrow, the light goes out and they are found mired at the bottom of a ditch. These are the men of temporary celebrity. . . . Every civilised nation is full of them. . . . They sacrifice their consistency for the sake of power, and surrender their future fame in exchange for the applause of their own day."

This lesson was not lost either on the fourth generation of eminent Adamses. Henry had a deep suspicion of democracy. "Like Henry," Brooks wrote in 1919, "I inherited a belief in the great democratic dogma, as I inherited my pew in the church at Quincy, but . . . I reverted to the pure Calvinistic philosophy." When President Eliot of Harvard, having heard one of Brooks's lectures at the Law School, observed that Brooks seemed to have little respect for democracy, Brooks retorted, "Do you think I'm a damned fool!"

The only eminent Adams who professed respect for popular opinion was the only one who had deserted the Statehouse and the library
for the marketplace. Charles Francis Adams, Jr., explained in 1878
that the purpose of the Massachusetts Railroad Commission, a pioneer regulatory agency which he helped create, was to serve "as a
sort of lens by means of which the scattered rays of public opinion
could be concentrated to a focus and brought to bear upon a given
point." The foundation of his lifelong effort at railroad reform in the
heyday of the railroad buccaneers was his faith in "the eventual
supremacy of an enlightened public opinion." But he had only contempt for his successful business associates. "Business success—
moneygetting," he remarked, ". . . comes from a rather low instinct.
. . . it is rarely met with in combination with the finer or more
interesting traits of character. I have known, and known tolerably
well, a good many 'successful' men—'big' financially—men famous
during the last half-century; and a less interesting crowd I do not care
to encounter. Not one that I have ever known would I care to meet
again, either in this world or in the next; nor is one of them associated
in my mind with the idea of humor, thought or refinement."

The compromising world of public opinion was not a natural
habitat for Adamses. They felt at home only in a world of moral
purposes, where compromise was weakness and the battle was between Virtue and Vice. "In every civilization," Brooks Adams concluded in 1919, "there are, as Saint Paul pointed out, two principles
in conflict—the law, or the moral principle, and the flesh, or the evil
principle."

In the mind of the fighting Adamses there was, of course, never
any doubt of the side on which they were destined to be generals.
"Your father and grandfather," John Quincy wrote to his son Charles
Francis in 1840, "have fought their way through the world against
hosts of adversaries, open and close, disguised and masked; with
many lukewarm and more than one or two perfidious friends. The
world is and will continue to be prolific of such characters. Live in
peace with them; never upbraid, never trust them. But—'don't give
up the ship!' Fortify your mind against disappointments—*aequam
memento rebus in arduis servare mentem*—keep up your courage,
and go ahead!" This conviction of personal rectitude saved one
Adams after another from the temptation to give public answer to
enemies. They took a lofty attitude to those very electoral bodies
whose favor they needed, they refused to build a patronage machine,

and when slandered chose not to collect and publish the documents they possessed that would exonerate them. As a consequence, they bottled up their hatreds, and wrote off their opponents as the unregenerate cohorts of evil. In the ceaseless war between Virtue and Vice, the defeat of any one generation of Adamses was only a minor skirmish. "I believe," declared John Adams, "no effort in favor of virtue is lost."

While this obstinacy—their Puritan forebears would have called it a stiff-necked pride—at one time actually helped make them statesmen, it made them poor politicians. The lifeblood of an increasingly democratic America was competition and compromise. But, beginning with John Adams, the family constructed its own Rogue's Gallery of Public Enemies. John Adams could not tolerate Benjamin Franklin, he came to detest Alexander Hamilton; and he became friendly to Thomas Jefferson only after both had retired from active life. John Quincy Adams (then an unmellow fifty-nine) wrote in his diary for November 23, 1835, after complaining of the "conspiracy against me" at the conference at Ghent:

> Among the dark spots in human nature which, in the course of my life, I have observed, the devices of rivals to ruin me have been sorry pictures of the heart of man. They first exhibited themselves at college, but in the short time that I was there their operation could not be of much effect. But from the day I quitted the walls of Harvard, Harrison Gray Otis, Theophilus Parsons, Timothy Pickering, James A. Bayard, Henry Clay, Jonathan Russell, William H. Crawford, John C. Calhoun, Andrew Jackson, Daniel Webster, and John Davis, W. B. Giles, and John Randolph, have used up their faculties in base and dirty tricks to thwart my progress in life and destroy my character.

Passionate enmities, though shifting from generation to generation, were an Adams inheritance.

It is not surprising, then, that the great-grandsons of John Adams, Henry and Brooks, who had given up the political battle, translated the penchant for personal enmity into cosmic terms. Brooks, who saw "the flesh . . . incarnated in the principle of competition . . . rooted in the passions of greed, avarice, and cruelty," cast bankers, the centralizing moneyed interests, in a Satanic role. Henry, too, fell prey to his own version of the Protocols of the Elders of Zion, and felt compelled to believe that the forces of Evil were well organized in some conspiracy. At the same time both Henry and Brooks, in remarkable feats of intellectual acrobatics, balanced the dogmas of nineteenth-century physics on the dogmas of seventeenth-century morality. In nineteenth-century America, the sharp moral edges of the Puritan world were being dissolved. When the Adamses became confused, they took refuge in the cosmos.

The large forces of an increasingly democratic America, which made it harder than ever for Adamses to play an active role on the national political scene, also explained why the family's aristocratic tradition—its tradition of noblesse oblige—became a burden. Charles Francis Adams, Jr., noted the resentment that his father, Charles Francis, had come to feel. The "constant reference" to John and John Quincy

> in connection with himself annoyed and at times irritated him. He could not habituate himself to it, nor learn to take it lightly and as matter of course,—at one time the commonplace utterance of some not unkindly man, devoid of good taste, and at another the obvious retort of a coarse and commonplace opponent, quick to avail himself of a telling personal allusion. For all such it was so very easy to refer to a noticeable family deterioration,—"sharp decline" was the approved form of speech—and the reference was sure to elicit a sneering laugh, and round of blockhead applause from the benches of the groundlings. . . . To have one's ancestors unceasingly flung in one's face is unpleasant, and listening to the changes incessantly rung upon them becomes indubitably monotonous.

The weight of the family inheritance accumulated through the century. But the future of that inheritance had been revealed to the prophetic vision of John Adams himself. "I must study politics and war," he wrote, "that my sons may have liberty to study mathematics and philosophy. My sons ought to study mathematics and philosophy, geography, natural history and naval architecture, navigation, commerce and agriculture, in order to give their sons a right to study painting, poetry, music, architecture, statuary, tapestry and porcelain." John Adams' generation was peculiarly posterity-conscious. Jefferson, too, was haunted by his duty to the future. But while Jefferson was preoccupied with Man in general, Adams saw in his own descendants the representatives of a developing nation.

In societies less committed to judge each generation on its own merit, the accumulated glory of the Adams family could have provided an increasingly solid foundation for the public careers of later generations. But the United States was a nation of the uprooted. "We may consider each generation as a distinct nation," declared Jefferson, "with a right, by the will of its majority, to bind themselves, but none to bind the succeeding generation, more than the inhabitants of another country."

By the fourth generation, the family had become preoccupied with itself, entangled in its own past, in a fashion characteristically un-American. As early as 1860, Henry Adams, who had been reading Gibbon, concluded, "Our house needs a historian in this generation and I feel strongly tempted by the quiet and sunny prospect." But even before Henry the House of Adams had begun to write its own history. Charles Francis Adams spent seven years editing ten volumes of the letters and papers of his grandfather John and another ten years editing twelve volumes of the diary of his father John Quincy. Charles Francis, Jr., spent his last years writing about Colonial Massachusetts, as well as a biography of his father. But in his own *Autobiography*, Charles Francis, Jr., records, with masochistic delight, how he disposed of the diaries of his youth:

> In those years I kept a diary. So doing was enjoined on me by my father; and I kept it from my Latin School days until the time I went into the army, in my twenty-fifth year. Later on I kept the volumes sealed up in a package, with directions that they should be destroyed in the event of my death. A few years ago . . . I opened the parcel, and looked through the volumes. I did this during my Sundays, passed in the house at Quincy while living in Boston—very charming Sundays they were, too. . . . During those days I exhumed the sealed package, and thirty years later, read over that old diary. The revelation of myself to myself was positively shocking. Then and there I was disillusioned. Up to that time—and I was then about fifty-five—I had indulged in the pleasing delusion that it was in me . . . to do, or be, something rather noticeable. I have never thought so since. . . . I saw myself in a looking-glass, and I said—"Can that indeed be I!" and, reflecting, I then realized that the child was father of the man! It was with difficulty I forced myself to read through that dreadful record; and, as I finished each volume, it went into the fire; and I stood over it until the last leaf was ashes. It was a tough lesson; but a useful one. I had seen myself as others had seen me. I have never felt the same about myself since. I now humbly thank fortune that I have almost got through life without making a conspicuous ass of myself.

At the opening of the twentieth century, the Adamses had made a profession of their family history, and were jealous, resentful, even uncharitable to their forebears. Henry was deeply pained when he read his brother Charles's biography of their father. "Now I understand," he exclaimed, "why I refused so obstinately to do it myself. These biographies are murder, and in this case, to me, would be both patricide and suicide. They belittle the victim and the assassin equally. They are like bad photographs and distorted perspectives. . . . I have sinned myself, and deeply, and am no more worthy to be called anything, but, thank my diseased and dyspeptic nervous wreck, I did not assassinate my father."

When Charles Francis, Jr., the eldest of his generation, thought of joining the Union Army to fulfill the family's patriotic tradition, he consulted his father. "My father, with the coldness of temperament natural to him, took a wholly wrong view of the subject and situation, did not believe in any one taking a hand in actual fight, and wholly failed to realize that it would have been an actual disgrace had his family, of all possible families American, been wholly unrepresented in the field. And I was the one to go!" When Charles Francis, Jr., had put the question, his father had simply replied, "But none of his predecessors had been soldiers. Why should he?" To preserve the family's reputation, Charles Francis, Jr., broke a family tradition. He served in the Union cavalry with bravery and distinction, reaching the rank of brevet brigadier-general.

To reveal the special relations of Family to Democracy, the fourth generation—that of John Quincy II, Charles Francis, Jr., Henry, and Brooks—is the most articulate. In that generation, men of large talents found themselves conspicuously unable to come to terms with their noble inheritance. They spent themselves in quarreling with one another, in debunking their Puritan ancestry, and, finally, in maligning the human race. This is all worth reflecting on as a parable of the impossibility of noblesse oblige ("A noble inheritance obliges noble actions") in a democracy. That fourth generation, it is also worth noticing, was actually the first in which all the family started with a comfortable money inheritance.

The Adams saga, then, unfolded with a providential American irony. The most distinguished American family inheritance, after only *four* generations (which would have been a brief chapter in the lives of the Cecils, the Percys, the Churchills, or other distinguished Old World families), had already become a burden. In a nation which idolized the self-made man, anything could be embarrassing that kept a man from standing on his own feet. Later Adamses might survive the burden by finding each for himself his own path.

By the end of the nineteenth century, these most articulate Adamses had begun to luxuriate in their decadence. They made a literary profession of crying nay to the world around them. This was the same family whose founder John, in the era of the American Revolution, had rejoiced that his generation was to be the vanguard of a new civilization. Brooks Adams ended his *Law of Civilization and Decay* (1896) in a purple lament:

> No poetry can bloom in the arid modern soil, the drama has died, and the patrons of art are no longer even conscious of shame at profaning the most sacred of ideals. The ecstatic dream, which hallowed by the presence of his God, is reproduced to bedizen a warehouse; or the plan of an abbey, which Saint Hugh may have consecrated, is adapted to a railway station.

To make his civilization less like the Rome of Caracalla and more like the Athens of Pericles, he called for the infusion of a "stream of barbarian blood." But Brooks's was the wail of a narcissistic generation, not the swan song of a civilization. The Adamses had long enjoyed the illusion of confusing themselves with the cosmos. The fourth-generation scions proved unqualified to recognize new creative forces. Dazzled by their own ancestors, they were disappointed in themselves. How could they understand that the civilization which Adamses had helped build had flourished only because it found ways for new John Adamses to spring out of each anonymous generation?

CHAPTER 4

The Intimacy of Gibbon's
Decline and Fall

THERE ARE MANY REASONS to admire Edward Gibbon's *History of the Decline and Fall of the Roman Empire*. Since it was first published in several volumes between 1776 and 1788, few books of history have been so widely or so indiscriminately praised. His twentieth-century editor, historian J. B. Bury, calls him "one of those few writers who hold as high a place in the history of literature as in the roll of great historians." Most students of history and of literature would agree.

Praise of Gibbon (1737–1794) has become especially fashionable with the rise of liberal and Marxist prejudices against religion. And, as pessimism has become increasingly fashionable about the future of our Western civilization, the *Decline and Fall of the Roman Empire* has become a handy guide to the sources of decay in other empires and civilizations. I will not enter the debate over the adequacy of Gibbon's explanations of the fall of Rome. Nor will I explore the easy—or uneasy—analogies between the career of the ancient Roman Empire and that of our modern Western civilization.

My interest in Gibbon's work is quite different. I will not assess it as a "great" book. Rather I will consider it as an "intimate" book. By this I mean a book that has something personal to say to us today. I am aware that it may seem odd to characterize a man of Gibbon's grandiloquence of phrase and a multivolume work on such a grandiose subject as "intimate."

For me personally Gibbon's book has an especially intimate significance. It was the first extensive work of English literature (or of history) which I read and reread. It occupied much of my thought during my university years as an undergraduate. And the engraving of Gibbon's rotund face, made by Chapman in 1807, a dozen years after his death, hangs on the wall of my study. Gibbon's face has been with me ever since I first made his acquaintance.

Gibbon's work can have an intimate, personal significance for all history readers and history writers in our age. He may help us discover some of the peculiar weaknesses and strengths of our way of looking at the past. To discover this intimacy we must try to see Gibbon not simply as a spokesman for the Enlightenment, nor his work as an effort to perfect one genre in the social sciences. Rather, let us think of him as an original, giving his own form to a large chunk of the past.

Toward this end it will help us at the outset to recognize a distinctive, if not entirely unique, feature of his place in the roll of great Western historians. Despite the wide popularity and continuity of Gibbon's audience, he seems not to have founded a "Gibbonian" school of historical interpretation. For example, the authoritative *International Encyclopedia of the Social Sciences,* which includes extensive articles on such lesser figures as Bryce, Burckhardt, Huizinga, Maitland, Ranke, Savigny, and Spengler, gives no such attention to Gibbon. Serious scholars do not doubt the originality or the significance of Gibbon's work. Still, he has not become the founder of a "school." He has not taken a place as the originator of any large new conceptual framework, or any novel way of pigeonholing the human past. I will suggest that this is a clue to the intimacy of his message about that past, and what he can tell each of us about the role of people in the grand chronicle of empires and civilizations.

The historical profession, with all its paraphernalia of learned societies and prestigious academic specialties, has grown up only since Gibbon's day. Not until the early nineteenth century did professional historians reach beyond the techniques of classical scholarship and textual criticism, to draw on the new disciplines of archaeology and philology, anthropology, sociology, and economics, to create new vocations of searchers for facts and movements and forces.

It is doubtful if there is another example in the social sciences of a work of similar longevity, respectability, and popularity, which has had so small a dogmatic or doctrinaire ingredient. The comprehensive historical works of recent years—those which are taken seriously by students of the social sciences—are heavily laced with dogma. I am thinking of the potent works, for example, of Macaulay, Carlyle, Marx, Pareto, Tawney, and Toynbee. These seem to owe much of their fame and their influence to the special charm of some new formulas to explain or contain historical experience.

How, then, can we explain the power and longevity and appeal of Gibbon, despite his lack of substantial original conceptual content?

In the first place, we must remember that Gibbon had the advantage of being an amateur. Unlike some other great interpreters of the past, many of whom were also amateurs, he was not enticed or driven to his subject by the urgencies of his time, or by a revolutionary, a religious, or a patriotic passion. In the original sense of the word "amateur," he was simply a lover of his subject. And in a famous passage in his memoirs he recalls the precise moment when, as he sat in the Colosseum in Rome, he first felt that passion. In another, less famous passage, he recalled his mixed emotions as that exacting love affair came to an end:

> It was on the night of June 27, 1787, between the hours of eleven and twelve, that I wrote the last lines of the last page, in a Summerhouse garden.... I will not dissemble the first emotions of joy on the recovery of my freedom, and perhaps, the establishment of my fame. But my pride was soon humbled, and a sober melancholy was spread over my mind, by the idea that I had taken an everlasting leave of an old and agreeable companion, and that whatsoever might be the future date of my History, the life of the historian must be short and precarious.

Like other great amateurs—and other lovers—he had taken his plunge without really being ready for it. He was not equipped by formal training for his work as a historian of the Roman Empire. His fourteen "unprofitable months" at Magdalen College, in an Oxford which, according to him, was "steeped in port and prejudice," did not give him the academic tools he needed. He lamented that his desultory training in Greek left him without the "scrupulous ear of the well-flogged critic." His work as an ancient historian was never part of the perfunctory duties of an academic post.

Except for this one passion, he was not a man of passionate commitment. At the age of sixteen he did commit himself to the Roman Catholic Church, but when he was sent to Lausanne by his father, his tutor there quickly brought him back to Protestantism. Despite his skepticism of established Christianity, he found it natural to be a

Tory. He had the advantage of some political experience—as a member of Parliament and a commissioner of trade and plantations. His politics were prudent and pragmatic. He was a friend and admirer of Lord North, for whom he wrote a state paper against France in the years before the Revolution. When the American colonies protested the power of Parliament and began a civil war to break away, he believed that they were wrong. But, after the Battle of Saratoga made it plain that the ocean and independent enthusiasms had already separated the American colonies, he confessed that Lord North's costly efforts to subject the Americans were hopeless.

In an age that was filled with sycophants and that rewarded sycophancy, he did not dedicate his work to anyone—a fact for which he has not received the credit that is his due. He helps us understand why, and incidentally helps us share his vision of the significance of *people* in the vicissitudes of empire. He wrote these words in the preface to his fourth and final volume, published soon after Lord North had fallen from power:

> Were I ambitious of any other Patron than the Public, I would inscribe this work to a Statesman, who in a long, a stormy, and at length an unfortunate administration, had many political opponents, almost without a personal enemy: who has retained, in his fall from power, many faithful and disinterested friends; and who, under the pressure of severe infirmity, enjoys the lively vigour of his mind, and the felicity of his incomparable temper. Lord North will permit me to express the feelings of friendship in the language of truth: but even truth and friendship should be silent, if he still dispensed the favours of the crown.

Gibbon remained uncommitted to any but his own opinions. The shrewd observer Horace Walpole, as he greeted the first volume of Gibbon's history with surprise as "a truly classic work," also noted that in Parliament Gibbon had been called "a whimsical because he votes variously as his opinion leads him. I . . . never suspected the extent of his talents, he is perfectly modest."

Gibbon's amorous commitments also were dominated by prudence and propriety. As a young man of twenty in Lausanne (1757) he became infatuated by the beautiful and witty Suzanne Curchod (1739–1794), then only eighteen. But when Gibbon's father objected, he broke off the engagement. Later she married Jacques Necker, the French financier and statesman, and established one of the celebrated salons of modern Paris. (*Their* daughter, incidentally, was the saloniste and prolific author, Madame de Staël!) Gibbon's broken engagement took place seven years before he conceived the *Decline and Fall.* What might Gibbon have done with his talents if, instead of listening to his father, he had shared his life with the charming Suzanne?

Gibbon once modestly declared that "diligence and accuracy are the only merits which an historical writer may ascribe to himself; if any merit indeed can be assumed from the performance of an indispensable duty." Yet the product of his twenty years' passion showed that a historical masterpiece required much more. Not least was his inexhaustible sense of wonder and his tolerant curiosity about the foibles of the human race. The cast of an eye, the excess of an appetite, the perversity of tastes, the beauty or deformity of stature—he witnessed all these with delight.

He managed with deceptive ease to translate the catastrophes of nature into parables of human nature. The earthquakes which shook the eastern Mediterranean on A.D. July 21, 365, led him to observe:

> . . . their affrighted imagination enlarged the real extent of a momentary evil. . . . And their fearful vanity was disposed to confound the symptoms of a declining empire and a sinking world. It was the fashion of the times to attribute every remarkable event to the particular will of the Deity; the alterations of nature were connected, by an invisible chain, with the moral and metaphysical opinions of the human mind; and the most sagacious divines could distinguish, according to the colour of their respective prejudices, that the establishment of heresy tended to produce an earthquake, or that a deluge was the inevitable consequence of the progress of sin and error. Without presuming to discuss the truth or propriety of these lofty speculations, the historian may content himself with the observation, which seems to be justified by experience, that man has much more to fear from the passions of his fellow-creatures than from the convulsions of the elements.

The daily habits of remote and unfamiliar peoples help us understand their life-and-death commitments. Of the Scythians or Tartars he noted "with some reluctance" that "the pastoral manners which have been adorned with the fairest attributes of peace and innocence are much better adapted to the fierce and cruel habits of a military life." Their diet (not corn, but freshly slaughtered meat) and their light and easily moved tents both help us grasp that it was easy for them to behave as they did. "The exploits of the hunters of Scythia are not confined to the destruction of timid or innoxious beasts; they boldly encounter the angry wild boar, when he turns against his pursuers, excite the sluggish courage of the bear, and provoke the fury of the tiger, as he slumbers in the thicket." And so the nuances of human nature are newly revealed to us "on the immense plains of Scythia or Tartary."

Gibbon was fortunate to be born into an age when men of letters were expected to provide "amusement and instruction." The world of science—despite our clichés of an Age of Reason—was newly liberated from the medieval demand for meaning. In the Royal Society and other "invisible colleges" scientists, virtuosi, and amateurs were expanding the world with tiny increments of knowledge. Of course there were a few dazzlers, like Sir Isaac Newton. But the most important shift in attitude toward knowledge was from the interest in the cosmos to the interest in facts. Now it seemed possible for every man to become his own scientist. The telescope, the "flea glass" (microscope), the thermometer, and scores of other measuring devices were transforming experience into experiment. This new incremental approach to the physical world—spawning a wonderful newgrown wilderness of facts and contraptions—was also Gibbon's approach to the world of human nature. The time had not yet come when scientific quest for meaning threatened to transform the social world into another cosmos of dogmatic simplicities. Gibbon gives us incremental history on a grand scale.

For Gibbon, while human nature is anything but unintelligible, it remains only partly explicable. For him the menace to understanding was not so much ignorance as the illusion of knowledge. His explanations of rise and fall, of prosperity and decline are always *lists*. What he recounts is "the triumph of barbarism *and* religion." He recounts the quirks and quibbles of theologians, the rivalries of Eastern monarchs, their wives and mistresses and sons and daughters, not simply because they are amusing, but also because they are instructive. Without such trivia we cannot understand what the Eastern Empire was or what it became.

It is more accurate to insist that for Gibbon there are no trivia. Human habits, utterances, exclamations, and emotions are the very essence of his history—not mere raw material for distilling "forces" and "movements." The more vividly we see them, the better we know our subject. Inevitably, then, he must remain a skeptic about our capacity finally to grasp the whole story.

But despite—perhaps because of—this recognition, he is not a pessimist. The spectacle which he has unfolded of "the greatest, perhaps, and the most awful scene in the history of mankind" rewards us. He sees the whole planet as a stage for more grand spectacles, which will also be a stage for renewal. "If a savage conqueror should issue from the deserts of Tartary, he must repeatedly vanquish the robust peasants of Russia, the numerous armies of Germany, the gallant nobles of France, and the intrepid freemen of Britain; who, perhaps, might confederate for their common defence. Should the victorious Barbarians carry slavery and desolation as far as the Atlantic Ocean, ten thousand vessels would transport beyond their pursuit the remains of civilized society; and Europe would revive and flourish in the American world which is already filled with her colonies and institutions."

In his optimism Gibbon seems a spokesman for the Age of the Enlightenment. He seems, sometimes, to speak for a faith, burgeoning in his lifetime, that man's uninhibited critical faculties can grasp the world. I once thought of Gibbon in precisely that way. He spoke to me from and for a *period* of history. But in the years since Gibbon first spoke to me, he has come to say something more. He has become a more personal historian and hence more intimate, both in what he said and in what I hear.

Some eloquent outspoken prophets of the Age of Reason make it easy for historians to confine the epoch in that epithet. Among historians the great systematizers include such authors as Montesquieu (1689–1755) and Vico (1668–1744) and Voltaire (1694–1778). Of course these men—who are copiously treated in encyclopedias of the social sciences—still interest their fellow systematizers. Among the writers of narrative history in his epoch, Voltaire still speaks vividly to some of us. But his most popular contemporary competitors in narrative history—David Hume and William Robertson—have become historiographical antiques. Gibbon still can and does speak to all of us.

What he saw and what he accomplished was possible, he gladly acknowledged, only because of the peculiar opportunities of his place and time. "I shall ever glory in the name and character of an Englishman," he observed gratefully at the conclusion of his work, "I am proud of my birth in a free and enlightened country; and the approbation of that country is the best and most honourable reward for my labours." If he had not exploited the new opportunities and shared the new vistas of his age, he could not have given us his history. Yet his greatness, the intimate ingredient in his work, is his peculiar talent at transcending the characteristic enthusiasms of his age. Nowadays John Dryden and Alexander Pope and Jonathan Swift, and even Laurence Sterne and Henry Fielding, seem to have a certain quaintness. It is doubly remarkable that Edward Gibbon, whose style was at least as idiosyncratic as theirs, somehow manages to talk to us in our own idiom.

This is what I mean by the intimacy of Gibbon's *Decline and Fall.* Gibbon succeeds in this intimacy precisely because he does not offer us obsolescing parables of science or the social sciences. Nor is he stultified by the etiquette of a particular genre of literature. The chronological lopsidedness of his work—which gives more space to the first few centuries than to the last millennium of his thirteen-century tale—is itself a witness to his determination to shape the story, not by the a priori dimensions of centuries, but by his own concerns. He has the courage to juxtapose his lists of large causes with the minutiae of persons and places. He reminds us of our ties to the cosmos without pretending to unlock its secrets. He remains a modest man, refusing to carve neat channels where the course of history must flow. He lacks the conceit of the system builder, whose naïveté is revealed only with the centuries.

No historian has seen more vividly how nettlesome is the texture of the human past. Yet few have been bolder or more successful at grasping the nettle. He helps us share his pleasure at touching the random prickliness of experience. All this he does because he does not overestimate the dogmatic capacities of his own "enlightened age" nor does he underestimate the mystery of what remains untold and untellable.

At the end of his twenty years' voyage into the Roman Empire, he asks himself whether he should try another such voyage. With characteristic prudence he concludes that "in the repetition of similar attempts a successful Author has much more to lose, than he can hope to gain." Yet he insists that "the annals of ancient and modern times may afford many rich and interesting subjects. . . . To an active mind, indolence is more painful than labor." So he cheers us on, both readers and writers of history. For he, as much as any other writer in our language, reminds us that, even across the centuries and the oceans, people can talk to people about people. Just as Gibbon was not imprisoned in the jargon and special conceits of his age, so perhaps we need not be imprisoned in ours.

CHAPTER 5

Timetables of History

"TIME," WROTE the famous American philosopher-idler Henry David Thoreau, "is but the stream I go fishing in." Each of us—with the help of parents, grandparents, friends, teachers, historians, and others—goes fishing in that stream. And we usually come up with what we knew, or strongly suspected, was already there. One of the purposes of any book of history is to make it possible for us to go fishing and come up with some surprises.

The historian's neat categories parse experience in ways never found among living people. For people in the past, just as for us, experience has had no academic neatness. For example, 1776, the year of the United States' Declaration of Independence, was also the year of publication of the first volume of Gibbon's *Decline and Fall of the Roman Empire* and of Adam Smith's *Wealth of Nations,* the year of the death of the Scottish philosopher David Hume, the year when Fragonard made one of his best-known paintings and when the English landscape painter John Constable was born, the year of Mozart's Serenade in D Major, K. 250 (the "Haffner"), of Cook's third voyage to the Pacific, and of military ski competitions in Norway. Or 1927, the year when Lindbergh flew the Atlantic, was also the year when Trotsky was expelled from the Communist Party, when *Show Boat* opened in New York, when Sigmund Freud published *The Future of an Illusion* and Thornton Wilder *The Bridge of San Luis Rey,* when Pavlov did his work on conditioned reflexes, Al Jolson starred in the epoch-making "talkie" *The Jazz Singer,* the German economic system collapsed, and the Harlem Globetrotters basketball team was organized. Which of these items was most vivid to anyone living in Western Europe or America at the time must have depended on where that person lived, and on his education, interests, social class, and prejudices. How polychromatic and how iridescent is the experience of any age!

A number of peculiarities in our thinking and teaching have made "chronology"—the study of the arrangement of events in time—seem less interesting than it really is.

First is the time cliché. This is the notion that history mainly consists of certain "key" dates—"1066 and All That!" Dates, then, seem the rigid skeleton of history, which historians flesh out. And early Anglo-American history would be everything that happened between "1066" (the Norman Conquest) and "1776" (the American Revolution). "Crucial dates," we are told, are the Landmarks of History. But if we teach history as chronology the landmarks overshadow the landscape.

It is not surprising, then, that the unwilling student thinks of history as little more than lists of numbers (and names) to be memorized. A more profound consequence, for those of us who did our homework and learned the lists, was to shape—or rather pervert—our notions of human experience in the long past. History was not a broad stream of many eddies, but a neat and narrow road with sharp turns, unambiguous starting points, and clearly marked dead ends. Roman civilization "ended" when Alaric and the Visigoths sacked Rome in A.D. 410. Then the Dark Ages "began." Favorite examination questions asked: When did the Renaissance commence? Was it with the birth of Petrarch in 1304? or of Shakespeare in 1564? A sophisticated student was one who had become adept at marshaling and juggling dates to mark off one or another sharply bounded expanse of time.

Such a date-oriented history was inevitably a story of sudden beginnings and instant endings. The great eras and grand movements of history seemed to arrive with fanfare and to depart with formal valedictory. People who lived "in advance of their age" were "prophets." The past was peopled with figures of transition "wandering between two worlds, one dead, the other powerless to be born." It was such thinking that led an imaginative student to describe Dante (1265–1321) as "the Italian poet who had one foot in the Middle Ages, and with the other saluted the rising star of the Renaissance."

While these time clichés pervert our view of the *processes* of history, another peculiarity of our date-oriented thinking perverts our view of the *experience* of history. For we have been trained to think of the past as a *sequence,* and to think of history as consequences. We learn about the American Revolution because a great nation came out of it. Among its other consequences we may count the French revolutions of 1789 (1830?, 1848?) and too, indirectly, the Paris Commune of 1871, the Russian Revolution of 1917, and the myriad anticolonial revolutions of our age. We have been so overwhelmed and dazzled by this sequence-oriented view of the past that we have failed even to notice what we have been missing—History as Experience.

One of the obvious features of the experience that fills *our* lives every day is that we never can know what will flow out of it. But the historian is the scientist of hindsight. Since he knows (or thinks he knows) how it all turned out, he is preoccupied with the question: What chain of events made it come out that way? On the other hand, we, the people, live in a world of the contemporary. We see ourselves dominated by the events that happen at one time—in *our* time. We are charmed and enticed and threatened by the uncertainties of the future. The historian in his library and at his leisure can focus in turn on one kind of event after another—the political, the economic, the intellectual. He has the opportunity to sort out origins and consequences. But the citizen is the simultaneous target of all sorts of events. How numerous and how diverse are the events which make up the experience of living men and women!

Another effect of our common way of viewing the historical past is to reinforce our habits of thinking in ways that make us feel at home where we already are. We actually use our chronology to narrow our historical vision. We do this, for example, when we make the birth of Jesus the turning point of historical dating. The signs of A.D. and B.C. proclaim the central importance of an event which is actually believed to be central by only a small proportion of mankind. The cumbersome designation of early events by a subtractive system of B.C. simply adds to the problem of finding our bearings in strange and ancient societies. Muslims, naturally enough, date their events A.H. *(Annus Hegirae)* from the crucial event in the history of *their* religion.

All such ways of looking at chronology inhibit our thinking about the whole human past. In addition, the decimal system and the celebration of centuries and their multiples induce us to give the fluid past an unnatural neatness and rigidity. Among the ancient Jews, a "jubilee" when slaves were manumitted and debts were forgiven was celebrated every fifty years. Then the Roman Catholic Church began the practice of proclaiming a Holy Year (generally once every twenty-five years, when special privileges were given by the Church for pilgrimage to Rome, and there was an unusual jubilee indulgence), the first of which was proclaimed by Pope Boniface VIII in 1300. Since the rise of the historical profession in Western countries this slicing of the past into "centuries" has dominated us in ways difficult to overestimate. At first a hundred years was described as "a century of years." Then by the middle of the seventeenth century the word "century" itself had come to mean a period of a hundred years. Ever since then the units of academic instruction and scholarship have been wrapped in parcels, each one hundred years long.

We must try to remember how much of the historian's awareness of the contemporaneity of happenings all over the world was beyond the consciousness of people living at the time. The events and achievements that are contemporary by the calendar are not contemporary in experience unless people know of them. During nearly all history, communications have been limited, slow, and desultory. We must therefore be wary of assuming that because different events occurred in the same year they were *known* to contemporaries at about the same time. For example, Adam Smith's *Wealth of Nations* (probably the first comprehensive treatment of political economy in a Western language) had first been delivered as lectures in Glasgow, was first published in Britain in 1776, and did not appear in an American edition until 1789. It was not translated into French or German until 1794. The writings of John Locke, which were first published in England in the late seventeenth century, and were frequently referred to by the authors of the Declaration of Independence and the Constitution, remained scarce on American shores throughout the eighteenth century. One of the more tantalizing questions for the historian is how, when, and where knowledge of an event occurring in one place reached other parts of the earth.

In many cases this inability to communicate promptly, so that people in one part of the earth remained ignorant of some of the contemporaneity later revealed to historians, has itself been a crucial fact shaping the course of history. And there are a number of familiar examples in the history of the United States. If James Monroe, President Thomas Jefferson's special envoy, and Robert R. Livingston, then the United States Minister in Paris, had been able to consult President Jefferson about the urgent and surprising terms that Napoleon offered in 1803 for the sale of the whole of Louisiana, Jefferson and the Congress of the United States might have balked. Both the history and the boundaries of this nation might then have been quite different. These envoys' inability to keep their President currently informed forced them to strike a bargain on their own. Faced not with the question but with their answer, Jefferson put his constitutional scruples behind him, and the Congress ratified what they would not have initiated.

Similarly, Andrew Jackson's reputation as a military hero was in no small part due to the lack of communications. At the famous Battle of New Orleans on the morning of January 8, 1815, General Andrew Jackson, then commander of the American army in the Southwest, repulsed a superior British force, which lost more than 2,000 men, at a cost of only seventy-one Americans. So he "saved" New Orleans and the Mississippi Valley from a British invasion. But this battle had no effect on the outcome of the war with Britain, because the peace terms had been settled two weeks earlier by the Treaty of Ghent (signed December 24, 1814), a fact which neither Jackson nor his British opponents knew. If communications had been speedier, the battle might have been forestalled, and Andrew Jackson would never have been given the opportunity to become "The Hero of New Orleans"—with consequences for American politics and the rise and demise of Jacksonian Democracy on which we can only speculate.

Among the crucial features of our human experience, then, we must count not only the vast range of events and achievements that make up a contemporary life, but the accessibility of the events and achievements of one place to people living elsewhere. Contemporaneity—as a quality not of the calendar but of living human experience—is a relative and variable term. It depends not only on what happens when and where, but on who knows what, when, and where. Among the grand changes in human experience few have been more drastic than our changing and suddenly enlarging sense of the contemporary. In the most recent times we can begin to take it for granted that dominant events and achievements which occur in a particular year enter the experience of larger and larger numbers of people in that very year, or even on the very day of their occurrence.

The calendar of dates and the reach of experience come closer and closer together. To millions of citizens in our Televised States of America, an increasing number of events are known (and of course many are actually seen and heard) at the moment when they happen. This flood of confused contemporaneity has itself become a dominant and bewildering feature of life in our time.

As we read history for the years before the late twentieth century, we should not forget that we are seeing "contemporary" events as only God could have seen them. And so we can discover what men of the Pre-Television Age were missing about life in their own time. This too can help us see in a lively new perspective what we thought we already knew.

PART II

A BY-PRODUCT NATION

We know what we are,
But know not what we may be.

SHAKESPEARE

CHAPTER 6

The Therapy of Distance

THE STORY of American civilization gives us an opportunity to see what happens when a prospering old culture detaches a piece of itself to a great distance. On the other side of a broad ocean, the civilization of Englishmen became something it never could have become within their little island. "Not a place upon earth might be so happy as America," Thomas Paine observed in 1776. "Her situation is remote from all the wrangling world, and she has nothing to do but to trade with them." But that was not the whole story. The American colonies were not, of course, the first settlements of Englishmen outside England. There was an ancient distinction in constitutional law, as Charles H. McIlwain has shown, between the *realm* of England (England itself) and the *dominions* (other lands "belonging to" England). The American colonies were not the first testing ground of the capacity of the English Constitution to provide machinery for self-government beyond the island.

In the seventeenth century, while Englishmen in America were building colonies, the Irish, separated by only a few miles of water, were trying without success to assert their right to legislate for themselves. The English Commonwealth Parliament of 1649, with the arrogance of a parvenu, declared that the English Parliament alone ("the People . . . without any King or House of Lords") should have the power to govern England and "all the Dominions and Territories thereunto belonging." The very same Declaration which proclaimed England "to be a Commonwealth and Free-State" thus silently declared that Ireland had no right to govern itself. Free Englishmen asserted their right to make laws for all those whom they "possessed." For the first time there emerged into constitutional parlance the notion of British Possessions. The irony of this situation, which escaped most English statesmen, was vivid enough to the dyspeptic Irishman Jonathan Swift, who called "government without the consent of the governed . . . the very definition of slavery." The Irish, Swift noted, were well enough equipped with arguments, "but the love and torrent of power prevailed. . . . In fact, eleven men well armed will certainly subdue one single man in his shirt."

Ireland was too close to England, and the stakes of the Irish Empire too great, for the Irish prophets of Revolution to prevail. The Irish proponents of self-government lost. Before the settlement of the American colonies, the only place in the English dominions (i.e., outside England) where the right to self-government was successfully asserted was in the tiny Channel Islands, which neither threatened nor promised enough to justify a battle. The doughty Channel Islanders had the gall to argue that if *anyone* was dependent on anyone else, the English were dependent on *them,* since they were the remaining fragment of the Dukedom of Normandy, whose William had conquered England.

While Cromwell's Army could master next-door Ireland, neither he nor his successors could preserve the power of the English Parliament over these thirteen colonies of transatlantic Americans. Three thousand miles of ocean accomplished what could not be accomplished by a thousand years of history. The Atlantic Ocean proved a more effective advocate than all the constitutional lawyers of Ireland.

The significance of sheer distance appears from the earliest settlement of Englishmen in the New World. Here is how William Bradford describes what happened in mid-November 1620 when he and the other Pilgrim Fathers had their first view of the American coast:

> . . . after longe beating at sea they fell with that land which is called Cape Cod; the which being made and certainly knowne to be it, they were not a little joyfull. After some deliberation had amongst them selves and with the master of the ship, they tacked aboute and resolved to stande for the southward (the wind and weather being faire) to finde some place aboute Hudsons river for their habitation. But after they had sailed that course aboute halfe the day, they fell amongst deangerous shoulds and roring breakers, and they were so farr intangled ther with as they conceived them selves in great danger; and the wind shrinking upon them withall, they resolved to beare up againe for the Cape, and thought them selves

hapy to gett out of those dangers before night overtooke them, as by Gods providence they did. And the next day they gott into the Cape-harbor wher they ridd in saftie.

If the Pilgrim Fathers had been closer to home or more accurate in their navigation or luckier in their weather, it is most unlikely that there ever would have been any need for the Mayflower Compact. That document, which Bradford called "the first foundation of their govermente in this place," was to be the primary document of self-government in the British colonies in North America.

The legal right of these English separatists to settle in the New World came from a patent which they had received from the Virginia Company of London, who authorized them to establish "a particular plantation" wherever they wished within the domain of the Company. The Pilgrims had intended to settle at the mouth of the Hudson River, which was still well within the Virginia Company's northern boundaries. If they had landed there, their patent from the Virginia Company would have sufficed, and they would have had no need for a fundamental instrument of government.

But Cape Cod, where the Pilgrims actually found themselves, was too far north and so outside the Virginia Company's domain. By settling at Plymouth they put themselves in a state of nature. Their patent was not valid there. They were now within the jurisdiction of the Northern Virginia Company (at that time being reorganized into the Council for New England), from whom they had no patent. They would have to create their own government. This they did with the Mayflower Compact, written on board their vessel and signed on November 11, 1620, by forty-one men, including every head of a family, every adult bachelor, and most of the menservants. The only males who did not affix their names were two sailors who had signed on the voyage for a single year, and the other passengers who happened to be under the legal age of discretion.

The accident of misnavigation, as Bradford reported, had been noticed by some of the more legalistic and libertarian *Mayflower* passengers and became an urgent reason for hastily creating some document of self-government. The Compact which they wrote so quickly was "occasioned partly by the discontented and mutinous speeches that some of the strangers amongst them had let fall from them in the ship; Thate when they came a shore they would use their owne libertie; for none had power to command them, the patente they had being for Virginia, and not for New-england, which belonged to an other Government, with which the Virginia Company had nothing to doe."

The government which the *Mayflower* colonists created by their Compact was, according to Bradford, "as firme as any patent, and in some respects more sure." They wrote a new chapter in the history of self-government. For in other places the roots of civil government had been buried deep under the debris of time. America laid bare the birth of government where it would be plain for all to see. In 1802 at Plymouth, in an often reprinted oration, John Quincy Adams extolled the Mayflower document as "perhaps the only instance, in human history, of that positive, original social compact, which speculative philosophers have imagined as the only legitimate source of government."

It was appropriate that the occasion for the primeval document of American self-government should have come not from ideology but from a simple fact of life. That was what New England historians have straightforwardly called "the missing of the place." In America, need and opportunity upstaged ideology.

In their American remoteness the New Englanders created simple new forms of self-government. The New England town meetings had an uncertain precedent in the vestry meetings of rural England, but American circumstances gave town meetings comprehensive powers and a new vitality. Once again, Americans relived the mythic prehistory of government. Tacitus had sketched that prehistory in his account of popular assemblies among the Germanic tribes. It also could be glimpsed in the direct democracy of the Swiss Landsgemeinde (the popular assembly of the self-governing canton) which flourished from the thirteenth till the seventeenth century. Even as the direct democracy of the Swiss cantons was declining, it was being reborn in New England.

From the beginning, New England facts transcended Old English forms. The New England town meetings, which met first weekly, then monthly, came to include all the men who had settled the town. At first, the meetings seem to have been confined to so-called freemen, those who satisfied the legal requirements for voting in the colony. Soon the towns developed their own sort of "freemen"—a group larger than those whom the General Court of the colony recognized as grantees of the land. While the town meetings proved to be lively and sometimes acrimonious debating societies, they were more than that. They distributed town lands, they levied local taxes, they made crucial decisions on schools, roads, and bridges, and they elected the selectmen, constables, and others to conduct town affairs between the meetings.

The laws of Massachusetts Bay Colony gradually gave form to the town meetings. A law of 1692 required that meetings be held annually in March and enumerated the officers to be elected. A law of 1715 required the selection of moderators, gave them the power to impose fines on those who spoke without permission during meetings, and authorized any ten or more freeholders to put items on the agenda. But as the movement for Independence gathered momentum, Britain's Parliamentary Act of 1774 decreed that no town meeting should be held to discuss affairs of government without written permission from the royal Governor.

The transatlantic distance had given to these transplanted Englishmen their opportunity and their need to govern themselves. The tradition of self-government, which had been established in England by the weight of hundreds of years, was being established in America by the force of hundreds of miles.

What the Mayflower Compact and the town meetings did for the earliest New England settlers, the State constitutions and numerous State legislatures accomplished for later Americans spreading across the continent. The United States would have its Civil War, its war for secession. But, significantly, that war was fought between segments of the original seaboard colonies, and was involved with deep moral issues and the conflict of economic interests. Of the more remote States, only Utah—the Mormon community—would offer any substantial threat of secession.

In the growing United States, paradoxically, distance itself had nourished institutional safeguards against rebellion. Because the States grew in the American Void, as they grew they were free to develop and had to develop their own forms of self-government. The American Add-a-State plan was not confused by ancient imperial ties. The government of each new unit was shaped by and for the new settlers. The main sufferers from this system were the American Indians, who were already there and whom the new settlers treated as mere obstacles to be removed. The "mother country" headquartered in Washington speedily abandoned efforts to impose its will on remote parts. Paradoxically, the American federal system, and especially the equality of States in the United States Senate, made it possible for these western "colonies" gradually to dominate the politics of the Eastern Seaboard "mother country."

Just as the American remoteness dissolved the powers of the imperial bureaucrats in London over the lives of transplanted Englishmen, so too it dissolved numerous petty bureaucracies. Daily life in the English homeland was a domain of specialized monopolies. The nation labored under the burden of privileged guilds and chartered companies which had divided all the subjects' needs into profitable satrapies.

In seventeenth-century England, the command of armies had become an aristocratic monopoly. While the private soldiers tended to be the social dregs drawn from jails and taverns, the officers were usually aristocratic gentlemen who had bought or inherited their commands. This feature of European armies had certain wholesome and even pleasant consequences. It helped produce an Age of Limited Warfare that might equally have been called an Age of Ceremonial Warfare. Members of an international aristocracy were versed in the "rules" of war for civilized nations which were recorded in the writings of Hugo Grotius and Emmerich de Vattel.

The conduct of battles was a real-life version of chess. "Now it is frequent," Daniel Defoe observed in 1697, "to have armies of fifty thousand men of a side stand at bay within view of one another, and spend a whole campaign in dodging, or, as it is genteelly called, observing one another, and then march off into winter quarters. The difference is in the maxims of war, which now differ as much from what they were formerly as long perukes do from piqued beards, or as the habits of the people do now from what they then were. The present maxims of war are—

> Never fight without a manifest advantage,
> And always encamp so as not to be forced to it.

And if two opposite generals nicely observe both these rules, it is impossible they should ever come to fight." It is not surprising that between engagements the officers of opposing sides entertained one another with balls, concerts, and dinner parties.

In America, the profession of arms was being dissolved into communities of citizen-soldiers—not through force of dogma, but through force of circumstances. Firearms were a daily necessity—both for gathering food and skins, and for defense against the Indians. "A well grown boy at the age of twelve or thirteen years," a settler observed in the Valley of Virginia in the 1760s, "was furnished with a small rifle and shot-pouch. He then became a fort soldier, and had his porthole assigned him. Hunting squirrels, turkeys and raccoons, soon made him expert in the use of his gun."

Of course, the American Indians had never read Grotius or Vattel and were ignorant of European military etiquette. They were skilled, courageous, and ruthless guerrilla fighters, and the colonists had to follow their example. Backwoods warfare was nothing like the polite game of military chess described by Defoe. It was individualistic warfare, warfare without rules, which dissolved all sorts of distinctions—between officer and private, and even between soldier and civilian.

The military profession was only one of the monopolies that dissolved in the American remoteness. "Besides the hopes of being safe from Persecution in this Retreat," William Byrd wrote in 1728, "the New Proprietors [of New Jersey] inveigled many over by this tempting account of the Country: that it was a Place free from those 3 great Scourges of Mankind, Priests, Lawyers, and Physicians. Nor did they tell a word of a Lye, for the People were as yet too poor to maintain these Learned Gentlemen." But as important as their poverty was the sheer distance of the colonists from the Old World citadels of privilege.

In religion, the remoteness of America and the vast spaces in America made it impossible to preserve the monopoly of the Established Church. The Puritans in New England were not noted for their toleration. They warned away all heretics and they harried the Quakers from their midst. Meanwhile, Rhode Island, Connecticut, and Pennsylvania gladly welcomed refugees. And the American backwoods proved to be a boundlessly tolerating landscape. There was room enough for everybody. "If New England be called a Receptacle of Dissenters, and an Amsterdam of Religion," the Reverend Hugh Jones of Virginia wrote in 1724, "Pennsylvania the Nursery of Quakers, Maryland the Retirement of Roman Catholicks, North Carolina the Delight of Buccaneers and Pyrates, Virginia may be justly esteemed the happy Retreat of true Britons and true Churchmen for the most part. . . ." But even in Virginia, as Jones observed, "the Parishes being of great Extent, Every Minister is a kind of Independent in his own Parish." Commonly, there was no nearby church where the prescribed ceremonies could be performed. "In Houses also there is Occasion, from Humour, Custom sometimes, from Necessity most frequently, to baptize Children and church Women, otherwise some would go without it. In Houses also they most commonly marry, without Regard to the Time of the Day or Season of the Year."

The wonderful independence and variety of American religions never ceased to amaze the visitors from abroad. In 1828, Mrs. Trollope found the churchgoing Americans "insisting upon having each a little separate banner, embroidered with a device of their own imagining." She wrote, "The whole people appear to be divided into an almost endless variety of religious factions."

In England, the higher learning as well as religion had been a monopoly of the Established Church. Nonconformists had difficulty securing admission to Oxford or Cambridge (the only English universities till the early nineteenth century), while Catholics and Jews were absolutely excluded. The dissenting academies, which set high scholarly standards, had no power to grant degrees. In America, by contrast, at the time of the Revolution, nearly every major Christian sect had a degree-granting institution of its own. By the early eighteenth century, New England Puritans and their secessionists had set up Harvard and Yale, while Virginia conformists of the Church of England had their College of William and Mary. The flourishing variety of sects nourished a variety of institutions. New-Side Presbyterians founded Princeton University; revivalist Baptists founded Brown University in Rhode Island; Dutch Reformed revivalists founded Queen's College (later Rutgers University) in New Jersey; a Congregational minister transformed an Indian missionary school into Dartmouth College in New Hampshire; Anglicans and Presbyterians joined in founding King's College (later Columbia University) in New York City and the College of Philadelphia (later the University of Pennsylvania).

Americans were happily distant from the metropolitan headquarters in London of the monopolies of the medical and the legal professions. That was where professional guilds guarded their antique silver, displayed their charters, and organized to keep out competitors. And where they preserved pedantic distinctions among their several branches. The aristocrats of the legal profession were the "barristers" fortified in their London Inns of Court which held the power to admit to the bar, and the monopoly of practice before the High Courts. "Attorneys," while not authorized to plead in court, set the machinery of the court in motion. Then there were the "solicitors," private legal agents whose province it was to look after routine legal matters. Besides these there were "notaries" (organized in their Scriveners' Company), who prepared the documents that required a notarial seal, in addition to patent agents, and still other specialists. Their English citadel was London—but there was no American London.

In America, legal specialties dissolved, and there were citizen-lawyers. When the young John Adams in 1758 sought the advice of a leading Boston lawyer on the requirements for the practice, he was advised that "a lawyer in this country must study common law, and civil law, and natural law, and admiralty law; and must do the duty of a counsellor [barrister], a lawyer, an attorney, a solicitor, and even of a scrivener." As the standard of technical competence was lower than in England, even the distinction between lawyer and layman was blurred. Of the nine Chief Justices of Massachusetts between 1692 and the Revolution, only three had specialized legal training. American businessmen were more inclined to be their own lawyers. Land, which in England was an heirloom and the most metaphysical of legal subjects, in America became a commodity. When landowner-ship was widely diffused, its mysteries seemed less arcane.

Few expressed the American suspicion of professional monopolists better than Samuel Livermore, who was Chief Justice of the New Hampshire Supreme Court in the late eighteenth century. He lacked legal learning himself, and as a contemporary reported he "did not like to be pestered with it in his courts." "When [counsel] attempted to read law books in a law argument, the Chief Justice asked him why he read them; 'if he thought that he and his brethren did not know as much as those musty old worm-eaten books?' " One of Livermore's brethren on the bench (himself a farmer and trader by occupation) charged a jury "to do justice between the parties not by any quirks of the law out of Coke or Blackstone—books that I never read and never will—but by common sense as between man and man."

We must keep all this in mind when we recall that of the fifty-six signers of the Declaration of Independence twenty-five were self-styled "lawyers," and of the fifty-five members of the Constitutional Convention in Philadelphia thirty-one were lawyers. These facts were not so much evidence of the peculiar importance of legal learning as they were symptoms of the decline of monopolies in America. "In no country perhaps in the world," Edmund Burke observed in his speech *On Conciliation with the American Colonies* (1775), "is the law so general a study. . . . all who read, and most do read, endeavor to obtain some smattering in that science." The multiplying American legislatures, enough to provide a seat for nearly any citizen who was so inclined, helped bring into being the citizen-lawyer.

A similar American catharsis occurred in the medical professions. The eighteenth-century English patient suffered from the doctors' many submonopolies. At the top of the social scale, corresponding to the barrister, was the Doctor of Physick, who enjoyed the privileges of the Royal College of Physicians chartered by Henry VIII back in 1518. But his professional ethics, rooted in the clerical tradition of the two English universities, forbade him to shed blood or handle the human body. The "barber-surgeons," who had been organized in 1540, were later split by the distinction between the "barbers," who had a monopoly on cutting hair, shaving beards, and extracting teeth, and the "surgeons," who performed other operations. Besides these were the "apothecaries," who until 1617 had been the members of the grocers' guild, but thereafter had a monopoly on selling drugs. And in addition, there were the "midwives," who till the end of the seventeenth century were generally women and who had to be licensed by their bishop.

In colonial America, where distances were great and specialists scarce, all such monopolists gave way to the general practitioner. "I make use of the English word doctor," wrote the observant Marquis de Chastellux, who traveled the colonies in 1781, "because the distinction of physician is as little known in the army of Washington as in that of Agamemnon. We read in Homer, that the physician Macaon himself dressed the wounds. . . . The Americans conform to the ancient custom and it answers very well."

The therapy of distance worked in countless other ways. Distinctions of social classes, which in Europe had been reinforced by all these other distinctions, did not survive intact in the New World. Since the witty drawing rooms, learned libraries, genteel academies, and grand council-chambers of the Old World were an ocean away, Americans could not escape some provincial crudity and naïveté. But the ocean also separated them from the irrelevancies of a filigreed society, from Old World pomposity and pride and priggishness, from traditional conceits and familial arrogance. Americans would discover for themselves the wisdom in Jonathan Swift's ironic Irish view, "If a man makes me keep my distance, the comfort is, he keeps his at the same time." And American experience would show the world what a purging could do for ancient institutions.

CHAPTER 7

Why a Theory Seems Needless

T HE AMERICAN must go outside his country and hear the voice of America to realize that his is one of the most spectacularly lopsided cultures in all history. The marvelous success and vitality of our institutions is equaled by the amazing poverty and inarticulateness of our theorizing about politics. No nation has ever believed more firmly that its political life was based on a perfect theory. And yet no nation has ever been less interested in political philosophy or produced less in the way of theory. If we can explain this paradox, we shall have a key to much that is characteristic and much that is good in our institutions.

Perhaps the two sides of the paradox explain each other. The very same facts which account for our belief that we actually possess a theory also explain why we have had little interest in political theories and have never bothered seriously to develop them.

For the belief that an explicit political theory is superfluous precisely because we already somehow possess a satisfactory equivalent, I propose the name "givenness." "Givenness" is the belief that values in America are in some way or other automatically defined: *given* by

This and the following chapter, "Revolution Without Dogma," are adapted from my book *The Genius of American Politics*, whose theme was that "the genius of American democracy comes not from any special virtue of the American people but from the unprecedented opportunities of this continent and from a peculiar and unrepeatable combination of historical circumstances." Other chapters in that book deal with the New England Puritans, with the Civil War, with religion in the United States, and with "Our Cultural Hypochondria and How to Cure It."

certain facts of geography or history peculiar to us. The notion has three faces, which I shall describe in turn. First is the notion that we have received our values as a gift from the *past*, that the earliest settlers or Founding Fathers equipped our nation at its birth with a perfect and complete political theory, adequate to all our future needs.

The second is the notion that in America we receive values as a gift from the *present*, that our theory is always implicit in our institutions. This is the idea that the American Way of Life harbors an American Way of Thought which can do us for a political theory, even if we never make it explicit or never are in a position to confront ourselves with it. It is the notion that to Americans political theory never appears in its nakedness but always clothed in the peculiar American experience. We like to think that, from the shape of the living experience, we can guess what lies underneath and that such a guess is good enough—perhaps actually better than any naked theory. While according to the first axiom of "givenness" our values are the gift of our history, according to the second they are the gift of our landscape.

The third part of "givenness" is a belief which links these two axioms. It is a belief in the *continuity* or homogeneity of our history. It is the quality of our experience which makes us see our national past as an uninterrupted continuum of similar events, so that our past merges indistinguishably into our present. This sense of continuity is what makes it easy for us to accept the two first axioms at the same time: the idea of a preformed original theory given to us by the Founding Fathers, and the idea of an implicit theory always offered us by our present experience. Our feeling of continuity in our history makes it easy for us to see the Founding Fathers as our contemporaries. It induces us to draw heavily on the materials of our history, but always in a distinctly nonhistorical frame of mind.

The idea that values are a gift from our past may be likened to the obsolete biological notion of "preformation." That is the idea that all parts of an organism preexist in perfect miniature in the seed. Biologists used to believe that if you could look at the seed of an apple under a strong enough microscope you would see in it a minute apple tree. Similarly, we seem still to believe that if we could understand the ideas of the earliest settlers—the Pilgrim Fathers or Founding Fathers—we would find in them no mere seventeenth- or eighteenth-century philosophy of government but the perfect embryo of the theory by which we now live. We believe, then, that the mature political ideals of the nation existed clearly conceived in the minds of our patriarchs. The notion is essentially static. It assumes that the values and theory of the nation were given once and for all in the very beginning.

What circumstances of American history have made such a view possible? The first is the obvious fact that, unlike western European countries, where the coming of the first white man is shrouded in prehistoric mist, civilization in the United States stems from people who came to the American continent at a definite period in recent history. For American political thought this fact has had the greatest significance. We have not found it necessary to invent an Aeneas, for we have had our William Bradford and John Winthrop, or, looking to a later period, our Benjamin Franklin and James Madison. We have needed no Virgil to make a myth of the first settlement of our land or the first founding of the Republic; the crude facts of history have been good enough.

The facts of our history have thus made it easy for us to assume that our national life, as distinguished from that of the European peoples who trace their identity to a remote era, has had a clear purpose. Life in America—appropriately called the American Experiment—has again and again been described as the test or the proof of values supposed to have been clearly in the minds of the Founders. While, as we shall see, the temper of much of our thought has been antihistorical, it is nevertheless true that we have leaned heavily on history to clarify our image of ourselves. Perhaps never before, except conceivably in the modern state of Israel, has a nation so firmly believed that it was founded on a full-blown theory and hence that it might understand itself by recapturing a particular period in its past.

This idea is actually so familiar, so deeply imbedded in our thinking, that we have never quite recognized it as a characteristic, much less a peculiarity, of our political thought. Nor have we become aware of its implications. "Four score and seven years ago," Lincoln said at Gettysburg in 1863, "our fathers brought forth on this continent, *a new nation, conceived in Liberty, and dedicated to the proposition that all men are created equal.*" We have forgotten that these words are less the statement of a political theory than an affirmation that an adequate theory already existed at the first epoch of national life. This belief itself helps account for the way in which the traditional, conservative, and inarticulate elements of our Revolution have been forgotten. A few slogans have been eagerly grasped as if they gave the essence of our history. While the conservative and legal aspect of our Revolution has remained hidden from popular view, schoolboys and popular orators (who seldom read beyond the preambles of legal documents) have conceived the Declaration of Independence as written primarily, if not exclusively, to vindicate man's equality and his "inalienable rights to life, liberty, and the pursuit of happiness."

Our determination to believe in a single logically complete theory as our heritage from the earliest settlers has thus actually kept us from grasping the *facts* of the early life of our nation. Strenuous efforts have been made to homogenize all the fathers of our country. A great deal of the popular misunderstanding of the New England Puritans, for example, can be traced to this desire. Tradition teaches us to treat the history of our nation from 1620 to 1789 as a series of labor pains, varying only in intensity. The Puritans, we are taught, came here for religious and political liberty; and the American Revolutionaries are supposed to have shown a pilgrimlike fervor and clarity of purpose.

If we compare our point of view with that of the historically conscious peoples of Europe, we shall begin to see some of its implications. The Europeans have, of course, had their interludes of nostalgia for some mythical heroic age, some Wagnerian Götterdämmerung. Mussolini sought to reincarnate the Roman Empire, Hitler to revive a prehistoric "Aryan" community. But such efforts in Europe have been spasmodic. Europeans have not with any continuity attributed to their nameless "earliest settlers" the mature ideals of their national life. In contrast, we have been consistently primitivistic. The brevity of our history has made this way of thinking easy. Yet that is not the whole story. We find it peculiarly congenial to claim possession of a perfect set of political ideas, especially when they have magical elusiveness and flexibility. Their mere existence seems to relieve us of an unwelcome task.

Our firm belief in a perfectly preformed theory helps us understand many things about ourselves. In particular, it helps us see how it has been that, while we in the United States have been infertile in political theories, we have at the same time possessed an overweening sense of orthodoxy. The poverty of later theorizing has encouraged appeal to what we like to believe went before. In building an orthodoxy from sparse materials, of necessity we have left the penumbra of heresy vague. The inarticulate character of American political theory has thus actually facilitated heresy hunts and tended to make them indiscriminate. The heresy hunts which come at periods of national fear—the Alien and Sedition Acts of the age of the French Revolution, the Palmer raids of the age of the Russian Revolution, and similar activities of more recent times—are directed not so much against acts of espionage as against acts of irreverence toward that orthodox American creed, believed to have been born with the nation itself.

Among the factors which have induced us to presuppose an orthodoxy, to construct what I have called a "preformation" theory, none has been more important than the heterogeneous character of our population. Our immigrants, who have often been the outcasts, the déclassés and the persecuted of their native countries, are understandably anxious to become part of a new national life. Hence they are eager to believe that they can find here a simplicity of theory lacking in the countries from which they came. Immigrants, often stupidly blamed for breeding "subversive" or "un-American" ideas, have as much as any other group frenetically sought a "pure" American doctrine. Where else has there been such a naive sense of political orthodoxy? Who would think of using the word "un-Italian" or "un-French" as we use the word "un-American"?

The fact that we have had a written constitution, and even our special way of interpreting it, has contributed to the "preformation" notion. Changes in our policy or our institutions are read back into the ideas, and sometimes into the very words, of the Founding Fathers. Everybody knows that this has made of our federal Constitution an "unwritten" document. What is more significant is the way in which we have justified the adaptation of the document to current needs: by attributing clarity, comprehensiveness, and a kind of mystical foresight to the social theory of the founders. In Great Britain, where there is an "unwritten" constitution in a very different sense, constitutional theory has taken for granted the *gradual* formulation of a theory of society. No sensible Briton would say that his history is the unfolding of the truths implicit in Magna Charta and the Bill of Rights. Such documents are seen as only single steps in a continuing process of definition.

The difference is expressed in the attitudes of the highest courts in the two countries. In Great Britain the highest court of appeal, the House of Lords, has gradually come to the conclusion that it must be governed by its own earlier decisions. When the House of Lords decides a point of the constitution, it is thus frankly developing the constitution, and it must follow the line which it has previously taken, until the legislature marks out another. Not so in the United States. Our Supreme Court considers itself free to overrule its earlier decisions, to discover, that is, that the constitution which it is interpreting really has all along had a different meaning from what had been supposed.

The American view is actually closer to the British view during the Middle Ages, when the very idea of legislation was in its infancy and when each generation believed that it could do little more than increase its knowledge of the customs which already existed. In the United States, therefore, we see the strange fact that the more flexible we have made our constitution, the more rigid and unexperimental we have made our political theory. We are haunted by a fear that capricious changes in theory might imperil our institutions. This is our kind of conservatism.

Our theory of society is thus conceived as a kind of exoskeleton, like the shell of the lobster. We think of ourselves as growing *into* our skeleton, filling it out with the experience and resources of recent ages. But we always suppose that the outlines were rigidly drawn in the beginning. Our mission, then, is simply to demonstrate the truth—or rather the workability—of the original theory. This belief in a perfect original doctrine, one of the main qualities of which is practicality, may help us understand that unique combination of empiricism and idealism which has characterized American political life.

If we turn from our constitution to our political parties, we observe the same point of view. The authority of a particular past generation implies the impotence of later generations to reconstruct the theoretical bases of our national life. Today it is still taken for granted that the proper arena of controversy was marked off once and for all in the late eighteenth century: We are either Jeffersonians or Hamiltonians.

In no other country has the hagiography of politics been more important. The lives of our national saints have remained vivid and contemporary for us. In no other country—except perhaps in the Soviet Union, where people have been called Marxists, Leninists, or

Trotskyites—have statesmen so intimately embraced the image of early national heroes. Would an Englishman call himself a Walpolean or a Pittite? Yet in the United States the very names of our political parties—Republican and Democratic—are borrowed from the early age of our national life. This remarkable persistence of early labels offers the sharpest contrast to what we see in continental western Europe. There new parties—and new party labels—come and go with the seasons, and most of the parties, with double- or triple-barreled names, draw on the novel vocabulary of the nineteenth and twentieth centuries. It is a commonplace that no fundamental theoretical difference separates our American political parties. What need has either party for an explicit political theory when both must be spokesmen of the *original* American doctrine on which the nation was founded?

Political theory has been little studied in the United States. For example, departments of political science in many of our universities show more interest in almost anything else than in political theory. This, too, can be explained in part by the limitations imposed by the "preformation" point of view. If our nation in the beginning was actually founded on an adequate and sufficiently explicit theory revealed at one time, later theorists can have only the minor task of exegesis, of explaining the sacred texts. Constitutional history can, and in many ways has, become a substitute for political theory.

The unique role which our national past has played in constructing our image of ourselves and our standards for American life has made us hypersensitive about our own history. Because we have searched it for the substance of a political philosophy, we have been inclined to exaggerate its contemporary relevance. When Charles A. Beard in his *Economic Interpretation of the Constitution* in 1913 showed that members of the Constitutional Convention had a financial interest in the establishment of a stable federal government, he scandalized respectable scholars. Leaders of opinion, like Nicholas Murray Butler, thought the book a wholesale attack on the American creed. The explosive import of such a book would have been impossible had not the facts of political history already been elevated into an axiom of political philosophy. Any innuendo against the motives of the Founding Fathers was therefore seen as an implied attack on the American way of life. The British have never been so disturbed by the suggestion that the barons had a personal interest in extracting from King John the concessions written into Magna Charta.

During the 1930s, when the Communist party made a serious effort to appear a native American growth (using the slogan "Communism Is Twentieth-Century Americanism"), it too sought to reinterpret the American past. It argued that the American Revolution had really been a class war and not merely a colonial rebellion. The radical attack on the doctrine of judicial review, which then seemed to obstruct change in our institutions, was made by way of a labored two-volume historical treatise, Louis Boudin's *Government by Judiciary*. He sought to prove that the Founding Fathers had never intended the Supreme Court to have the power to declare federal laws unconstitutional.

The lives of our great men have played a peculiarly large role in our attempt at self-definition. Some of our best historical talent has gone into biography: Albert J. Beveridge's *Marshall*, Charles Van Doren's *Franklin*, Dumas Malone's *Jefferson*, and Douglas Southall Freeman's *Washington*. We have also the long filial tradition of Sparks's or Weems's or Marshall's *Washington* or Wirt's *Patrick Henry*. Such works are a kind of hybrid between what the lives of the saints or of the Church Fathers are for Catholics and what the lives of gods and goddesses were for the ancient Greeks. For us, biographies have taken on a special importance, precisely because we have had so little dogmatic writing. And our national history thus has a primary significance for Americans which is without parallel in modern nations. The quest for the meaning of our political life has been carried on through historical rather than philosophical channels.

It is not surprising, then, that much of our self-criticism has taken the form of historical reinterpretation. In periods of disillusionment we have expressed ourselves not so much in new philosophies, in dogmas of dictatorship or existentialism, as in earnest, if sometimes tortured, reinterpretations of the American past. In the 1920s and 1930s, for example, people who would not have looked twice at a revolutionary political theory or a nihilist metaphysic eagerly read W. E. Woodward's *New American History*, James Truslow Adams' *Founding of New England*, Edgar Lee Masters' *Lincoln*, or the numerous other iconoclastic works about Washington or Grant. The sharpest criticisms of contemporary America were the works of Sinclair Lewis and H. L. Mencken, which were hardly theoretical.

The mystic rigidity of our "preformation" theory has been consistent with great flexibility in dealing with practical problems. Confident that the wisdom of the Founding Fathers somehow made provision for all future emergencies, we have not felt bound to limit our experiments to those which we could justify with theories in advance. In the last century or so, whenever the citizens of continental western Europe have found themselves in desperate circumstances, they have had to choose among political parties, each of which was committed to a particular theoretical foundation for its whole program—"monarchist," "liberal," "catholic," "socialist," "fascist," or "communist." This has not been the case in the United States. Not even during the Civil War. Historians still argue over what, if any, political theory Lincoln represented.

In the crisis which followed the Great Depression, when Franklin D. Roosevelt announced his program for saving the American economy, he did not promise to implement a theory. Rather, he declared frankly that he would try one thing after another and would keep trying until a cure was found. "The country demands bold, persistent experimentation. It is common sense to take a method and try it: if it fails, admit it frankly and try another." Neither he nor his listeners doubted that whatever solution, within the limits of common-law liberties, might prove successful would also prove to have been within the prevision of the Founding Fathers. The people balked only when a proposal—like the Court-packing plan—seemed to imperil the independence of the judiciary, an ancient principle of the common law.

On second thought, it is not surprising that we who have been most sure of the basic structure of our political life should also have been most prodigal of legislation. Two remarkable and complementary facts are that the amendments to our federal Constitution have been so few during the last two centuries, and that at the same time our legal experiments have been so numerous. For us it is enough to recommend a piece of legislation if a considerable number of people want it, if there is no loud opposition, and if there seems a reasonable chance that it might reduce some present evil. Our laws have been abundant and ephemeral as the flies of summer. Conservatism about our basic institutions, and the faith that they will be vindicated in the national experience, have made us less fearful of minor legislation.

Our mystic belief in the "preformed" national theory has thus restrained theoretical vagaries without preventing particular experiments. Without having ever intended it, we have stumbled on an evolutionary approach to institutions. Yet at the same time we have

taken up a kind of social Freudianism; for the "preformation" concept of values implies belief that the childhood years of a nation's
history are crucial for the formation of its character. More than that,
we have given the national past a peculiarly normative significance.
Small wonder that we should seem complacent, if we judge ourselves
by whether we are true to our own character. Our American past and
the theories of politics which it is thought to imply have become the
yardstick against which national life is measured. This is the deeper
meaning of the criterion of "Americanism" which is so familiar in the
United States and sounds so strange to European ears.

Our first axiom, the "preformation" ideal, is the notion that, in the
beginning and once and for all, the Founding Fathers of the nation
gave us a political theory, a scheme of values, and a philosophy of
government. It is a static kind of "givenness"—a gift of orthodoxy,
the gift of the past.

Our second axiom is similar, in that it, too, is an excuse or a reason
for not philosophizing. It is the notion that a scheme of values is
given, not by traditions, theories, books, and institutions, but by present experience. It is the notion that our theory of life is embodied
in our way of life and need not be separated from it, that our values
are given by our condition. If this second part of the idea of "givenness" seems, in strict logic, contradictory to the first, from the point
of view of the individual believer it is actually complementary. For,
while the first axiom is ideal and static in its emphasis, the second is
practical and dynamic. "Preformation" means that the theory of
community was given, once and for all, in the beginning; the second
sense of "givenness" means that the theory of community is perpetually being given and ever anew.

Taken together with the idea of preformation, this second "givenness" makes an amazingly comprehensive set of attitudes. The
American is thus prepared to find in *all* experience—in his history
and his geography, in his past and his present—proof for his conviction that he is equipped with a hierarchy of values, a political theory.
Both axioms together encourage us to think that we need not invent
a political theory because we already possess one. The idea of "givenness" as a whole is, then, both as idealistic as a prophet's vision and
as hardheaded as common sense.

This second face of "givenness" is at once much simpler and
much more vague than the concept of preformation. It is simply the

notion that values are implicit in the American experience. The idea
that the American landscape is a giver of values is, of course, old and
familiar. It has long been believed that in America the community
values would not have to be sought through books, traditions, the
messianic vision of prophets, or the speculative schemes of philosophers but would somehow be the gift of the continent itself.

We Americans have always been much impressed by the simple
fact that we are children of a Brave New World. Even from the
earliest settlements, but especially since the formative era of the late
eighteenth and early nineteenth centuries, we have looked upon
ourselves as the lucky beneficiaries of an especially happy environment. In the pamphlets which Puritans wrote in the seventeenth
century to attract their brethren to New England, we read fantastic
tales of the abundance of crops and game, the magic of the air and
water; how life on the new continent cured consumption, gout, and
all sorts of fevers; how the old became young, the young became
vigorous, and barren women suddenly bore children. In the very
same pamphlet we can read how the wilderness would toughen the
effete and how the wealth of this unexploited paradise would enrich
the impoverished.

The myth was no less alive two centuries later, when Paul Bunyan, the giant woodsman of the forest frontier (as James Stevens
describes him),

> felt amazed beyond words that the simple fact of entering Real America
> and becoming a Real American could make him feel so exalted, so pure,
> so noble, so good. And an indomitable conquering spirit had come to him
> also. He now felt that he could whip his weight in wildcats, that he could
> pull the clouds out of the sky, or chew up stones, or tell the whole world
> anything.
>
> "Since becoming a Real American," roared Paul Bunyan, "I can look
> any man straight in the eye and tell him to go to hell! If I could meet a
> man of my own size, I'd prove this instantly. We may find such a man
> and celebrate our naturalization in a Real American manner. We shall
> see. Yay, Babe!"
>
> Then the two great Real Americans leaped over the Border. Free-
> dom and Inspiration and Uplift were in the very air of this country, and
> Babe and Paul Bunyan got more noble feelings in every breath.

We have been told again and again, with the metaphorical precision
of poetry, that the United States is the *land* of the free. Independence, equality, and liberty, we like to believe, are breathed in with

our very air. No nation has been readier to identify its values with the peculiar conditions of its landscape. We believe in *American* equality, *American* liberty, *American* democracy, or, in sum, the *American* way of life.

Our belief in the mystical power of our land has in this round-about way nourished an empirical point of view; and a naturalistic approach to values has thus, in the United States, been bound up with patriotism itself. What the Europeans have seen as the gift of the past, Americans have seen as the gift of the present. What the European thinks he must learn from books, museums, and churches, from his culture and its monuments, the American thinks he can get from contemporary life, from seizing peculiarly American opportunities.

It is surely no accident that the most influential, if not the only significant, general interpretation of our history has been that of Frederick Jackson Turner. In 1893 he found the special virtues of our institutions and of our national character in the uniquely recurrent conditions of our frontier. Turner translated Paul Bunyan into the language of sociology:

> Behind institutions, behind constitutional forms and modifications, lie the vital forces that call these organs into life and shape them to meet changing conditions. . . . All peoples show development. . . . But in the case of the United States we have a different phenomenon. . . . This perennial rebirth, this fluidity of American life, this expansion west-ward with its new opportunities, its continuous touch with the simplic-ity of primitive society, furnish the forces dominating American character. . . .
>
> The result is that to the frontier the American intellect owes its striking characteristics. That coarseness and strength combined with acuteness and inquisitiveness; that practical, inventive turn of mind, quick to find expedients; that masterful grasp of material things, lacking in the artistic but powerful to effect great ends; that restless, nervous energy; that dominant individualism, working for good and for evil, and withal that buoyancy and exuberance which comes with freedom—these are traits of the frontier, or traits called out elsewhere because of the existence of the frontier.

These words—indeed, much of the work of Turner and his follow-ers—are actually a theory to justify the absence of an American political theory.

How can we explain the origin, growth, and vitality of this idea of "givenness" in America? The most obvious and some of the most important explanations have escaped us for their very obviousness. To become aware of them it may be necessary to go to Europe, where some of us begin to discover America.

One fact which becomes increasingly difficult to communicate to the urban American, but which the automobile and our national parks have kept alive for some of us, is the remarkable grandeur of the American continent. Even for the early Puritan settlers the forest which hid savage arrows had a fascination. The magic of the land is a leitmotif throughout the eighteenth and nineteenth centuries. We hear it, for example, in Jefferson's ecstatic description of the confluence of the Potomac and the Shenandoah rivers, in Lewis and Clark's account of the far west, in the vivid pages of Francis Parkman's *Oregon Trail,* and in a thousand other places. It is echoed in the numberless travel books and diaries of those men and women who left the comfortable and dingy metropolises of the Atlantic seaboard to explore the Rocky Mountains, the prairies, or the deserts. Their simple emotions should not be underestimated, nor should we interpret them with too much subtlety. It is misleading to associate too closely the appeal of virgin America with the bookish romanticism of European belles lettres. The unspoiled grandeur of America helped men believe that here the Giver of values spoke to man more directly—in the language of experience rather than in that of books or monuments.

Our immigrant character has been an incentive toward this point of view. The United States has, of course, been peopled at widely distant times and for the most diverse reasons. Some came because they were Protestants, others because they were Catholics, still others because they were Jews, some because they were monarchists, others because they were opposed to monarchy. We have been too well aware of this diversity to try to seek our common values in our original cultures. It is true that we have developed a kind of generalized Christianity, which is probably what we mean by the "In God We Trust" on our coins. We have looked anxiously for some common faith. A few writers, like Louis Adamic, have even tried to make the motleyness itself a scheme of values: to make the patchwork seem the pattern. But the readiest solution, a necessary solution, perhaps the only possible solution for us, has been to assume, in the immigrant's own phrase, that ours is a "golden land," that values spring from our common ground. If American ideals are not in books or in the blood but in the air, then they are readily acquired; actually, it is almost impossible for an immigrant to avoid acquiring them. He does not need to learn a philosophy so much as to rid his lungs of the air of Europe.

The very commonness of American values has seemed their proof. They have come directly from the hand of God and from the soil of the continent. This attitude helps explain why the martyr (at least the *secular* martyr) has not been attractive to us. In the accurate words of our old popular song, "The Best Things in Life Are Free." Men in America have had to struggle against nature, against Indians, high mountains, arid deserts, against space itself. But these struggles have seemed required to make the continent livable or comfortable, not to make our society good. In Europe, on the other hand, the liberal could not make the plant of liberty grow without first cutting out the weeds of tyranny; and he took that for his task. But the American has preened himself on his good sense in making *his* home where liberty is the natural growth. Voltaire declared, "Where liberty is not, there is my home." This was a fitting and thoroughly un-American reply to Franklin's "Where liberty dwells, there is my country."

The character of our national heroes bears witness to our belief in "givenness," our preference for the man who seizes his God-given opportunities over him who pursues a great private vision. Perhaps never before has there been such a thorough identification of normality and virtue. A "red-blooded" American must be a virtuous American; and nearly all our national heroes have been red-blooded, outdoor types who might have made the varsity team. Our ideal is at the opposite pole from that of a German Superman or an irredentist agitator in his garret. We admire not the monstrous but the normal, not the herald of a new age but the embodiment of his own. In the language of John Dewey, he is the well-adjusted man; in the language of Arthur Miller's Salesman, Willy Loman, he is the man who is not merely liked but *well*-liked. Our national heroes have not been erratic geniuses like Michelangelo or Cromwell or Napoleon but rather men like Washington and Jackson and Lincoln, who possessed the commonplace virtues to an extraordinary degree.

The third part of the idea of "givenness" is actually a kind of link between the two axioms which I have already described: the notion that we have an ideal given in a particular period in the past (what I have called the idea of "preformation") and the idea that the theory of American life is always being given anew in the present, that values are implicit in the American experience. The third aspect helps us understand how we can at once appeal to the past and yet be fervently unhistorical in our approach to it.

By this I mean the remarkable continuity or homogeneity of American history. To grasp it, we must at the outset discard a European cliché about us, namely, that ours is a land without continuity or tradition, while in Europe man feels close to his ancestors. The truth of the matter is that anyone who goes to Europe nowadays cannot fail to be impressed by the amazing, the unique, continuity of American history and, in sharp contrast, the *dis*continuity of European history.

This is true in several senses. In the first place, there is the obvious fact that the recent history of Europe has seen violent oscillations of regime. Each new regime has taken on itself a task of historical amnesia: the fascists trying to deny their democratic past, the democrats trying to deny their fascist past, etc. But there is a subtler way in which the landscape and monuments which surround the European tend to impress on him the various possibilities of life in his place, while what the American sees confirms his sense of "givenness," his belief in the normality, if not the inevitability, of the particular institutions which he has evolved. "For the American tourist," Aldous Huxley has shrewdly observed, "the greatest charm of foreign travel is the very high ratio of European history to European geography. Conversely, for the European, who has come to feel the oppressive weight of a doubtless splendid, but often fatal past, the greatest charm of travel in the New World is the high ratio of its geography to its history."

In Sicily, for example, centuries of history are compacted in a single building. The visitor to the Capella Palatina in Palermo sees Christian mosaics of the twelfth century surmounted by a ceiling of Moslem craftsmanship. Throughout the island one comes upon pagan temples on the foundations of which rose churches, in the Middle Ages transformed into mosques, later again to be used as Christian chapels.

The capitals of Europe are rich in evidence of the unpredictability of human history. Of all cities in the world, Rome is perhaps richest in such evidence: the retaining walls which early Romans built to protect the road up the Palatine are made of fragments stolen from Greek and North African temples; columns standing in the

Forum bear witness not only to ancient Roman skill but also to the shattered schemes of the conquered peoples from whom they were taken. The fate which the Romans brought upon their predecessors was later, of course, visited upon Rome herself by the barbarians and Christians, who made the Forum into their stone quarry. The Colosseum, where Christians and Jews were once slaughtered to amuse the mob, is now divided by partitions which later Christians erected to support the stage of their Passion Play. Its walls are pocked by holes from which barbarian and Christian soldiers extracted iron for their weapons in the Middle Ages; large segments were removed by popes to add splendor to their churches. The magnificent roads which Julius Caesar built for his legions were traveled after World War II by little automobiles which, with appropriate irony, borrow their name from Mickey Mouse—in Italian, "Topolino."

In Europe one need not be an archaeologist or a philosopher to see that over the centuries many different kinds of life are possible in the same place and for the same people. Who can decide which, if any of these, is "normal" for Italy? It is hardly surprising, then, that the people of Europe have not found it easy to believe that their values are given by their landscape. They look to ideology to help them choose among alternatives.

In the United States, of course, we see no Colosseum, no Capella Palatina, no ancient roads. The effect of this simple fact on our aesthetic sense, though much talked of, is probably less significant than on our sense of history and our approach to values. We see very few monuments to the uncertainties, the motley possibilities, of history or, for that matter, to the rise and fall of grand theories of society. Our main public buildings were erected for much the same purpose for which they are now being used. The Congress of the United States is still housed in the first building expressly constructed for that purpose. Although the White House, like the Capitol, was gutted by fire during the War of 1812, it, too, was soon rebuilt on the same spot and to a similar design; in 1952 another restoration was completed. Our rural landscape, with a few scattered exceptions—the decayed plantation mansions of the South, the manor houses of upstate New York, and the missions of Florida and California—teaches us very little of the fortunes of history. Even our archaeology is republican, designed to make the past contemporary; you can spend a vacation at Colonial Williamsburg.

The impression which the American has as he looks about him is one of the inevitability of the particular institutions, the particular kind of society in which he lives. The kind of acceptance of institutions as proper to their time and place which tyrants have labored in vain to produce has in the United States been the result of the accidents of history. The limitations of our history have perhaps confined our philosophical imagination; but they have at the same time confirmed our sense of the continuity of our past and made the definitions of philosophers seem less urgent. We Americans are reared with a feeling for the unity of our history and an unprecedented belief in the normality of our kind of life to our place on earth.

No less important is the converse of this fact, namely, that our history has *not* been *dis*continuous, has not been punctuated by the kind of internal struggles which have marked the history of most of the countries of western Europe, and which have fed their awareness that society is shaped by men. The two apparent exceptions to this observation are the American Revolution and the Civil War, but our statesmen have deftly fitted these into the preformed pattern of our institutions. The important fact is what De Tocqueville observed a century ago, namely, that America somehow has reaped the fruits of the long democratic revolution in Europe "without having had the revolution itself." This was but another way of saying that the prize for which Europeans would have to shed blood would seem the free native birthright of Americans.

The history of the United States has thus had a unity and coherence unknown in Europe. Many factors—our geographical isolation, our special opportunities for expansion and exploitation within our own borders, and our remoteness from Europe—have, of course, contributed. Even our American Civil War, which shook us deeply and was one of the bloodiest wars anywhere in the century, can be understood with scant reference to the ideologies then sweeping Europe: to the intellectual background of 1848, of the Risorgimento, of the Paris Commune. It was not properly a counterpart of European struggles of the period, nor really an exception to the domestic continuity of our history.

But, whatever the causes, the winds of dogma and the gusts of revolution which during the last two centuries have blown violently over western Europe, making France, Italy, Germany, and now perhaps even England testing grounds for panaceas, have not ruffled our intellectual climate. The United States, with a kind of obstinate provincialism, has enjoyed relatively calm weather. While European politics became a kaleidoscope, political life in the United States has seemed to remain a window through which we can look at the life envisaged by our patriarchs. The hills and valleys of European history in the nineteenth century have had no real counterpart in the history of the United States. Because our road has been relatively smooth, we have easily believed that we have trod no historical road at all.

CHAPTER 8

Revolution Without Dogma

WE ARE ACCUSTOMED to think of the American Revolution as the great age of American political thought. It may therefore be something of a shock to realize that it did not produce in America a single important treatise on political theory. Men like Franklin and Jefferson, universal in their interests, active and spectacularly successful in developing institutions, were not fertile as political philosophers.

We have been slow to see some of the more obvious and more important peculiarities of our Revolution because influential scholars on the subject have cast their story in the mold of the French Revolution of 1789. Some of our best historians have managed to empty our Revolution of much of its local flavor by exaggerating what it had in common with that distinctively European struggle. This they have done in two ways.

First, they have stressed the international character of the intellectual movement of which the French Revolution was a classic expression—the so-called Enlightenment. They speak of it as a "climate of opinion" whose effects, like the barometric pressure, could no more be escaped in America than in Europe. As Carl Becker put

---

This and the preceding chapter, "Why a Theory Seems Needless," are adapted from my book *The Genius of American Politics,* whose theme was that "the genius of American democracy comes not from any special virtue of the American people but from the unprecedented opportunities of this continent and from a peculiar and unrepeatable combination of historical circumstances." Other chapters in that book deal with the New England Puritans, with the Civil War, with religion in the United States, and with "Our Cultural Hypochondria and How to Cure It."

it in his *Heavenly City of the Eighteenth-Century Philosophers:* "The Enlightenment . . . is not a peculiarly French but an international climate of opinion . . . and in the new world Jefferson, whose sensitized mind picked up and transmitted every novel vibration in the intellectual air, and Franklin of Philadelphia, printer and friend of the human race—these also, whatever national or individual characteristics they may have exhibited, were true children of the Enlightenment. The philosophical empire was an international domain of which France was but the mother country and Paris the capital."

Second, they have treated ours as only a particular species of the genus Revolution—of what should perhaps more properly be called *Revolutio Europaensis.* Since the French Revolution has been made the model, from that European revolution historians have borrowed the vocabulary in which ours is discussed and the calendar by which it is clocked. They even write of the "Thermidor" of our Revolution which, like that interlude in the French Revolution after 1789, was an era "when the people became tired of agitation and longed for peace and security." In our history, they say this era saw the framing of our Federal Constitution.

In so doing, historians have also exaggerated the significance of what is supposed to have been the ideology of the Revolution. Such an emphasis has had the further attraction to some "liberal" historians of seeming to put us in the main current of European history. It has never been quite clear to me why historians would not have found our revolution significant enough merely as a victory of constitutionalism.

The most obvious peculiarity of our American Revolution is that, in the modern European sense of the word, it was hardly a revolution at all. The Daughters of the American Revolution, who have been understandably sensitive on this subject, have always insisted in their literature that the American Revolution was no revolution but merely a colonial rebellion. The more I have looked into the subject, the more convinced I have become of the wisdom of their naïveté. "The social condition and the Constitution of the Americans are democratic," Alexis de Tocqueville observed a half-century after American independence. "But they have not had a democratic revolution." This fact is surely one of the most important of our history.

A number of historians have pointed out the ways in which a social revolution, including a redistribution of property, accompanied the American Revolution. These are facts which no student of the period should neglect. Yet these historians have by no means succeeded in showing that such changes were so basic and so far-reaching as actually in themselves to have established our national republican institutions. When we speak of the Revolution therefore, we are still fully justified in referring to something other than "the American Revolution as a social movement." If we consider the American Revolution in that sense, it would not be a great deal more notable than a number of other social movements in our history, such as Jacksonianism, populism, progressivism, and the New Deal. More-over, in so far as the American Revolution was a social movement, it was not much to be distinguished from European revolutions; and the increasing emphasis on this aspect of our history is but another example of the attempt to assimilate our history to that of Europe.

The Revolution, as the birthday of our nation, must mean something very different from all this. It is the series of events by which we separated ourselves from the British Empire and acquired a national identity. Looking at our Revolution from this point of view, what are some features which distinguish it from the French Revolution of 1789 or the other revolutions to which western European nations trace their national identity? And, especially, what are those peculiarities which have affected the place of theory in our political life?

First, and most important, the United States was born in a *colonial* rebellion. Our national birth certificate is a Declaration of Independence and not a Declaration of the Rights of Man. The vast significance of this simple fact is too often forgotten. Compared even with other colonial rebellions, the American Revolution is notably lacking in cultural self-consciousness and in any passion for national unity. The more familiar type of colonial rebellion—like that in India—is one in which a subject people vindicates its local culture against foreign rulers. But the American Revolution had very little of this character. On the contrary, ours was one of the few conservative colonial rebellions of modern times.

We should recall several of the peculiar circumstances (most of them obvious) which had made this kind of revolution possible. At the time of the Revolution, the greater part of the population of the American colonies was of British stock. Therefore, no plausible racial or national argument could be found for the superiority either of the inhabitants of the mother country or of the continental American colonies. Even when Jefferson, in his *Notes on Virginia,* went to some trouble to refute Buffon and the Abbé Raynal and others who had argued that all races, including man, deteriorated on the American continent, he did not go so far as to say that the American races were distinctly superior.

Since the climate and topography of substantial parts of the American colonies were similar to those of the mother country (and for a number of other reasons), there had been a pretty wholesale transplantation of British legal and political institutions to North America. Unlike the Spanish colonies in South America, which were to rebel, at least in part, because they had had so little home rule, the British colonies in North America were to rebel because, among other reasons, they had had so much. Finally, the North American continent was (except for sparse Indian settlements) empty of indigenous populations, hence barren of such local institutions and traditions as could have competed with what the colonists had brought with them.

All these facts were to make it easy, then, for the American Revolution to seem in the minds of most of its leaders an affirmation of the tradition of British institutions. The argument of the best theorists of the Revolution—perhaps we should call them lawyers rather than theorists—was not, on the whole, that America had institutions or a culture superior to that of the British. Rather their position, often misrepresented and sometimes simply forgotten, was that the British by their treatment of the American colonies were being untrue to the ancient spirit of their own institutions. The slogan "Taxation Without Representation Is Tyranny" was clearly founded on a British assumption. As James Otis put it in his pamphlet, *The Rights of the British Colonies* (1764), he believed "that this [British] constitution is the most free one, and by far the best, now existing on earth: that by this constitution, every man in the dominions is a free man: that no parts of His Majesty's dominions can be taxed without their consent: that every part has a right to be represented in the supreme or some subordinate legislature: that the refusal of this would seem to be a contradiction in practice to the theory of the constitution."

According to their own account, then, the Americans were to have forced on them the need to defend the ancient British tradition, to be truer to the spirit of that tradition than George III and Lord North and Townshend knew how to be. They were fighting not so much to establish new rights as to preserve old ones: "for the preservation of our liberties . . . in defence of the freedom that is our birthright, and which we ever enjoyed till the late violation of it" (Declaration of Causes of Taking up Arms, July 6, 1775). From the colonists' point of view, until 1776 it was Parliament that had been revolutionary, by exercising a power for which there was no warrant in English constitutional precedent. The ablest defender of the Revolution—in fact, the greatest political theorist of the American Revolution—was also the great theorist of British conservatism, Edmund Burke.

Second, the American Revolution was *not* the product of a nationalistic spirit. We had no Bismarck or Cavour or any nationalist philosophy. We were singularly free from most of the philosophical baggage of modern nationalism.

Perhaps never was a new nation created with less enthusiasm. To read the history of our Revolution is to discover that the United States was a kind of *pis aller.* This fact explains many of the difficulties encountered in conducting the Revolution and in framing a federal constitution. The original creation of a United States was the work of doubly reluctant men: men reluctant, both because of their local loyalties—to Virginia, Massachusetts, Rhode Island, and New York—and because of their imperial loyalty. The story of the "critical period" of American history, of the Articles of Confederation and the Constitution, tells of the gradual overcoming of this reluctance. It was overcome not by any widespread conversion to a nationalist theory—even the *Federalist* papers are conspicuously lacking in such a theory—but by gradual realization of the need for effective union.

In the period of the American Revolution we do discover a number of enthusiasms: for the safety and prosperity of Virginia or New York, for the cause of justice, for the rights of Englishmen. What is missing is anything that might be called widespread enthusiasm for the birth of a new nation: the United States of America. Until well into the nineteenth century, Jefferson—and he was not alone in this—was using the phrase "my country" to refer to his native state of Virginia.

Our Revolution was successful at the first try. This is equally true whether we consider it as a revolt against British rule or as a movement for republican federalism. There was no long-drawn-out agitation, no intellectual war of attrition, of the sort which breeds dogmas and intransigence. Thomas Paine's *Common Sense,* which is generally considered "the first important republican tract to be issued in

America . . . the first to present cogent arguments for independence," did not appear until January 10, 1776. Down to within six
months of the break, few would have considered independence; and
even then the colonists had only quite specific complaints. There had
been no considerable tradition in America either of revolt against
British institutions or of republican theorizing.

The political objective of the Revolution, independence from
British rule, was achieved by one relatively short continuous effort.
More commonly in modern history (for example, in the European
revolutions of the nineteenth century) any particular revolt has been
only one in a long series. Each episode, then, ends on a note of
suspense which comes from the feeling that the story is "to be continued." Under those circumstances, challenges to constituted authority follow one another, accumulating their ideological baggage.

In France, for example, 1789 was followed by 1830 and 1848 and
1870; a similar list could be made for Italy, Germany, and perhaps
Russia. Such repetition creates a distinctive revolutionary tradition,
with continued agitation keeping alive certain doctrines. Repeated
efforts provide the dogmatic raw material for a profusion of later
political parties, each of which rallies under the banner of one or
another of the defeated revolutions or of a revolution yet to be made.
But, properly speaking, 1776 had no sequel, and needed none. The
issue was separation, and separation was accomplished.

If we understand the "conservatism" of the Revolution, we will
begin to see that it illustrates the remarkable continuity of American
history. And we will also see how the attitude of our Revolutionary
thinkers has engraved in our national consciousness a belief in the
inevitability of our particular institutions, or, in a word, our sense of
"givenness."

The character of our Revolution has nourished our assumption
that whatever institutions we happened to have here (in this case the
British constitution) had the self-evident validity of anything that is
"normal." We have thus casually established the tradition that it is
superfluous to the American condition to produce elaborate treatises
on political philosophy or to be explicit about political values and the
theory of community.

I shall confine myself to two topics. First, the manifesto of the
Revolution, the Declaration of Independence, and, second, the man
who has been generally considered the most outspoken and system-

atic political philosopher of the Revolution, Thomas Jefferson. Obviously, no one could contend that there is either in the man or in the document nothing of the cosmopolitan spirit, nothing of the world climate of opinion. But we do find another spirit of at least equal, and perhaps overshadowing, importance and this spirit may actually be more characteristic of our Revolution.

First, then, for the Declaration of Independence. Its technical, legalistic, and conservative character will appear at once by contrast with the comparable document of the French Revolution. Ours was concerned with a specific event, namely, the separation of these colonies from the mother-country. But the French produced a "Declaration of the Rights of *Man* and the Citizen." When De Tocqueville, in his *Ancien Régime* (Book I, chap. iii), sums up the spirit of the French Revolution, he is describing exactly what the American Revolution was not:

> The French Revolution acted, with regard to things of this world, precisely as religious revolutions have acted with regard to things of the other. It dealt with the citizen in the abstract, independent of particular social organizations, just as religions deal with mankind in general, independent of time and place. It inquired, not what were the particular rights of the French citizens, but what were the general rights and duties of mankind in reference to political concerns.
>
> It was by thus divesting itself of all that was peculiar to one race or time, and by reverting to natural principles of social order and government, that it became intelligible to all, and susceptible of simultaneous imitation in a hundred different places.
>
> By seeming to tend rather to the regeneration of the human race than to the reform of France alone, it roused passions such as the most violent political revolutions had been incapable of awakening. It inspired proselytism, and gave birth to propagandism; and hence assumed that quasi religious character which so terrified those who saw it, or, rather, became a sort of new religion, imperfect, it is true, without God, worship, or future life, but still able, like Islamism, to cover the earth with its soldiers, its apostles, and its martyrs.

In contrast to all this, our Declaration of Independence is essentially a list of specific historical instances. It is directed not to the regeneration but only to the "opinions" of mankind. It is closely tied to time and place; the special affection for "British brethren" is freely admitted; it is concerned with the duties of a particular king and certain of his subjects.

Even if we took only the first two paragraphs or preamble, which are the most general part of the document, and actually read them as a whole, we could make a good case for their being merely a succinct restatement of the Whig theory of the British revolution of 1688. To be understood, the words of the Declaration must be annotated by British history. This is among the facts which have led some historians (Guizot, for example) to go so far as to say that the English revolution succeeded twice, once in England and once in America.

The remaining three-quarters—the unread three-quarters—of the document is technical and legalistic. That is, of course, the main reason why it remains unread. For it is a bill of indictment against the king, written in the language of British constitutionalism. "The patient sufferance of these Colonies" is the point of departure. It deals with rights and franchises under British charters. It carefully recounts that the customary and traditional forms of protest, such as "repeated Petitions," have already been tried.

The more the Declaration is reread in context, the more plainly it appears a document of imperial legal relations rather than a piece of high-flown political philosophy. The desire to remain true to the principles of British constitutionalism up to the bitter end explains why, as has been often remarked, the document is directed against the king, despite the fact that the practical grievances were against Parliament; perhaps also why at this stage there is no longer an explicit appeal to the rights of Englishmen. Most of the document is a bald enumeration of George III's failures, excesses, and crimes in violation of the constitution and laws of Great Britain. One indictment after another makes sense only if one presupposes the framework of British constitutionalism. How else, for example, could one indict a king "for depriving us in many cases, of the benefits of Trial by Jury"?

We can learn a great deal about the context of our Revolutionary thought by examining Jefferson's own thinking down to the period of the Revolution. We need not stretch a point or give Jefferson a charismatic role, to say that the flavor of his thought is especially important for our purposes. He has been widely considered the leading political philosopher of the Revolution. Among other things, he was, of course, the principal author of the Declaration of Independence itself; and the Declaration has been taken to be the climax of the abstract philosophizing of the revolutionaries. Because he is sup-

posed to be the avant-garde of revolutionary thought, evidence of
conservatism and legalism in Jefferson's thought as a whole is especially significant.

Neither in the letters which Jefferson wrote nor in those he received do we discover that he and his close associates—at least down
to the date of the Revolution—showed any conspicuous interest in
political theory. We look in vain for general reflections on the nature
of government or constitutions. The manners of the day did require
that a cultivated gentleman be acquainted with certain classics of
political thought; yet we lack evidence that such works were read
with more than a perfunctory interest. To be sure, when Jefferson
prepares a list of worthy books for a young friend in 1771, he includes
references to Montesquieu, Sidney, and Bolingbroke; but such references are rare. Even when he exchanges letters with Edmund Pendleton on the more general problems of institutions, he remains on
the level of legality and policy, hardly touching political theory.
Jefferson's papers for the Revolutionary period (read without the
hindsight which has put the American and the French revolutions in
the same era of world history) show little evidence that the American
Revolution was a goad to higher levels of abstract thinking about
society. We miss any such tendency in what Jefferson and his associates were reading or in what they were writing.

On the other hand, we find ample evidence that the locale of
early Jeffersonian thought was distinctly *colonial;* we might even say
provincial. And we begin to see some of the significance of that fact
in marking the limits of political theorizing in America. By 1776,
when the irreversible step of revolution was taken, the colonial period in the life of Jefferson and the other Revolutionary thinkers was
technically at an end; but by then their minds had been congealed,
their formal education completed, their social habits and the cast of
their political thinking determined. The Virginia society of the pre-
Revolutionary years had been decidedly derivative, not only in its
culture, its furniture, its clothes, and its books, but in many of its ideas
and—what is more to our purpose—in perhaps most of its institutions.

It is an important and little-noted fact that for many American
thinkers of the period (including Jefferson himself) the cosmopolitan
period in their thought did not begin until several years *after* their
Revolution. Then, as representatives of the new nation, some of them
were to enter the labyrinth of European diplomacy. Much of what

we read of their experiences abroad even in this later period would confirm our impression of their naïveté, their strangeness to the sophisticated Paris of Talleyrand, the world of the *philosophes.* In Jefferson's particular case, the cosmopolitan period of his thought probably did not begin much before his first trip abroad as emissary to France in 1784.

When John Adams had gone, also to France, a few years earlier on his first foreign mission, he thought himself fresh from an "American Wilderness." Still more dramatic is the unhappy career of John Marshall, who was an innocent abroad if there ever was one. The career of Franklin, who was at least two generations older than these Revolutionary leaders, is something of an exception; but even in his case much of his charm for the salons of Paris consisted in his successful affectation of the character of a frontiersman.

The importance of this colonial framework in America was to be enormous, not only from the point of view of Revolutionary thought, but in its long-run effect on the role of political theory in American life. The legal institutions which Americans considered their own and which they felt bound to master were largely borrowed. Jefferson and John Adams, both lawyers by profession, like their English contemporaries, had extracted much of their legal knowledge out of the crabbed pages of Sir Edward Coke's *Institutes of the Lawes of England.*

Now there were the elegant lectures of Sir William Blackstone, published as the four-volume *Commentaries on the Laws of England,* appearing between 1765 and 1769. It was this work of the ultraconservative interpreter of English law that for many years remained the bible of American lawyers and, for several generations of them, virtually their whole bookish education. Blackstone's *Commentaries,* as Burke remarked in his Speech on Conciliation, had even by 1775 sold nearly as many copies in America as in England. American editions were numerous and popular; despite copious emendations and contradicting footnotes, Blackstone's original framework was faithfully preserved. Lincoln (as Carl Sandburg describes him), sitting barefoot on a woodpile in Illinois, fifty years later, reading the volumes of the conservative English lawyer—which he called the foundation of his own legal education—is a symbol of that continuity which has characterized our thinking about institutions. For our present purposes, the significant fact is that such a work as the *Commentaries* and the institutions which it expounded could continue to dominate the legal thinking of a people who were rebelling against the country of its origin.

During the very years when the Revolution was brewing, Jefferson was every day talking the language of the common law. We cannot but be impressed not only at the scarcity in the Jefferson papers for these years of anything that could be called fresh inquiry into the theory of government but also by the legalistic context of Jefferson's thought. We begin to see that the United States was being born in an atmosphere of legal rather than philosophical debate. Even apart from those technical legal materials with which Jefferson earned his living, his political pieces themselves possess a legal rather than a philosophical flavor.

A Summary View of the Rights of British America (July 1774), which first brought Jefferson wide notice and which was largely responsible for his momentous choice on the committee to draft a declaration of independence, is less a piece of political theory than a closely reasoned legal document. He justifies the American position by appeal to the Saxon precedent: "No circumstance has occurred to distinguish materially the British from the Saxon emigration." It was from this parallel of the Americans with the Saxons, who also had once conquered a wilderness, that Jefferson draws several important legal consequences.

Jefferson's draft of the "new" Virginia Constitution of 1776 reveals a similar legalistic spirit: his Preamble comprised no premises of government in general, but only the same specific indictments of George III which were to be the substance of the Declaration of Independence. Jefferson actually describes the powers of the chief administrator as, with certain exceptions, "the powers formerly held by the king."

Jefferson's solid achievements in the period up to the Revolution were thus mainly works of legal draftsmanship. The reputation which he first obtained by his *Summary View,* he was to substantiate by other basic documents like the Virginia Constitution and by a host of complex public bills like those for dividing the county of Fincastle, for disestablishing the Church of England, for the naturalization of foreigners, and for the auditing of public accounts. Jefferson was equally at home in the intricacies of real-property law and in the problems of criminal jurisdiction. One of the many consequences of the neglect of American legal history has been our failure to recognize the importance of this legal element in our Revolutionary tradition. Jefferson's chef d'oeuvre, a most impressive technical performance, was his series of Bills for Establishing Courts of Justice in Virginia. These bills, apparently drafted within about ten days in late 1776, show a professional virtuosity which any lawyer would envy.

The striking feature of these lawyerly accomplishments to those of us fed on clichés about the Age of Reason is how they live and move and have their being in the world of the common law, in the world of estates tail, bills in chancery, writs of supersedeas, etc., and not in the plastic universe of an eighteenth-century *philosophe*. Our evidence is doubly convincing, for the very reason that Jefferson was something of a reformer in legal matters. Yet even in his extensive projects of reform, he was eager to build on the foundation of the common law, for example, in his plan for the reform of the law of crimes and punishments. His tenacious conservatism appears in bold relief when we remind ourselves that Jefferson was a contemporary of Jeremy Bentham, whose first important work, the *Fragment on Government*, also appeared in 1776.

But Jefferson, unlike Bentham, did not found his reforms on any metaphysical calculus—rather on legal history and a continuity with the past. Even when he opposed feudal land tenures, he sought support from British sources. In the *Summary View* he had noted that feudal tenures were unknown to "our Saxon ancestors." "Has not every restitution of the antient Saxon laws had happy effects?" To have preserved the feudal tenures would actually have been, in Jefferson's words, "against the practice of our wise British ancestors." And on August 13, 1776, he asked, "Have not instances in which we have departed from this in Virginia been constantly condemned by the universal voice of our country?" "Is it not better now that we return at once into that happy system of our ancestors, the wisest and most perfect ever yet devised by the wit of man, as it stood before the 8th century?"

It is worth noting that Jefferson, who was to be the principal political philosopher of the Revolution, was given leadership in the important technical project of legal codification and reform in his native state of Virginia. Had he died at the end of 1776, he would probably have been remembered as a promising young lawyer of reformist bent, especially talented as a legal draftsman. In both houses of the Virginia legislature he had received the highest number of ballots in the election of members of the committee of legal revisers. The gist of the report of that committee (which included

Edmund Pendleton, George Wythe, and George Mason, three of the ablest legal scholars on the continent, all active in the Revolution) is significant for our purposes. Jefferson himself recalled some years later that the commission had determined "not to meddle with the common law, i.e., the law preceding the existence of the statutes, further than to accommodate it to our new principles and circumstances."

Jefferson's philosophic concern with politics by the time of the outbreak of the Revolution (actually only the end of his thirty-third year) was the enthusiasm of a reflective and progressive colonial lawyer for the traditional rights of Englishmen. To be sure, Jefferson did go further than some of his fellow lawyers in his desire for legal reform—of feudal tenures, of entails, of the law of inheritance, of criminal law, and of established religion—yet even these projects were not, at least at that time, part of a coherent theory of society. They remained discrete reforms, "improvements" on the common law.

Jefferson's willingness to devote himself to purification of the common law must have rested on his faith in those ancient institutions and a desire to return to their essentials. This faith shines through those general maxims and mottoes about government which men took seriously in the eighteenth century and which often imply much more than they say. Jefferson's personal motto, "Rebellion to Tyrants Is Obedience to God," expresses pretty much the sum of his political theory—if, indeed, we should call it a "theory"—in this epoch. It was this motto (which Jefferson probably borrowed from Franklin, who offered it in 1776 for the Seal of the United States) that Jefferson himself proposed for Virginia and which he used on the seal for his own letters. But when we try to discover the meaning of the slogan to Jefferson, we find that it must be defined by reference less to any precise theology than to certain clear convictions about the British constitution. For who, after all, was a "tyrant"? None other than one who violated the sacred tenets of the ancient common law. Jefferson made his own view clear in the device which he suggested for the obverse of the United States seal: figures of "Hengist and Horsa, the Saxon chiefs from whom we claim the honor of being descended, and whose political principles and form of government we have assumed."

In the Revolutionary period, when the temptations to be dogmatic were greatest, Jefferson did not succumb. The awareness of the peculiarity of America had not yet by any means led Jefferson to a rash desire to remake all society and institutions. What we actually discern is a growing tension between his feeling of the novelty of the American experience, on the one hand, and his feeling of belonging to ancient British institutions, on the other.

The tension was admirably expressed in Du Simitière's design for a coat of arms for Virginia. How large a hand Jefferson, who seems to have counseled Du Simitière, had in inventing the design is actually uncertain. But, regardless of authorship, the design eloquently portrays—almost caricatures—the current attitude. The indigenous glories of the New World were represented on the four quarters of the shield by a tobacco plant, two wheat sheafs, "a stalk of Indian corn full ripe," and "four fasces . . . alluding to the four gr[e]at rivers of Virginia." The background, the supporting and decorative elements—in fact, all parts of the arms that have any reference to institutions—emphasize the continuity of the British tradition. This was in August 1776, after the date of the Declaration of Independence.

> Field a cross of St. george gules (as a remnant of the ancient coat of arms [showing] the origin of the Virginians to be English). . . . Supporters Dexter a figure dressed as in the time of Queen Elizabeth representing Sir Walter Rawleigh planting with his right hand the standard of liberty with the words MAGNA CHARTA written on it, with his left supporting the shield. Senester a Virginian rifle man of the present times compleatly accoutr[ed.]
>
> Crest. the crest of the antient arms of Virginia, the bust of a virgin naked and crowned with an antique crown. alluding to the Queen Elizabeth in whose reign the country was discover'd.
>
> Motto. "Rebellion to Tyrants is Obedience to God," or "Rex est qui regem non habet."

We begin to see how far we would be misled, were we to cast American events of this era in the mold of European history. The American Revolution was in a very special way conceived as both a vindication of the British past and an affirmation of an American future. The British past was contained in ancient and living institutions rather than in doctrines; and the American future was never to be contained in a theory. The Revolution was thus a prudential decision taken by men of principle rather than the affirmation of a theory. What British institutions meant did not need to be articulated; what America might mean was still to be discovered. This continuity of American history was to make a sense of "givenness" easier to develop; for it was this continuity which had made a new ideology of revolution seem unnecessary.

Perhaps the intellectual energy which American Revolutionaries economized because they were not obliged to construct a whole theory of institutions was to strengthen them for their encounter with nature and for their solution of practical problems. The effort which Jefferson, for example, did not care to spend on the theory of sovereignty he was to give freely to the revision of the criminal law, the observation of the weather, the mapping of the continent, the collection of fossils, the study of Indian languages, and the doubling of the national area.

The experience of our Revolution may suggest that the sparseness of American political theory, which has sometimes been described as a refusal of American statesmen to confront their basic philosophical problems, has been due less to a conscious refusal than to a simple lack of necessity. As the British colonists in America had forced on them the need to create a nation, so they had forced on them the need to be traditional and empirical in their institutions. The Revolution, because it was conceived as essentially affirming the British constitution, did not create the kind of theoretical vacuum made by some other revolutions.

The colonial situation, it would seem, had provided a *ne plus ultra* beyond which political theorizing did not need to range. Even Jefferson, the greatest and most influential theorist of the Revolution, remained loath to trespass that boundary, except under pressure: the pressure of a need to create a new federal structure. Mainly in the realm of federalism were new expedients called for. And no part of our history is more familiar than the story of how the framers of the federal Constitution achieved a solution: by compromise on details rather than by agreement on a theory.

There is hardly better evidence of this fact than the character of *The Federalist* papers themselves. Nearly everything about them illustrates or even symbolizes the way of political thinking which I have tried to describe. *The Federalist or, The New Constitution* consists of essays written by Alexander Hamilton, James Madison, and John Jay and published one at a time in certain New York journals between late 1787 and early 1788. They had a simple practical purpose: to persuade the people of the state of New York to ratify the recently drawn federal Constitution. The eighty-five numbers were written, like any series of newspaper articles, to be read separately, each essay being a unit. Their object is summarized by Hamilton in No. 1:

> I propose, in a series of papers, to discuss the following interesting particulars:—The utility of the UNION to your political prosperity—The insufficiency of the present Confederation to preserve that Union—The necessity of a government at least equally energetic with the one proposed, to the attainment of this object—The conformity of the proposed Constitution to the true principles of republican government—Its analogy to your own State constitution—and lastly, The additional security which its adoption will afford to the preservation of that species of government, to liberty, and to property.

If, indeed, *The Federalist* may be considered a treatise on political theory, it differs from other important works of the kind by being an argument in favor of a particular written constitution. In this it is sharply distinguished from the writings of Plato, Aristotle, Hobbes, Locke, Rousseau, and J. S. Mill, which give us either systematic theories of the state or wide-ranging speculation. The organization of *The Federalist* papers is practical rather than systematic. They proceed from the actual dangers which confronted Americans to the weaknesses of the existing confederation and the specific advantages of the various provisions of the new constitution.

The Federalist essays are too often treated as if they comprised a single logical structure. They were a collaborative work mainly in the sense that their authors agreed on the importance of adopting the new constitution, not in the sense that the authors start from common and explicit philosophic premises. Hamilton, Madison, and Jay differed widely in personality and in philosophic position. Individually they had even favored some other institutions than those embodied in the Constitution. But they had accepted the compromises and were convinced that what was being offered was far superior to what they already had. To read *The Federalist* is to discover the wisdom of John C. Calhoun's observation that "this admirable federal constitution of ours . . . is superior to the wisdom of any or all of the men by whose agency it was made. The force of circumstances, and not foresight or wisdom, induced them to adopt many of its wisest provisions."

The Revolution itself, as we have seen, had been a kind of affirmation of faith in ancient British institutions. In the greater part of the institutional life of the community the Revolution thus required no basic change. If any of this helps to illustrate or explain our characteristic lack of interest in political philosophy, it also helps to account for the value which we still attach to our inheritance from the British constitution: trial by jury, due process of law, representation before taxation, habeas corpus, freedom from attainder, the independence of the judiciary, and the rights of free speech, free petition, and free assembly, as well as our narrow definition of treason and our antipathy to standing armies in peacetime. It also explains our continuing—sometimes bizarre, but usually fortunate—readiness to think of these traditional rights of Englishmen as if they were indigenous to our continent. In the proceedings of the San Francisco Vigilance Committee of 1851, we hear crude adventurers on the western frontier describing the technicalities of habeas corpus as if they were fruits of the American environment, as natural as human equality.

CHAPTER 9

The Equality of the Human Species

Iᴛ ɪs ᴇᴀsʏ to forget that the assertion of human equality in the Declaration of Independence was not a direct statement of a moral principle, but rather of a scientific and historical fact from which the principle was supposed to follow: "All men are created equal." The truth which the authors declared self-evident was not simply that men ought to be treated as equals nor that they were *born* equal. They actually had been *created* equal. The equality of men was to be confirmed by the evidence of natural history. That this way of stating human equality was not a verbal accident is evidenced in the less ambiguous words of Jefferson's earlier draft: "We hold these truths to be sacred & undeniable; that all men are created equal & independent, *that from that equal creation* they derive rights inherent & inalienable. . . ."

To demonstrate the unity of the human species, it was incumbent on Jefferson—by the canons of his own anthropology—to prove somehow that all men were descended from a single pair of original

---

This chapter is adapted from my book, *The Lost World of Thomas Jefferson,* which aimed to re-create the world of science and nature in which Jefferson's political ideas developed. In that book I describe a Jeffersonian Circle of "natural philosophers" centered in the American Philosophical Society at Philadelphia. This Society was another of Benjamin Franklin's community projects. He conceived it and began to round up its members as early as 1743, and it became the forum for scientific ideas in the last colonial years and in the first years of the Republic. Jefferson himself was elected its President in 1796 and was regularly reelected until 1815. In this chapter I describe some notions widely accepted by the American scientific community at the time from the writings of leading members of the Society, and I try to see how Jefferson's own ideas fitted in.

parents. Lacking details of the dispersion of mankind and the adaptation of its branches to different continents, the Jeffersonian had to find other evidence of a single cradle of mankind. The believers in the inequality of man and in its corollary, the multiplicity of the human species, had of course avoided this historical task. They simply assumed that the Creator had in the beginning made several unequal species of man, each with different physical and social characteristics.

Captain Bernard Romans, for example, in his *Concise Natural History of East and West Florida*, published in New York in 1775, asserted "that God created an original man and woman in this part of the globe, of different species from any in the other parts." It is significant that these opponents of human equality supported their argument by denying the peculiarly cosmopolitan, adaptive and pioneering quality of man. They argued that because among plants and lower animals different species had been created for the different continents, the symmetry of nature required that there should similarly have been created several species of man.

Probably the most eminent and convincing American exponent of this doctrine of "separate creation" was the physician Benjamin Smith Barton, the greatest American botanist of his age who developed the argument in his widely read *New Views of the Origin of the Tribes and Nations of America*. The presence in America of fourteen species of the *Caprimulgus Europaeus* (nighthawk) which were not seen in Europe he found "an interesting fact, which does not favour the opinion of those writers who have imagined, that all animals and all vegetables were originally created in the old world, from whence they have spread over every portion of the earth: an opinion which ought never to have been advanced by philosophers; and which it is not likely will prevail among those naturalists who observe with attention, and deliver their sentiments without reserve or timidity."

Barton's knowledge of a strange jumping rodent which he found to be peculiarly American, together with a great deal of other information, confirmed his belief "that with respect to *many* of the living existences, there has been a separate creation in the old and in the new world." Numerous observers, according to Barton, had made the mistake of identifying American with European animals simply because of superficial resemblances. He admitted, of course, that several species of quadrupeds had come (or had been transported) to America from Asia or from Europe—just as some American species had migrated to those continents. But many animals had never been found outside America and these he considered exclusively American. Upon any other supposition than that of a separate creation, Barton thought it impossible to explain the presence here of such creatures as the raccoon, the opossum, the woodchuck, the alpaca, and the bison.

It may at first seem surprising that the American philosopher should have been willing to admit a separate creation of any animals on this continent. For if unique species of plants and animals had been created for America, then why not of man too? Might not the Indian have been created for this continent, the Negro for Africa—and what then of the unity of the human species? This, of course, was the implication which anti-equalitarians like Captain Romans had drawn. But the course of the Jeffersonian argument actually confirmed the concept of the uniqueness of man. His belief that man was a peculiarly cosmopolitan species, destined for adaptation, pioneering, and conquest on new continents, predisposed the Jeffersonian to consider the existence of endemic species of plants and lower animals irrelevant to the number of *human* species. He could squarely face the fact that the Creator had made some lower species expressly for America, and feel that this did not increase the probability of such a separate creation of man. Jefferson himself, who showed great interest in the peculiarly American species of the lower creation, could not conceive the possibility of a "separate creation" of man on this continent.

The Jeffersonian betrayed no doubt that there had been a single original source for all mankind, from which men had anciently emigrated. Its precise location, however, seemed a matter over which intelligent men might differ. Barton, for example, in his *New Views of the Origin of the Tribes and Nations of America,* sharply contrasted the two classes of anthropologists: first, those superficial students who thought the American Indians were strictly speaking the aborigines of the soil, and not emigrants from other parts of the world; and second, the men of great learning and wisdom, including the clergy, and those like Joseph Acosta, Edward Brerewood, John de Laet, Hugo Grotius, George de Hornn and many others, who asserted that the American Indians were anciently derived from another continent. The men of this latter group understandably disagreed among themselves as to the residence of the parents of the species (some placing it in Asia, while others found it in Europe, in

Africa, or in the unknown Atlantis). What according to Barton distinguished them from the other school was not where they had discovered the cradle of mankind, but that they all refused to doubt that there had been such a cradle.

Jefferson himself categorically denied the separate creation of the American Indians, but he was too cautious to swallow any of the simplistic theories of Indian origin. He could not accept Moreton's deduction of the American Indians from the fugitive Trojans, Adair's derivation from the Hebrews, Reinold Foster's theory of their descent from the soldiers sent by Kouli Khan to conquer Japan, nor Brerewood's doctrine of their Tartar ancestry. While finding all these much less absurd than Romans' doctrine of separate creation, Jefferson was forced finally to admit that "the question of Indian origin, like many others, pushed to a certain height must receive the same answer, 'Ignoro.'"

It was a desire to confirm the common origin of men that drew Jefferson's own energies into linguistic studies. In his *Notes on Virginia*, he distinguished the different original stocks of Indians on the basis of their languages; he established the connection of American Indians with the eastern inhabitants of Asia; and he cataloged the Indian tribes for the benefit of future scholars. The strikingly large number of radical tongues found on this continent had led him to the novel conjecture that the American Indians might be older than the Asiatic peoples and that the original home of man might therefore have been in America. Throughout his life he studied Indian languages, always with an eye to the light they might throw on the source of mankind. He never reached an answer which satisfied him in detail.

The Jeffersonian of course noticed among men, as among other representatives of any fixed biological type, the existence of varieties. By "varieties" he meant something quite definite: variations not created in the beginning as a part of the original scheme of creation, but which had come into being more recently from environmental causes. This meaning of "variety," still in use when the first edition of the *American Dictionary* appeared in 1828, was succinctly stated by Noah Webster under the word *Species*:

1. In *zoology*, a collection of organized beings derived from one common parentage by natural generation, characterized by one peculiar form,

liable to vary from the influence of circumstances only within certain narrow limits. These accidental and limited variations are *varieties*. Different races from the same parents are called *varieties*.

This was precisely the sense in which Jefferson himself used the words. In his *Notes on Virginia,* for example, he explained that there were "varieties in the race of man, distinguished by their powers both of body and mind," just as in the case of other animals. "It is not against experience," he added, "to suppose that different species of the same genus, or varieties of the same species, may possess different qualifications. Will not a lover of natural history then, one who views the gradations in all the races of animals with the eye of philosophy, excuse an effort to keep those in the department of man as distinct as nature has formed them?" Since these different "varieties" were by definition nothing but accidental variations of a single primeval type, the American philosopher was prepared against allowing the existence of "varieties" of man in any way to impugn the unity of the human species.

In this he was supported by the best authority. For his usage was plainly authorized by Carolus Linnaeus' *Systema Naturae* (1735) which had provided the vocabulary for his natural history. Opening the first volume of the *Systema Naturae,* we find beneath the Order of Primates the *Genus Homo* which is divided into two species: *Homo (sapiens) diurnus* which includes all humankind; and *Homo (troglodytes) nocturnus,* illustrated by the orang-outang *(Homo sylvestris Orang Outang).* Within the human species Linnaeus distinguished several varieties: *Ferus, Americanus, Europaeus, Asiaticus, Afer,* and *Monstrosus.* Each of these (except "Monstrosus," which was a kind of sport of nature) was designated by the environment in which it had developed. The "Ferus" was a man who had become wild or savage by growing up alone in the wilderness; the others were distinguished by the continents which had brought them into being.

The large numbers of Indians and Negroes made this continent a nearly perfect laboratory of anthropology and enabled the Jeffersonian to scrutinize at least three *(Homo sapiens Americanus, Homo sapiens Europaeus,* and *Homo sapiens Afer)* of the six principal "varieties" of the human species. Moreover, the axiomatic symmetry of the cosmos made it superfluous to examine the causes of every variation among men. The Jeffersonian was therefore ready to assume that if the peculiarities of the red man (probably a migrant from Asia) and of the black man (surely a migrant from Africa), which distinguished them both from the white man of Europe, could be shown to have arisen recently and through the influence of environment—if there was no difference of species among these—then evidence pertaining to unexamined varieties would not be likely to disprove the unity of mankind.

The American philosopher built his generalizations on personal experience—in Jefferson's phrase, "on what I have seen of man, white, red, and black." The extensive studies of the Indian by Dr. Benjamin Rush, the eminent physician and pioneer psychiatrist, were based on contemporary observations. It is hard to believe that Benjamin Smith Barton and his uncle, David Rittenhouse, had not actually encountered Indians on their surveying expedition to western Pennsylvania. Numerous articles in the *Transactions* of the Philosophical Society were illustrated by personal anecdotes of Indian manners and customs.

John Adams recollected clearly the "forms and figures" of the Indians who frequented his father's house in Massachusetts. Such observations were especially valuable because in western Europe, even at the time of the Declaration of Independence, reliable information about the physique, the nature and the habits of non-European races was extremely scarce. Two centuries earlier, Shakespeare had been attracted by tales of anthropophagi whose heads grew beneath their shoulders. In the eighteenth century, travel books told the even more marvelous tales of beautiful virgins who grew on trees.

When Jefferson undertook his study of the American Indian, he made it his first task to clear away the inventions of fanciful writers. He revealed a piquant satisfaction in showing how his predecessors (and particularly the opponents of human equality) had distorted the facts of anthropology. Most European tales about the Indian, he said, were no more true than Aesop's Fables—and, he implied, no less guided by the preconceptions of their authors. From his ample firsthand experience he refuted each of the allegedly innate deficiencies of the Indian. In the Appendix to his *Notes on Virginia*, he disproved them one by one.

Monsieur Buffon has indeed given an afflicting picture of human nature in his description of the man of America. But sure I am there never was a picture more unlike the original. He grants indeed that his stature is the same as that of the man of Europe. He might have admitted, that the Iroquois were larger, and the Lenopi, or Delawares, taller than people in Europe generally are. But he says their organs of generation are smaller and weaker than those of Europeans. Is this a fact? I believe not; at least it is an observation I never heard before.—"They have no beard." Had he known the pains and trouble it costs the men to pluck out by the roots the hair that grows on their faces, he would have seen that nature had not been deficient in that respect. Every nation has its customs. I have seen an Indian beau, with a looking-glass in his hand, examining his face for hours together, and plucking out by the roots every hair he could discover, with a kind of tweezer made of a piece of fine brass wire, that had been twisted round a stick, and which he used with great dexterity.—"They have no ardor for their females." It is true they do not indulge those excesses, nor discover that fondness which is customary in Europe; but this is not owing to a defect in nature but to manners. Their soul is wholly bent upon war.

European philosophers said that because the Indian had little sexual passion, he felt less family affection, was less philanthropic than the white man, and ought for that reason to be distinguished as an inferior species.

To support this, their main evidence was the alleged lack of the body hair which the European associated with strong sexual instincts. But even if their facts had been correct, Jefferson objected, their conclusion was unwarranted: Negroes, for example, actually had less hair than white men, and yet were notoriously more ardent. If philosophers would only gather enough facts, would weigh them impartially, and would take full account of the influence of environment, Jefferson believed that they would probably find the American Indian to be "formed in mind as well as in body, on the same module with 'Homo sapiens Europaeus.' " To avoid any vagueness about his intention to speak in precise biological terms, he referred his reader to the "Definition of a Man" in Linnaeus' *Systema Naturae*.

Most Jeffersonian philosophers, including Jefferson himself, were not much troubled by the characteristic color of the Indian. They somehow found the Indian's copper skin so much like that of the white man as to suggest nothing more than a difference of "variety."

Yet the difference of complexion between white man and red man was nothing compared with the difference between their stages of civilization. Opponents of human equality simply asserted that the

Indian had been created a species inferior to the European in intellectual and social endowments. But the equalitarian was committed to a more elaborate explanation. There was, for example, Dr. Samuel Stanhope Smith's sociological account. After the Deluge, he observed, men found themselves in an immense wilderness where beasts multiplied faster than the human race. Although agriculture had been the employment of Noah and his immediate descendants (from whom the civilized states traced an uninterrupted descent), this was too laborious a mode of subsistence to satisfy all men. The less industrious, seeing the wilderness filled with beasts, readily abandoned the toils of clearing and cultivating the ground and sought an easier and more adventurous living from the chase. Hunting soon dispersed them over extensive regions; and single families, or collections of a few families, became independent tribes. Their remoteness from one another and their mode of procuring subsistence rendered them savage and made progress impossible.

While most of the Jeffersonians found the general features of this account acceptable, they were more reluctant than the pious Dr. Smith to adopt the Biblical history of the Deluge with all its consequences. Again, instead of attempting to reconstruct the details of ancient history, they preferred to interpret recent facts so as to disprove the strictures on the contemporary Indian. Barton, for example, easily refuted the charge that the Indians' unfriendliness to Christianity was evidence of their intellectual inferiority. The true explanation, he said, was the natural reluctance of rude nations to forsake the religions of their ancestors, and the improper means of persuasion used by Jesuit missionaries.

The Negro presented the Jeffersonian anthropologist with a more difficult problem. The Indian was observed in autonomous communities which displayed a gamut of talents, including powers of organization and leadership. The white man perforce met him as an equal, if only in battle. But, in America at least, the Negro's servile condition concealed his talents. It would not be so easy to prove that the Negro's physical peculiarities and his primitive social development were nothing but environmental modifications on the original type of man. Virtually nothing was recorded of his African civilizations, and little could be learned from the Negro himself, or from buried relics like those which told of an ancient Indian culture. Since little was known of the native African languages, the student lacked still another kind of information that had been useful in demonstrating the Indian's membership in the single tribe of mankind.

It is not surprising then that the Jeffersonian who had committed his moral science to the data of natural history should betray uncertainty whether the Negro was the equal of other races of man. But these American philosophers showed a remarkable facility at explaining away the most obvious and troublesome peculiarity of the Negro—his color. In his "Observations intended to favour a supposition that the Black Color (as it is called) of the Negroes is derived from the Leprosy," Jefferson's friend, Dr. Benjamin Rush, reasoned, partly from his clinical observations in the Pennsylvania Hospital and partly from common experience, toward the conclusion that the so-called black color of the Negro was the effect not of any original difference in his nature, but of the affliction of his ancestors with leprosy. This disease, he noted, was accompanied in some instances by a black color of the skin. The big lips and flat nose typical of Negroes were actually symptoms of leprosy, which Rush himself had more than once observed. The inhabitants of the leper islands of the South Pacific possessed thick lips and woolly hair; and albinism (also found among American Negroes) was not unknown there.

The same morbid insensibility of the nerves which was induced by leprosy was found peculiarly in Negroes, who, compared to white people, were able to endure surgical operations with ease. Rush recalled cases where Negroes had actually held the upper part of a limb during amputation. Such pathological insensibility was also apparent in the apathy with which Negroes exposed themselves to great heat, and the indifference with which they handled hot coals. Lepers were remarkable for their strong venereal desires; and so strong were these desires in Negroes that even the depressing circumstances of slavery had not prevented their extraordinary fruitfulness.

When asked to account for the duration of the Negro's color through long centuries, Rush answered that leprosy was of all diseases the most permanently inherited. According to Rush, the fact that in the eighteenth century Negroes seldom infected others with the disease could not be held against his theory, because by now leprosy had nearly ceased to be infectious. And actually there were even instances where something like an infectious quality had appeared in the skin of Negroes. Since local diseases of the skin seldom affected the general health of the body or the duration of human life, the present health and longevity of the Negro were no objection to his thesis.

If the black color of the Negro had really been caused by leprosy, Rush found certain conclusions inevitable:

1. That all the claims of superiority of the whites over the blacks, on account of their color, are founded alike in ignorance and inhumanity. If the color of the negroes be the effect of a disease, instead of inviting us to tyrannise over them, it should entitle them to a double portion of our humanity, for disease all over the world has always been the signal for immediate and universal compassion.

2. The facts and principles which have been delivered, should teach white people the necessity of keeping up that prejudice against such connections with them, as would tend to infect posterity with any portion of their disorder. This may be done upon the ground I have mentioned without offering violence to humanity, or calling in question the sameness of descent, or natural equality of mankind.

3. Is the color of the negroes a disease? Then let science and humanity combine their efforts, and endeavor to discover a remedy for it. Nature has lately unfurled a banner upon this subject. She has begun spontaneous cures of this disease in several black people in this country.

When cured of the disease, the Negroes would be much happier, for however well they sometimes appeared to be satisfied with their color, there were many proofs of their preferring that of the white people. And most important, Rush concluded, "We shall render the belief of the whole human race being descended from one pair, easy, and universal, and thereby not only add weight to the Christian revelation, but remove a material obstacle to the exercise of that universal benevolence which is inculcated by it."

Through this whole argument ran the assumption (the more significant because not explicitly avowed) that the norm for the color of a healthy member of the human species was *white*. It was inconceivable to Rush that when the Negro had been cured of his affliction and returned to his pristine condition, he would have the red complexion of the American Indian or the yellow of the Asiatic. One of his final arguments for redoubling the effort to perfect a cure was that the Negro might have the happiness of wearing the proper white color of the human skin. Jefferson himself betrayed this assumption in the *Notes on Virginia* (Query XIV) when he judged the color of the Negro to be aesthetically inferior to that of the white man: "Are not the fine mixtures of red and white, the expressions of every passion by greater or less suffusions of color in the one, preferable to that eternal monotony, which reigns in the countenances, that immovable veil of black which covers the emotions of the other race?"

Jefferson's anthropological judgments on the Negro all betray a suspicion that color might very well have been among "the real distinctions which nature has made." We must not forget that Jefferson, unlike Rush, was a Virginian. Although he was theoretically opposed to the institution of slavery, he had been reared in a society where there seemed little to confirm the equal talents of the Negro. While his relevant statements were uniformly and perhaps designedly ambiguous, Jefferson seemed inwardly driven to suggest that some original differences in color must have been indelible in the Creator's design. Yet he never quite dared say that color variations were actually indices of a difference of species. He was not sure enough of the irrelevance of the Negro's color to assign him the same ancient parents as the white man; yet he was too much of an equalitarian to suggest that the Negro might have been created a distinct species.

Partly because of this inner uncertainty, Jefferson's comments on the Negro were written in the optative mood, and therefore admirably illustrate the relation between his theology and his science. While he insisted that the axiomatic unity of the human species had to be confirmed by facts, he was willing finally to rely on a general presumption in favor of human equality.

> The opinion that they [Negroes] are inferior in the faculties of reason and imagination, must be hazarded with great diffidence. To justify a general conclusion, requires many observations, even where the subject may be submitted to the anatomical knife, to optical glasses, to analysis by fire or by solvents. How much more then where it is a faculty, not a substance, we are examining; where it eludes the research of all the senses; where the conditions of its existence are various and variously combined; where the effects of those which are present or absent bid defiance to calculation; let me add too, as a circumstance of great tenderness, where our conclusion would degrade a whole race of men from the rank in the scale of beings which their Creator may perhaps have given them.

The reader of such warnings cannot but be bewildered. On the one hand, Jefferson urged, be careful lest by overhasty conclusions from scanty evidence you assume that the present peculiarities of the Negro show an original difference of species. For this might mistake the Creator's design and thereby degrade a whole race from their destined rank. On the other hand, he insisted with barely less emphasis, be careful that you do not hastily ignore any visible distinctions, for these all may have a divine claim to social recognition.

In his *Notes on Virginia,* Jefferson concluded after examining the evidence:

> I advance it, therefore, as a suspicion only, that the blacks, whether originally a distinct race [Jefferson significantly does not say "species"] or made distinct by time and circumstances, are inferior to the whites in the endowments both of body and mind. It is not against experience to suppose that different species of the same genus, or varieties of the same species, may possess different qualifications. Will not a lover of natural history then, one who views the gradations in all the races of animals with the eye of philosophy, excuse an effort to keep those in the department of man as distinct as nature has formed them?

It would be hard to imagine a statement more tentative or ambiguous than this and still couched in the language of Linnaean natural history. Jefferson thus revealed both his determination to confirm his concept of man by the data of biology; and, at the same time, his reluctance to confide his feelings, where they were really uncertain, to the strict arbitration of unfriendly facts.

Similar doubts appear in his attempts to assess the effects of slavery on the Negro. In order fairly to judge the influence of environment on the Negro's capacities, Jefferson compared him, not with his white master, nor with his free Indian neighbor, but with the ancient Roman slave. Only after a long and circumstantial comparison, in which he considered the poetic and philosophic accomplishments of slaves in Roman times, did he conclude that the inferiority of the Negro might not be explained by his servile status. "It is not their condition then," Jefferson said, "but nature, which has produced the distinction." To say that the Negro lacked the genius of an Epictetus, a Terence, or a Phaedrus was, of course, highly ambiguous dispraise, and probably was meant as such. Yet Jefferson felt compelled to mitigate even these gentle strictures by adding that, whether or not further observations would verify "the conjecture, that nature has been less bountiful to them in the endowments of the head . . . in those of the heart she will be found to have done them justice."

He defended the Negroes against their allegedly congenital disposition to theft. After an ingenious evasion in which Jefferson questioned whether the slave might not be justified in taking a little property from his master when his master had already taken everything from him, he summed up the "factual" foundation of his belief: "That a change in the relations in which a man is placed should change his ideas of moral right or wrong, is neither new, nor peculiar to the color of the blacks. Homer tells us it was so two thousand six hundred years ago."

What he always expressed was an open-minded hopefulness that the facts would some day produce unambiguous proof of the equality of the Negro. He never lost his eagerness for an entirely satisfactory demonstration "that the want of talents observed in them is merely the effect of their degraded condition, and not proceeding from any difference in the structure of the parts on which intellect depends." On this he expected the Santo Domingo experiment to throw some light. "Be assured," he wrote to a correspondent who had sent him a disappointing anthology of Negro literature, "that no person living wishes more sincerely than I do, to see a complete refutation of the doubts I have myself entertained and expressed on the grade of understanding allotted to them by nature, and to find that in this respect they are on a par with ourselves."

PART III

THE RHETORIC OF DEMOCRACY

Human speech is like a cracked
kettle on which we tap out tunes
for bears to dance to, while we
long to make music that will
melt the stars.

FLAUBERT, *Madame Bovary*

CHAPTER 10

The Rhetoric of Democracy

ADVERTISING, of course, has been part of the mainstream of American civilization, although you might not know it if you read the most respectable surveys of American history. It has been one of the enticements to the settlement of this New World, it has been a producer of the peopling of the United States, and in its modern form, in its worldwide reach, it has been one of our most characteristic products.

Never was there a more outrageous or more unscrupulous or more ill-informed advertising campaign than that by which the promoters for the American colonies brought settlers here. Brochures published in England in the seventeenth century, some even earlier, were full of hopeful overstatements, half-truths, and downright lies, along with some facts which nowadays surely would be the basis for investigation by a Better Business Bureau. Gold and silver, fountains of youth, plenty of fish, venison without limit, all these were promised, and of course some of them were actually here. How long might it have taken to settle this continent if there had not been such promotion by enterprising advertisers? How has American civilization been shaped by the fact that there was a kind of natural selection here of those people who were willing to believe advertising?

Advertising has taken the lead in promising and exploiting the new. This was a new world, and one of the advertisements for it appears on the dollar bill on the Great Seal of the United States, which reads *novus ordo seclorum,* one of the most effective advertising slogans to come out of this country. "A new order of the centuries"—belief in novelty and in the desirability of opening novelty to everybody has been important in our lives throughout our history and especially in this century. Again and again advertising has been an agency for inducing Americans to try anything and everything from the continent itself to a new brand of soap. As one of the more literate and poetic of the advertising copywriters, James Kenneth Frazier, a Cornell graduate, wrote in 1900 in "The Doctor's Lament":

> This lean M.D. is Dr. Brown
> Who fares but ill in Spotless Town.
> The town is so confounded clean,
> It is no wonder he is lean,
> He's lost all patients now, you know,
> Because they use *Sapolio*.

The same literary talent that once was used to retail Sapolio was later used to induce people to try the Edsel or the Mustang, to experiment with Lifebuoy or Body All, to drink Pepsi-Cola or Royal Crown Cola, or to shave with a Trac II razor.

And as expansion and novelty have become essential to our economy, advertising has played an ever-larger role: in the settling of the continent, in the expansion of the economy, and in the building of an American standard of living. Advertising has expressed the optimism, the hyperbole, and the sense of community, the sense of reaching which has been so important a feature of our civilization.

Here I wish to explore the significance of advertising, not as a force in the economy or in shaping an American standard of living, but rather as a touchstone of the ways in which we Americans have learned about all sorts of things.

The problems of advertising are of course not peculiar to advertising, for they are just one aspect of the problems of democracy. They reflect the rise of what in *The Americans: The Democratic Experience* I have called Consumption Communities and Statistical Communities, and many of the special problems of advertising have arisen from our continuously energetic effort to give everybody everything.

If we consider democracy not just as a political system, but as a set of institutions which do aim to make everything available to everybody, it would not be an overstatement to describe advertising as the characteristic rhetoric of democracy. One of the tendencies of democracy, which Plato and other antidemocrats warned against a long time ago, was the danger that rhetoric would displace or at least overshadow epistemology; that is, *the temptation to allow the problem of persuasion to overshadow the problem of knowledge.* Democratic societies tend to become more concerned with what people believe than with what is true, to become more concerned with credibility than with truth. All these problems become accentuated in a large-scale democracy like ours, which possesses the apparatus of modern industry. And the problems are accentuated still further by literacy, by instantaneous communication, and by the daily plague of words and images.

In the early days it was common for advertising men to define advertisements as a kind of news. The best admen, like the best journalists, were supposed to be those who were able to make their news the most interesting and readable. This was natural enough, since the verb "to advertise" originally meant, intransitively, to take note or to consider. For a person to "advertise" meant originally, in the fourteenth and fifteenth centuries, to reflect on something, to think about something. Then it came to mean, transitively, to call the attention of another to something, to give notice, to notify, admonish, warn or inform in a formal or impressive manner. And then, by the sixteenth century, it came to mean: to give notice of anything, to make generally known.

It was not until the late eighteenth century that the word "advertising" in English came to have a specifically "advertising" connotation as we might say today. And not until the late nineteenth century that it began to have a specifically commercial connotation. By 1879 someone was saying, "Don't advertise unless you have something worth advertising." But even into the present century, newspapers continue to call themselves by the title "Advertiser"—for example, the Boston *Daily Advertiser,* which was a newspaper of long tradition and one of the most dignified papers in Boston until William Randolph Hearst took it over in 1917. Newspapers carried "Advertiser" on their mastheads, not because they sold advertisements but because they brought news.

Now, the main role of advertising in American civilization came increasingly to be that of persuading and appealing rather than that of educating and informing. By 1921, for instance, one of the more popular textbooks, Blanchard's *Essentials of Advertising,* began: "Anything employed to influence people favorably is advertising. The mission of advertising is to persuade men and women to act in a way that will be of advantage to the advertiser." This development—in a country where a shared, a rising, and a democratized standard of living was the national pride and the national hallmark—meant that advertising had become the rhetoric of democracy.

What, then, are some of the main features of modern American advertising as a form of rhetoric? First, and perhaps most obvious, is *repetition*. It is hard for us to realize that the use of repetition in advertising is not an ancient device but a modern one, which actually did not come into common use in American journalism until just past the middle of the nineteenth century.

The development of what came to be called "iteration copy" was a result of a struggle by a courageous man of letters and advertising pioneer, Robert Bonner, who bought the old New York *Merchant's Ledger* in 1851 and turned it into a popular journal. He then had the temerity to try to change the ways of James Gordon Bennett, who of course was one of the most successful of the American newspaper pioneers, and who was both a sensationalist and at the same time an extremely stuffy man when it came to things that he did not consider to be news. Bonner was determined to use advertisements in Bennett's wide-circulating New York *Herald* to sell his own literary product, but he found it difficult to persuade Bennett to allow him to use any but agate type in his advertising. Agate was the smallest type used by newspapers in that day, only barely legible to the naked eye. Bennett would not allow advertisers to use larger type, nor would he allow them to use illustrations except stock cuts, because he thought it was undignified. He said, too, that to allow a variation in the format of ads would be undemocratic. He insisted that all advertisers use the same size type so that no one would be allowed to prevail over another simply by presenting his message in a larger, more clever, or more attention-getting form.

Finally Bonner managed to overcome Bennett's rigidity by leasing whole pages of the paper and using the tiny agate type to form larger letters across the top of the page. In this way he produced a message such as "Bring home the New York Ledger tonight." His were unimaginative messages, and when repeated all across the page, they technically did not violate Bennett's agate rule. But they opened a new era and presaged a new freedom for advertisers in their use of the newspaper page. Iteration copy—the practice of presenting prosaic content in ingenious, repetitive form—became common, and nowadays of course is commonplace.

A second characteristic of American advertising which is not un-related to this is the development of *an advertising style*. We have histories of most other kinds of style—including the style of many unread writers who are remembered today only because they have been forgotten—but we have very few accounts of the history of advertising style, which of course is one of the most important forms of our language and one of the most widely influential.

The development of advertising style was the convergence of several very respectable American traditions. One of these was the tradition of the "plain style," which the Puritans made so much of and which accounts for so much of the strength of Puritan literature. The "plain style" was of course much influenced by the Bible and found its way into the rhetoric of American writers and speakers of great power like Abraham Lincoln.

When advertising began to be self-conscious in the early years of this century, the pioneers urged copywriters not to be too clever, and especially not to be fancy. One of the pioneers of the advertising copywriters, John Powers, said, for example, "The commonplace is the proper level for writing in business; where the first virtue is plainness, 'fine writing' is not only intellectual, it is offensive." George P. Rowell, another advertising pioneer, said, "You must write your advertisement to catch damned fools—not college professors." He was a very tactful person. And he added, "And you'll catch just as many college professors as you will of any other sort." In the 1920s, when advertising was beginning to come into its own, Claude Hopkins, whose name is known to all in the trade, said, "Brilliant writing has no place in advertising. A unique style takes attention from the subject. Any apparent effort to sell creates corresponding resistance. . . . One should be natural and simple. His language should not be conspicuous. In fishing for buyers, as in fishing for bass, one should not reveal the hook." So there developed a characteristic advertising style in which plainness, the phrase that anyone could understand, was a distinguishing mark.

At the same time, the American advertising style drew on an-other, and what might seem an antithetic, tradition—the tradition of hyperbole and tall talk, the language of Davy Crockett and Mike Fink. While advertising could think of itself as 99.44 percent pure, it used the language of "Toronado" and "Cutlass." As I listen to the radio in Washington, I hear a celebration of heroic qualities which would make the characteristics of Mike Fink and Davy Crockett pale, only to discover at the end of the paean that what I have been hearing is a description of the Ford dealers in the District of Columbia neighborhood. And along with the folk tradition of hyperbole and tall talk comes the rhythm of folk music. We hear that Pepsi-Cola hits the spot, that it's for the young generation—and we hear other products celebrated in music which we cannot forget and sometimes don't want to remember.

There grew somehow out of all these contradictory tendencies—combining the commonsense language of the "plain style," and the fantasy language of "tall talk"—an advertising style. This characteristic way of talking about things was especially designed to reach and catch the millions. It created a whole new world of myth. A myth, the dictionary tells us, is a notion based more on tradition or convenience than on facts; it is a received idea. Myth is not just fantasy and not just fact but exists in a limbo, in the world of the Will to Believe, which William James has written about so eloquently and so perceptively. This is the world of the neither true nor false—of the statement that 60 percent of the physicians who expressed a choice said that our brand of aspirin would be more effective in curing a simple headache than any other leading brand.

That kind of statement exists in a penumbra. I would call this the "advertising penumbra." It is not untrue, and yet, in its connotation it is not exactly true.

Now, there is still another characteristic of advertising so obvious that we are inclined perhaps to overlook it. I call that *ubiquity*. Advertising abhors a vacuum and we discover new vacuums every day. The parable, of course, is the story of the man who thought of putting the advertisement on the other side of the cigarette package. Until then, that was wasted space, and a society which aims at a democratic standard of living, at extending the benefits of consumption and all sorts of things and services to everybody, must miss no chances to reach people. The highway billboard and other outdoor advertising, bus and streetcar and subway advertising, and skywriting, radio and TV commercials—all these are of course obvious evidence that advertising abhors a vacuum.

We might reverse the old mousetrap slogan and say that anyone who can devise another place to put another mousetrap to catch a consumer will find people beating a path to his door. "Avoiding advertising will become a little harder next January," the *Wall Street Journal* reported on May 17, 1973, "when a Studio City,

California, company launches a venture called StoreVision. Its product is a system of billboards that move on a track across supermarket ceilings. Some 650 supermarkets so far are set to have the system." All of which helps us understand the observation attributed to a French man of letters during his visit to Times Square. "What a beautiful place, if only one could not read!" Everywhere is a place to be filled, as we discover in a *Publishers Weekly* description of one advertising program: "The paperback edition of Dr. Thomas A. Harris' million-copy best seller, *I'm O.K., You're O.K.,* is in for full-scale promotion in July by its publisher, Avon Books. Plans range from bumper stickers to airplane streamers, from planes flying above Fire Island, the Hamptons and Malibu. In addition, the $100,000 promotion budget calls for 200,000 bookmarks, plus brochures, buttons, lipcards, floor and counter displays, and advertising in magazines and TV."

The ubiquity of advertising is of course just another effect of our uninhibited efforts to use all the media to get all sorts of information to everybody everywhere. Since the places to be filled are everywhere, the amount of advertising is not determined by the *needs* of advertising, but by the *opportunities* for advertising, which become unlimited.

But the most effective advertising, in an energetic, novelty-ridden society like ours, tends to be "self-liquidating." To create a cliché you must offer something which everybody accepts. The most successful advertising therefore self-destructs because it becomes cliché. Examples of this are found in the tendency for copyrighted names or trademarks to enter the vernacular—for the proper names of products which have been made familiar by costly advertising to become common nouns, and so to apply to anybody's products. Kodak becomes a synonym for camera, Kleenex a synonym for facial tissue, when both begin with a small *k,* and Xerox (now, too, with a small *x*) is used to describe all processes of copying, and so on. These are prototypes of the problem. If you are successful enough, then you will defeat your purpose in the long run by making the name and the message so familiar that people won't notice them, and then people will cease to distinguish your product from everybody else's.

In a sense, of course, as we will see, the whole of American civilization is an example. When this was a "new" world, if people succeeded in building a civilization here, the New World would survive and would reach the time, in our age, when it would cease to be new.

And now we have the oldest written constitution in use in the world. This is only a parable of which there are many more examples.

The advertising man who is successful in marketing any particular product then is apt to be diluting the demand for his product in the very act of satisfying it. But luckily for him, he is at the very same time creating a fresh demand for his services as advertiser.

And as a consequence, there is yet another role which is assigned to American advertising. This is what I call "erasure." Insofar as advertising is competitive or innovation is widespread, erasure is required in order to persuade consumers that this year's model is superior to last year's. In fact, we consumers learn that we might be risking our lives if we go out on the highway with those very devices that were last year's lifesavers but without whatever special kind of brake or windshield wipers or seat belt is on this year's model. This is what I mean by "erasure"—and we see it on our advertising pages or our television screen every day. We read in the *New York Times* (May 20, 1973), for example, that "For the price of something small and ugly, you can drive something small and beautiful"—an advertisement for the Fiat 250 Spider. Or another, perhaps more subtle example is the advertisement for shirts under a picture of Oliver Drab: "Oliver Drab. A name to remember in fine designer shirts? No kidding . . . Because you pay extra money for Oliver Drab. And for all the other superstars of the fashion world. Golden Vee [the name of the brand that is advertised] does not have a designer's label. But we do have designers. . . . By keeping their names *off* our label and simply saying Golden Vee, we can afford to sell our $7 to $12 shirts for just $7 to $12, which should make Golden Vee a name to remember. Golden Vee, you only pay for the shirt."

The special role of advertising in our life gives a clue to a pervasive oddity in American civilization. A leading feature of past cultures, as anthropologists have explained, is the tendency to distinguish between "high" culture and "low" culture—between the culture of the literate and the learned on the one hand and that of the populace on the other. In other words, between the language of literature and the language of the vernacular. Some of the most useful statements of this distinction have been made by social scientists at the University of Chicago—first by the anthropologist Robert Redfield in his several pioneering books on peasant society, and then by Milton Singer in his remarkable study of Indian civilization, *When a Great Tradition Modernizes* (1972). This distinction between the great tradition and the little tradition, between the high culture and the folk culture, has become a commonplace of modern anthropology.

Some of the obvious features of advertising in modern America offer us an opportunity to note the significance or insignificance of that distinction for us. Elsewhere I have tried to point out some of the peculiarities of the American attitude toward the *high* culture. There is something distinctive about the place of thought in American life, which is not quite what it has been in certain Old World cultures.

But what about distinctive American attitudes to *popular* culture? What is our analogue to the folk culture of other peoples? Advertising gives us some clues to a characteristically American democratic folk culture. Folk culture is a name for the culture which ordinary people everywhere lean on. It is not the writings of Dante and Chaucer and Shakespeare and Milton, the teachings of Machiavelli and Descartes, Locke or Marx. It is, rather, the pattern of slogans, local traditions, tales, songs, dances, and ditties. And of course holiday observances. Popular culture in other civilizations has been for the most part both an area of continuity with the past, a way in which people reach back into the past and out to their community, and at the same time an area of local variations. An area of individual and amateur expression in which a person has his own way of saying, or notes his mother's way of saying or singing, or his own way of dancing, his own view of folk wisdom and the cliché.

And here is an interesting point of contrast. In societies outside the United States, it is the *high* culture that has generally been an area of centralized, organized control. In Western Europe, for example, universities and churches have tended to be closely allied to the government. The institutions of higher learning have had a relatively limited access to the people as a whole. This was inevitable, of course, in most parts of the world, because there were so few universities. In England, for example, there were only two universities until the early nineteenth century. And there was central control over the printed matter that was used in universities or in the liturgy. The government tended to be close to the high culture, and that was easy because the high culture itself was so centralized and because literacy was relatively limited.

In our society, however, we seem to have turned all of this

around. Our high culture is one of the least centralized areas of our culture. And our universities express the atomistic, diffused, chaotic, and individualistic aspect of our life. We have in this country more than 3,000 colleges and universities, institutions of so-called higher learning. We have a vast population in these institutions.

But when we turn to our popular culture, what do we find? We find that in our nation of Consumption Communities and emphasis on Gross National Product (GNP) and growth rates, advertising has become the heart of the folk culture and even its very prototype. And as we have seen, American advertising shows many characteristics of the folk culture of other societies: repetition, a plain style, hyperbole and tall talk, folk verse, and folk music. Folk culture, wherever it has flourished, has tended to thrive in a limbo between fact and fantasy, and of course, depending on the spoken word and the oral tradition, it spreads easily and tends to be ubiquitous. These are all familiar characteristics of folk culture and they are ways of describing our folk culture, but how do the expressions of our peculiar folk culture come to *us?*

They no longer sprout from the earth, from the village, from the farm, or even from the neighborhood or the city. They come to us primarily from enormous centralized self-consciously "creative" (an overused word, for the overuse of which advertising agencies are in no small part responsible) organizations. They come from advertising agencies, from networks of newspapers, radio, and television, from outdoor-advertising agencies, from the copywriters for ads in the largest-circulation magazines, and so on. These "creators" of folk culture—or pseudo–folk culture—aim at the widest intelligibility and charm and appeal.

But in the United States, we must recall, the advertising folk culture, like all advertising, is also confronted with the problems of self-liquidation and erasure. These are by-products of the expansive, energetic character of our economy. And they, too, distinguish American folk culture from folk cultures elsewhere.

Our folk culture is distinguished from others by being discontinuous, ephemeral, and self-destructive. Where does this leave the common citizen? All of us are qualified to answer.

In our society, then, those who cannot lean on the world of learning, on the high culture of the classics, on the elaborated wisdom of the books, have a new problem. The University of Chicago, for example, in the 1930s and 1940s was the center of a quest for a "common discourse." The champions of that quest, which became a kind of crusade, believed that such a discourse could be found through familiarity with the classics of great literature and especially of Western European literature. I think they were misled; such works were not, nor are they apt to become, the common discourse of our society. Most people, even in a democracy, and a rich democracy like ours, live in a world of popular culture, our special kind of popular culture.

The characteristic folk culture of our society is a creature of advertising, and in a sense it *is* advertising. But advertising, our own popular culture, is harder to make into a source of continuity than the received wisdom and commonsense slogans and catchy songs of the vivid vernacular. The popular culture of advertising attenuates and is always dissolving before our very eyes. Among the charms, challenges, and tribulations of modern life, we must count this peculiar fluidity, this ephemeral character of that very kind of culture on which other peoples have been able to lean, the kind of culture to which they have looked for the continuity of their traditions, for their ties with the past and with the future.

We are perhaps the first people in history to have a centrally organized mass-produced folk culture. Our kind of popular culture is here today and gone tomorrow—or the day after tomorrow. Or whenever the next semi-annual model appears! And insofar as folk culture becomes advertising, and advertising becomes centralized, it becomes a way of depriving people of their opportunities for individual and small-community expression. Our technology and our economy and our democratic ideals have all helped make that possible. Here we have a new test of the problem that is at least as old as Heraclitus—an everyday test of man's ability to find continuity in his experience. And here democratic man has a new opportunity to accommodate himself, if he can, to the unknown.

CHAPTER 11

A Nationally Advertised President

IN EUROPE the history-making political leaders have usually been set apart from the crowd by qualities of the artist and the prophet. But ours have generally been respectable spokesmen for the respectable community. Compare Queen Elizabeth I, Cromwell, Robespierre, Napoleon, Bismarck, Hitler, Garibaldi, Mussolini, Lenin, or Stalin with William Bradford, John Winthrop, Benjamin Franklin, George Washington, Thomas Jefferson, Andrew Jackson, Abraham Lincoln, Woodrow Wilson, and Franklin D. Roosevelt. The most remembered and most adored European leaders have been erratic and charismatic, with at least a touch of the daemonic. Claiming the inspiration of God, they avow their desire to change the course of history. They are remembered as makers and not merely reflectors of the spirit of their age. By contrast ours have been simply "representative men," possessing the commonplace virtues in extraordinary degree. Washington embodied the sober judgment and solid character of the Virginia planter. Jackson was only one of many elevated by the rise of the West. "This middle-class country," Emerson shrewdly remarked in his oration on Lincoln, "had got a middle-class president, at last."

As the power of the President and of the Federal Government increase, we should be troubled by whether the affairs of a great nation can be conducted by no better than a "typical" American. Perhaps we can no longer rely on that remarkable Providence (first observed by an enemy of Lincoln who foresaw Lincoln's election but had faith the nation would survive him) which has helped our nation outlive the most insipid leaders. We cannot look complacently on our temptations to apotheosize the commonplace in the most powerful office in the land.

Yet a number of facts, so recent and so peripheral to the familiar topics of political history that they have hardly begun to enter our textbooks, actually add up to just this. They offer new temptations for our national political leader to be a passive spokesman for the Voice of the People. They make it easier and more necessary than ever before that any candidate for the Presidency should seem constantly to have his finger on the public pulse. And they make it easier than ever for Americans to confuse vigorous leadership with adept follow-ership.

These new tendencies could be described as the rise of the Nationally Advertised President. Franklin Delano Roosevelt was our first. The attitude of the vast majority of the American people to him was as different from that of their grandfathers to the Presidents of their day as our attitude to General Motors is different from that of our great-grandfathers to the village harness maker. Like other "nationally advertised brands," FDR could not, of course, have been successful if he had not had something to offer. But he might not have been able to sell himself to the American public on such a scale, and for twice as many terms as any of his predecessors, without the aid of certain revolutionary changes in our system of public communication.

During the nineteenth century the telegraph transformed American journalism. Until the 1830s and the coming of the telegraph, the reporting of political news in the United States was a bitterly partisan business. Newspapers were owned body and soul by one or another political party, and, generally speaking, lacked moderation, conscience, or decency. The practice of ignoring or misrepresenting the opposition's statements was pushed to a point unknown today even among the most partisan of our large daily papers. Not until the last years of the age of Jackson did news begin to be sold in the open market, and as it became a commodity, its quality began to improve. With the rise of the cheap newspaper—the "penny press" in those days—addressed to a vast audience, newspapers tended to become financially independent of political parties. The growing volume of advertising they carried further encouraged them to assert their political independence.

It was the telegraph, of course, that made possible the establishment of enterprises such as the wire services selling news to newspapers. The AP was founded in 1848. And these wire services had a financial interest in seeing a crudely partisan press supplanted by an independent one. The wire services sold a nonpartisan product; very early they set a standard of impartial reporting that still distinguishes our press from that of most of the rest of the world.

Technical and economic developments made it possible to communicate news to more and more people more rapidly than ever before. The Fourdrinier machine for producing paper in a continuous strip instead of in sheets, and the Hoe presses, which by 1900 could produce up to 144,000 sixteen-page newspapers per hour, acted as both cause and effect in making the news big business. By the turn of the century, major newspaper chains like Scripps's and Hearst's were going strong. The great rise in newspaper circulation set in soon after 1892; in that year there were only ten papers in four cities that had a circulation of over 100,000; by 1914 there were over thirty of that size in a dozen cities. During this period, the average circulation of daily newspapers in the United States doubled. The combined circulation of daily newspapers in 1930 amounted to 44 million; by 1955 the figure was nearly 55 million.

To this growing business the government, and especially the federal government in Washington, offered the richest single source of raw material. At the beginning of this century there were fewer than two hundred Washington correspondents. The number increased sharply during the First World War, but even in 1929 the Washington press bureaus were only about five hundred. By 1950 about 1,500 people in Washington made their living directly from collecting and reporting national news.

We sometimes forget that the Presidential press conference is an institution of very recent date. Under President Wilson, something like the present formal and regular White House press conferences came into being. Although interrupted by the First World War, the institution was continued in one form or another by all presidents after him. The figure any one of these cut in newspapers all over the country depended very much on how he "handled himself" during these periodic interviews. FDR was the first President to appoint a special press secretary, and the power of that office has steadily increased.

By the early twentieth century a continual, ever-widening current of news was flowing from the White House. The news-gathering agencies themselves began to become self-appointed representatives of public opinion who put point-blank questions to the President, and from whom the President could learn what was troubling the public mind. Communication was now constant and two-way. No longer did the press await "statements" from the White House; it could prod the President when he was reticent, and focus attention on embarrassing questions. The corps of Washington correspondents became a more flexible, more regular, more direct, and at times more successful means than Congress itself of calling the President to public account.

The new continuity, informality, and immediacy of relations between people and President were furthered by the radio, which, with catastrophic suddenness, became a major factor in American political life during the twenties. The first Presidential election whose results were publicly broadcast was that of November 2, 1920: between five hundred and one thousand Americans were wearing earphones on that night to learn whether Harding or Cox had been elected. By 1922 about 400,000 radio sets were in use in the United States; by 1928 the number had increased more than twenty-fold to 8.5 million; in 1932 to 18 million; by 1936 to 33 million; and by 1950 to well over 80 million. It was in the elections of 1924, however, that the radio began to acquire real political significance. In that year, for the first time, the proceedings of the two national party conventions were broadcast to the public. But not until 1928 did the major parties make extensive use of the radio in their campaigning. Then for the first time millions of Americans in their own homes heard the candidates' voices. The inauguration of President Hoover, on March 4, 1929, was broadcast over a network of 120 stations.

These and other changes still to come in American political life were, of course, intimately connected with the rising American standard of living. For the ever accelerating need to cultivate the market to increase the wants of the people, and to attract them to specific products, was served by both press and radio. Advertising had begun to become big business by the 1880s. Until about 1890 most dailies still received more revenue from the sale of papers than from advertising. By 1914 advertising was providing many with two thirds of their income, by 1929 with three fourths. The bills that advertising clients received from radio stations amounted only to about $5 million in 1927; the sum shot up to over $107 million in 1936; by 1945 it was nearly $480 million; and in 1949 had increased by nearly another third, to the phenomenal figure of $637 million. Advertising agencies in the United States, which handled a business of nearly $600 million dollars in 1930, had an annual business in the neighborhood of a billion dollars about fifteen years later.

It is not surprising that the self-conscious and scientific study of public opinion, which was to become important in national political calculations by midcentury, had its roots in the efforts of advertisers to evaluate the reach of their advertising dollars. The first public opinion surveys were made by advertising managers to discover who was reading their copy. In 1919 there appeared the first survey department within an advertising agency, and the first independent surveying agency. It was not until 1935 that the representative sample method was used in public opinion surveys. In July of that year, in the middle of FDR's first administration, Elmo Roper published his first survey in *Fortune;* a few months later Dr. George Gallup began releasing his surveys as director of the American Institute of Public Opinion.

A new philosophy and science of public opinion came into being. Walter Lippmann's *Public Opinion* (1922), soon followed by his *Phantom Public* (1925), advanced the important idea of "stereotypes" and explored some theoretical consequences of the new publicity. For the citizen was now becoming more and more like the customer. With characteristic American directness, a new profession of "public relations" developed. The anti-big-business sentiment of the 1880s and 1890s and the rise of muckraking had disposed big-business men to offer high prices for skillful press-agentry. Ivy Lee, by paying some attention to the public interest and to the legitimate curiosity of newspaper reporters, helped put this new activity on a respectable and profitable footing. "This profession," observed Edward L. Bernays in the foreword to his *Crystallizing Public Opinion* (1923), "in a few years has developed from the status of circus agent stunts to . . . an important position in the conduct of the world's affairs."

By the time Franklin Delano Roosevelt came into office on March 4, 1933, technological and institutional innovations had in many ways prepared the way for a transformation of the relation between President and people. Communications from the President to the reading or listening public, which formerly had been ceremonial, infrequent, and addressed to small audiences, could now be constant, spontaneous, and directed to all who could read or hear (sometimes whether they wished to or not). And now through the questions put to the President at his regular press conferences, and through the telegrams and mail received after his radio addresses or public statements, he could sense the temper and gauge the drift of public opinion and so discover what the sovereign people wanted. He could even send up trial balloons to get some advance idea of public response to his future decisions. The President was no longer simply dealing with the "people," but with "public opinion."

There is no denying that FDR possessed a genius for using these means of communication. Without them he could hardly have developed that novel intimacy between people and President which marked his administrations. In the little memorial miscellany published by Pocket Books on April 18, 1945 (less than a week after FDR's death), we read in Carl Carmer's verse dialogue:

> Woman:
> . . . Come home with me
> If you would think of him. I never saw him—
> But I knew him. Can you have forgotten
> How, with his voice, he came into our house,
> The President of these United States,
> Calling us friends. . . .
> Do you remember how he came to us
> That day twelve years ago—a little more—
> And you were sitting by the radio
> (We had it on the kitchen table then)
> Your head down on your arms as if asleep.

For the first time in American history the voice of the President was a voice from kitchen tables, from the counters of bars and lunchrooms, and the corners of living rooms.

FDR's relaxed and informal style, both in writing and speaking, enabled him to make the most of the new informal circumstances under which people heard him. That he was compelled by his infirmity to sit while giving his radio talks only added to the informality. A whole world separates FDR's speeches from those of his immediate predecessors—from the stilted rhetoric of the oratory collected in such volumes as Calvin Coolidge's *Foundations of the Republic* (1926) or Herbert Hoover's *Addresses upon the American Road* (1938). Earlier Presidential speeches had too often echoed the style

and sentiments of commencement addresses; FDR could say something informal and concrete even in such an unpromising State
Paper as a Mother's Day Proclamation.

Perhaps never before had there been so happy a coincidence of
personal talent with technological opportunity as under his administrations. In the eight volumes of the *Public Papers and Addresses of
Franklin D. Roosevelt,* which cover the era of the New Deal, we
discover two new genres of political literature which were the means
by which a new relationship between President and people was
fashioned. The first genre was established in transcriptions of Presidential press conferences; the second, in FDR's radio talks, the "fireside chats." Both are distinguished by an engaging casualness and
directness; but this is not all that makes them new genres in the
literature of American politics. Here, for the first time among Presidential papers, we find an extensive body of public utterances that
are unceremonial yet serious.

Only a year after FDR assumed office, Theodore G. Joslin, who
had handled press relations for President Hoover, observed that
President Roosevelt had already come nearer than any of his predecessors "to meeting the expectations of the four hundred men and
women who, in these times of stress, write half a million words a day
to bring to our firesides news of developments at the seat of the
Government." FDR had already shown the camaraderie and the
willingness to make news which led some correspondents, not always
his political friends, to call his administration a "new deal for the
press." The unprecedented frequency of his press conferences established a continuity of relations with both correspondents and the
reading public. During Hoover's administration there had been only
sixty-six Presidential press conferences; but FDR held 337 press conferences during his first administration, and 374 during his second.
Thus, while Hoover met the press on an average of less than once in
every three weeks, Roosevelt would see them about five times in that
same period. The record of his conferences shows how this frequency
bred intimacy, informality, and a set of institutionalized procedures.
Before long the spirit of those press conferences became on both
sides much like that of any other responsible deliberative body.

Similarly, the frequency with which the President went on the air
effected a revolutionary change. Between March and October 1933,
FDR gave four "fireside chats." Through these, for the first time in
American history, a President was able to appeal on short notice and

in his own voice to the whole constituency. Neither the press conference nor the "fireside chat" was an occasion for ex cathedra pronouncements. On the contrary, they were designed to stimulate a more active "dialogue" between the people and the Chief Executive.

Perhaps the best index of the effect of FDR's radio talks was the volume of White House mail. In McKinley's time Presidential mail amounted to about a hundred letters a day, which were handled by a single clerk. Despite occasional flurries at inaugurations or crises, the daily flow remained small. Not until President Hoover's time did its volume increase significantly. Even then letters sometimes did not number more than a few hundred a day, and the system of handling them remained unchanged.

Under FDR, however, Presidential mail acquired a new and unprecedented volume, as we learn from the reminiscences of Ira R. T. Smith, for many years chief Presidential mail clerk *("Dear Mr. President . . .": The Story of Fifty Years in the White House Mail Room):*

> Mr. Roosevelt always showed a keen interest in the mail and kept close watch on its trend. Nothing pleased him more than to know that I had to build up a big staff and often had to work until midnight to keep up with a run of 5000 to 8000 letters a day, and on some occasions many more thousands. He received regular reports. . . . Whenever there was a decrease in the influx of letters we could expect to hear from him or one of his secretaries, who wanted to know what was the matter—was the President losing his grip on the public?

Before FDR came to the White House, Mr. Smith had handled all the mail by himself. But when, in response to his First Inaugural Address, FDR received more than 450,000 letters, it was plain that a new era had begun. During certain periods as many as fifty persons were required to open and sort the White House mail; before long an electric letter opener was installed, and instead of the old practice of counting individual pieces of mail, Mr. Smith and his helpers began measuring stacked-up letters by the yard.

Also, a new self-consciousness governed FDR's communications to the public; the era of "public relations" had begun. It was not enough that the President (or someone else for him) should state what he really believed. He had to consider all the "angles." Andrew Jackson had had his Amos Kendall and his Frank Blair; and it had not been uncommon for Presidents to employ ghost writers and close personal advisers who, in some cases, were responsible for both style and content. But perhaps never before did a President depend so consistently and to such an extent in his literary product on the collaboration of advisers. Among FDR's speech writers were men like Harry Hopkins, Robert Sherwood, Samuel Rosenman, Stanley High, Charles Michelson, Ernest Lindley, Sumner Welles, Raymond Moley, Rexford Tugwell, Archibald MacLeish, Tom Corcoran, Basil O'Connor, and Robert Jackson, and these are only a few.

FDR's speeches, even the most important and those seemingly most personal, were as much a cooperative product as a piece of copy produced by a large advertising agency. The President's genius consisted very much in his ability to give calculated, prefabricated phrases an air of casualness. It was, of course, remarkable that his speeches retained any personal flavor at all. And it was significant that this collaborative literary activity was not kept secret. The public began to take it as much for granted that the utterances of a President should be a composite product as that an advertisement of the Ford Motor Company should not be written by Henry Ford.

These changes that FDR, aided by technology, brought about in the conduct of the Presidency became permanent and took on the quality of mutations. They marked the decline in the periodicity of American political life.

In the early years of the Republic, politics, or at least national politics, was "a sometime thing." Political interest would rise to fever pitch before national elections or in times of crisis, and subside in between. The very vastness of the country reinforced this periodicity in American political life. And so our elections became notorious for their barbecue, holiday atmosphere: brief but hectic interruptions of the routine of life.

But technological developments increased the President's opportunity, and eventually his duty, to make news. Now headlines could be produced at an hour's notice. To oblige correspondents by making big stories frequently, and small stories constantly, became part of his job. In FDR's era the crises in economic life and international affairs were themselves rich raw material for the press. There had been crises and wars before, but never before had so large and steady a stream of announcements, information, "statements to the press," and descriptions of "problems facing the country" poured from the headquarters of government. The innocent citizen now found no respite from this barrage of politics and government. Even over a beer at his favorite bar he was likely to hear the hourly news broadcast, or the voice of his President.

The citizen was no longer expected to focus his attention only temporarily on a cluster of issues, conveniently dramatized by two rival personalities, at the time of national election. With the rise of weekly news magazines (*Time* was founded in 1923, *Newsweek* in 1933), of news quizzes, news broadcasts, and radio forums, the citizen was given the new duty to be "well informed." The complex of "alphabetical" agencies, the intricate and remote problems of foreign policy, and the details of the legislative process came now, as never before, to burden his mind and plague his conscience. Whether or not the American citizen was consciously becoming more "political," he was surely finding it more and more difficult to escape politics.

No longer was he granted the surcease of inter-election periods when his representatives were left to their own devices and he could turn to other things. Paradoxically, in spite of the great increase in population, the national government was becoming less and less republican, and more and more democratic; for elected officials were now in constant touch with their constituencies.

The very agencies that the President was now using to communicate his views to the public were also employed to elicit the public's response. Letters to the President and to Congressmen became a special American version of the ancient right of petition. As communications to public officials multiplied, the temptations increased for the public official, and especially the President, to trim his sails to the shifting winds of opinion, which now sometimes blew with hurricane force into Washington offices. The weak representative or the demagogue would find it easier to be weak and yet to seem to be strong by following the majority view at every turn. Here was still another force to prevent the realization of Edmund Burke's ideal of the independent representative.

The efflorescence of public relations techniques and of opinion polls increased the temptation, too, for the President to rely on experts in dealing with the public. Even if Presidential utterances would still have the appearance of casualness, it would be a studied casualness, or one that the people would suspect of being studied. The President would scrutinize surveys of press opinions and sometimes, within the very agencies of government, he would employ specialists in "opinion research" to inform him of what the people liked or disliked. He would employ theatrical advisers to help him find his most appealing voice and posture before the television cameras. In these ways, the citizen was more and more assimilated to the customer; he had to be "approached," his responses had to be measured so that he could be given what he wanted, or thought he wanted.

The new developments in communications made many of the oldest assumptions about the relations between geography and politics irrelevant. Jefferson and his "States Rights" disciples had started from the axiom that the citizen's knowledge and hence his capacity for an informed opinion were in inverse ratio to his geographic distance from the headquarters of decision. The closer he was to the scene, the more he would presumably know, and the more exact would be his knowledge. Thus the average citizen was expected to be best informed about the political affairs of his municipality, only a little less informed about those of his state, and considerably less informed about the affairs of the nation as a whole.

The changes that reached their climax under FDR not only exploded this assumption, they came close to making it the reverse of the truth. Both the multiplication of newscasts and the expansion of the profession of radio and television news commentator focused attention on national events, since these were sure to interest the largest number of listeners; and audience volume decided where money would be invested in communications. National affairs became more and more a good thing for the commercial sponsors of newscasts. Inevitably, many of the ablest reporters, too, were attracted to the national capital. The citizen, when he listens to the news from Washington, now has the benefit of sophisticated, well-informed, and competent interpreters who seldom have equals in the state capitals or on the local scene.

There thus has developed a new disparity between the citizen's information about national as contrasted with state or local matters. By about 1940, largely owing to the press and the radio, the citizens had already become better informed about national than about local issues. This reversal of a long-standing assumption would require revision of accepted notions about federalism, and about the competence of the average citizen to participate in government.

We are already far enough from the age of FDR to begin to see that the tendencies which I have just described were not ephemeral. American experience under FDR created new expectations that have continued to clamor for fulfillment. In the administrations of his successors these expectations became institutionalized. FDR had set a style that later Presidential candidates could only at their peril violate. While later Presidents might lack the vividness of FDR's personality, perhaps never again would any man attain the Presidency or discharge its duties satisfactorily without entering into an intimate and conscious relation with the whole public. This has opened unprecedented opportunities for effective and enlightening leadership—with unprecedented temptations. For never before has it been so easy for a statesman to seem to lead millions while in reality tamely echoing their every shifting mood and inclination.

CHAPTER 12

An American Style
in Historical Monuments

F OR NEARLY EVERY COUNTRY in Europe, the past is the store-house of greatness and romance, which declines into the prosaic, insoluble problems of the present. Aristocratic cultures recapture the glories of their history in the crumbling monuments of ancient castles, forts, and palaces. It becomes a patriotic act to leave the remains of that past in their surviving disarray. "There were giants in the earth in those days." Restoration would only cover up the masters' sure touch with the bungling brush strokes of latter-day amateurs. The ruins of the past must be left unrepaired because past magnificence (even in ruins) is more awe-inspiring than the glossy neatness of pigmy moderns. Better a sketch or a fragment by Michelangelo than a completed work done by one of us. In Europe ruins inspire and stimulate the present with confidence in the national genius and an avenging hatred against the barbarian who destroyed the grandeur. They stir unfulfillable yearnings toward the ancient greatness. A ruined Forum is the best propaganda for a Mussolini—and much better than a working model of the Forum would have been. Its every scar is a prod to national pride.

In older cultures nearly every monument was built from the half-crumbled ruins of earlier ones. The grand public buildings of the Forum and the Colosseum provided a stone quarry for medieval Christian churches, which were themselves often built on the foundation of pagan temples. Any wholehearted effort to restore the Forum would erase the footsteps of more recent momentous events, in the Middle Ages and the Renaissance. Therefore the typical pathway into the grand European past is the carefully preserved ruin; or the museum (often a defunct palace) crammed full of precious objets d'art, sculpture, and painting, which had been produced for a small aristocratic class.

Our American avenues to our past (our counterparts of ruins, museums, and monuments) are very different. For we view the present as the climax of history.

The unidirectional character of American history—with no lost imperial grandeur in our past—makes us unwilling to abase ourselves before the greatness of any earlier epoch. The great men and the great works of our national history seem great to us precisely because they are still alive. In the national folklore, the Founding Fathers, who fought and compromised for the ideals of religious conscience, political liberty, equality, independence, constitutionalism, and federalism, are great precisely because their ideals live in America today. They cannot stir irredentist movements or nostalgia for a lost empire; in the South we see some glimmering of such hopes, but they are not important, and they are now dying a permanent death. The federal constitution is adored because it still works. We view our national history—and the facts justify us—as a single broad stream, the unbroken living current of an American Way of Life, not as a miscellaneous series of great epochs. Partly for this reason we lean more heavily on our past than on our political ideology as a resource for discovering our present, and for defining our ideals. And we have a simpler problem than has the Old World. Our past, unlike theirs, contains fewer contradictions; and we demand that it explain itself to us by giving meaning to our present.

The traveler to Europe or the Orient spends much of his time viewing pyramids, tombs, and palaces: obtruding landmarks in which long-dead men asserted their greatness. All these monuments betray some doubt that the future will remember and understand the past by merely incorporating its ways of life. They express a belief in perfected permanent *things* rather than in persisting, improving *ways*. But there has been no American Ozymandias!

The remains of past aristocratic cultures, even those which were not constructed on purpose to impress us, are often well preserved because they were so little used. The elegant libraries found all over Europe, with their copies of sixteenth- and seventeenth-century books in mint condition attest to aristocracy more than to literacy. Often books were well preserved simply because they were rarely read and then usually by men of genteel manners. But ours is a culture of newspapers and magazines, which only professors and libraries preserve. Often the most widely used books leave the barest trace. The hornbook—the ABC which was in the hand of every New England child—was used up, and few remain from the seventeenth century. The New England Primer, the catechism in which children learned at the same time how to read and what to believe, was probably the commonest book in their houses in the seventeenth and eighteenth century; but from the early period we now possess few authentic examples. The inventories of the estates of eighteenth-century Virginians often list "pieces of books"—evidence not of their illiteracy but of their frequent use of books. The bibliophile, the curator of museums of fine arts, and the historian of the most impressive architectural monuments are often polishing the relics of a small aristocracy. Remnants of the widespread ways of life are gone with the wind.

In contrast to all this, the movement of Americans across the face of the continent led them to build only what would do until they could afford better. They hoped to move on and up to better things. Social mobility made most people in most parts of the country glad to tear down the old homestead in order to do better for their children, and to bury their humble ancestry. American technological progress in the nineteenth and twentieth century made the very idea of an heirloom obsolete. Any business that handed its heirs a "museum piece" was preparing for bankruptcy. Few American parents dream of passing down their house as a family headquarters; instead they hope that each of their children will afford something up to date. In America the "antique" is frequently confused with the "secondhand."

The self-consciously monumental character of many of the most important European remains has invited their destruction as a patriotic or an ideological duty in later ages. Down with the Bastille! Men who make icons prepare for the iconoclasts of the future. They are unwittingly preparing the most interestingly disfigured museum pieces. Protestant reformers dutifully defaced monuments of the Roman Catholic Church, fanatical rationalists in the time of the French Revolution smashed the heads off the statues of Notre Dame. Later emperors seek to erase the greater monuments of their predecessors—or, preferably, to carve their own names on them instead. Every ideologue tries to burn ideologues who have gone before. In nations with oscillating histories, it becomes a patriotic duty to destroy the embarrassingly inconsistent past. Street signs of "Hitlerstrasse" or "Stalinallee" are covered by names signaling the current ideology. Revolutions and reformations leave only the few relics which are too solid to be moved or too holy to be touched.

But the American past is erased in a more casual and goodnatured fashion. A house is removed to make way for a road; it is reconstructed to fit in the modern improvements: the two-car garage, the television room, or the air-conditioning ducts. Except for the Indian destruction of early settlements, or the few wanton destructions by British troops during the American Revolution and the War of 1812 (which happened to include the White House), and such Civil War episodes as the burning of Atlanta and Sherman's march to the sea, the relics of the American past have been removed not to deny the past, but to fulfill and improve it. It is no wonder that Americans feel the need to manufacture historical monuments.

These differences between our way of seeking our national past and of building our historical monuments and the European ways are vividly illustrated by a number of twentieth-century enterprises in historical reconstruction. Perhaps the most important of these is Colonial Williamsburg in Virginia, the project supported by about $50 million of Mr. John D. Rockefeller, Jr.'s money, and by a great deal of his personal enthusiasm. This effort to restore and reconstruct an American colonial capital is only the largest of an increasing number of efforts (New Salem, Sleepy Hollow, Jamestown, and Old Sturbridge Village are others) to discover our past by rebuilding the communities and the scenes of everyday activity of an earlier age. These are a special kind of historical reconstruction and popular interpretation. They are not entirely without precedent in Europe (for example in the Norwegian Folk Museums), but in this country they have taken on an unprecedented importance and influence. Colonial Williamsburg is not only a brilliant example of an American style in historical monuments; it has become a school for training skilled professional interpreters who will be devotees of this American attitude to our past.

Meanwhile, academic historians, disturbed by the heterodoxy, the boldness, and the popular appeal of Colonial Williamsburg, have generally not given it the significance it deserves. Some have been inclined to treat it as simply another example—like William Randolph Hearst's notorious imported castles—of a wealthy man indulging his whim. Some dismiss it as an educational "gadget" like the audiovisual aids to which they are unsympathetic. Or they treat it condescendingly as a harmless but amusing example of American vulgarity—a kind of patriotic Disneyland. But many visits there have persuaded me that it is significant in ways which its promoters did not advertise. Even before Colonial Williamsburg, the movies and radio had imposed specific tasks of historical verisimilitude on interpreters of our past which the historical novelist and stage dramatist had been able to evade. Television has only increased these challenges and further widens the unprecedentedly vast popular audience for vivid presentations of daily life in the past. As a historical monument, Colonial Williamsburg and others of its school make a comparable effort at popular interpretation of our history. They are almost as American in their method as in their subject matter.

In the first place, Colonial Williamsburg is a strikingly democratic kind of national monument. It presumes an unspecialized and unaristocratic kind of education. Unless one already knows a great deal, one cannot learn much from visiting the Roman Forum or the Athenian Acropolis. The Capitoline Museum, the Prado, and the National Gallery in London seem a jungle of canvas and marble to anyone not already instructed in the different arts and periods represented. Each room or department preserves the relics of only one kind of art, and usually of that art in only a single period. The European museum is a pretty esoteric place. The untutored visitor whose main sensations are of magnificence and discomfort considers himself lucky if he remembers the name of the museum. The numerous palace-museums—like the Louvre, Hampton Court, the Uffizi, the Pitti, or Schoenbrunn—are not any more comfortable, although they may be more interesting because they at least show the common visitor where the rich and powerful used to live.

But Colonial Williamsburg is a place where people often go "because of the children." And because it offers not a segment of the history of a particular fine art, but a model of a going community, it is intelligible and interesting to nearly everybody. Nobody is a specialist in daily life! It is a symbol of a culture where the fine arts have become much less important, where literacy is a higher ideal than literariness. The forbidding ribbon across the antique chair, the "Do Not Touch" sign, the somnolent guard (whose only qualification may be that he is a disabled war veteran)—these omnipresent features of the European museum have nothing to do with the American restored community. One of the most startling and impressive facts to anyone who has "done" Europe is that the guides of Colonial Williamsburg have no set speeches, and are actually giving the visitor their own interpretation of the rigorous course of lectures on colonial life which the director of interpretation expects them to attend. Visitors have some sense of using what the colonials themselves used; they see how things worked.

A Colonial Williamsburg would be impossible in a country that was not wealthy. It is made for the prosperous millions, for the "middling sort" of Americans, for a nation of paved roads and automobile owners and well-paid vacations, for a child-centered nation where families do things together. Colonial Williamsburg—like the American spelling bee, the strenuous effort to make college a "fun" experience, John Dewey's project method of education, *Sesame Street*, educational television shows, and quiz shows—symbolizes the American refusal to segregate any kind of activity: the refusal to believe that education need be a chore, or that learning need be confined to solemn and studious hours. Business and pleasure *ought* to be combined. Colonial Williamsburg acquired its fully American character with the completion of its vast motel (with cafeteria and swimming pool) and information center (offering free films about the colonial period). Americans like to learn together, they like to enjoy their education. For all these purposes Colonial Williamsburg is perfectly suited.

How did so appropriate an expression of national culture ever come into being? It was not the product of government initiative. Beginning partly as an imaginative private whim, it could not have been accomplished without shrewd real-estate dealings, architectural ingenuity, applied archaeology, and effective public relations. It is a spectacular example of private enterprise at work in the creation of a national monument. Dr. W. A. R. Goodwin, a single-minded Episcopal minister who loved Williamsburg, conceived the idea and in 1926 fired the imagination of John D. Rockefeller, Jr., who not only paid for it, but became foster father of the idea. It is not the product of legislative or other committees, of logrolling or boondoggling, but of a few individuals who had a queer and "impossible" idea. "Money was no object." On one occasion when a particular house, already partly reconstructed, had been built a few feet from its precise original position, Mr. Rockefeller did not hesitate to spend thousands of dollars to have it moved to its proper spot. Yet in the midst of the restored village a few islands were left to their owners, because the Committee considered the prices asked for the property to be exorbitant. The Virginia legislature cooperated, local historical societies helped. And in the end Colonial Williamsburg would vividly exemplify the paradox that only in a wealthy country can people care little about money.

Colonial Williamsburg is an American kind of sacred document. It asserts the belief in the continuity of past and present. Such an attempt to reconstruct the way of life of a whole past community and to interpret it to all living Americans is not only more expensive, but vastly more difficult and more taxing on the historical imagination, than to restore any particular ancient monument. The technical problems of archaeology have really turned out to be the least of all the problems.

A number of questions which Colonial Williamsburg has posed to its restorers have expressed some large peculiarities of American history. The restorers of such a community must, in the first place, be willing to break out of respected academic conventions; they must be willing to risk the objections, and even the ridicule of pedants, and the misunderstanding of scholars, of self-styled sophisticates, and of cosmopolites who are accustomed to the very different monuments of Europe. They must not be afraid to be at the same time archaeological precisionists, dramatic producers, advertisers, and promoters, and even occasionally to look a little silly to the humorless academic eye. They must combine the techniques of Hollywood, Madison Avenue, and P. T. Barnum with those of universities, museums, and research libraries. This is an extraordinary concoction. But American culture is extraordinary; and anyone who would provide us our kind of national monument must not be afraid to mix things which elsewhere have not seemed to go together.

In the course of this effort, the builders, managers, and promoters of Colonial Williamsburg have faced special temptations. These are, in one sense, only the temptations of all searchers for the past. But they are made especially seductive by the peculiarities of American history, and by the special role of our history in our effort to discover ourselves.

At any one time every community is actually a hodgepodge of the relics of different periods. The architectural "unity" of any period exists only in the minds of architectural historians. No age completely consumes its buildings; only in the oldest or the newest settlements, or after a great conflagration like the Fire of London or the Chicago Fire, or in projects of urban renewal or in suburban Levittowns and Park Forests and Restons are whole areas constructed in a single style. Thus the real look of a community in any particular period actually cannot be recaptured if its builders illustrate only one style.

The reconstructor's temptation is to be too pure; and in his effort to catch the special flavor of one age he may forget the admixture of earlier ages which was vivid to the men who lived then. Even in Colonial Williamsburg this temptation has not been wholly resisted, if only in choosing "typical" buildings of the immediate prerevolutionary period for restoration. In the code of restoration principles adopted at the beginning of the work in 1928, the advisory committee wisely recommended that "All buildings or parts of buildings in which the colonial tradition persists should be retained irrespective of their actual date." Ironically, the modern and unrestored parts of the village, by adding a note of variety, actually help us recover some of the heterogeneity of the once-living community.

But the very peculiarities of our history which focus our interest on the "middling sort" of men, put difficulties in the way of a fully appropriate restoration. The grander buildings tend to be the more durable; they are the ones for which we have blueprints, insurance records, and the detailed comments of colonial travelers. Yet to find the flavor of Williamsburg as an American community we must recapture the ways of living of slaves, servants, craftsmen, small businessmen, and others whose houses left the least trace. The restorers of Williamsburg, of course, have been aware of this difficulty, and in their reconstruction of many craft shops they have made an effort to overcome it. But inevitably they have been the victims of the ephemeral character of the life they are trying to recapture; a way of life is always more complex, more mixed, and more elusive than any particular grand monument.

The restorer faces a dilemma. If he tries to camouflage his work by artificial weathering and machine-made wormholes, he becomes a kind of forger. But if he does not, he misleads the viewer by making the past seem too shipshape. The restorers of Williamsburg have followed the rule that "where new materials must be used, they should be of a character approximating the old as closely as possible, but no attempt should be made to 'antique' them by theatrical means." Walking through restored Williamsburg, one finds many of these authentic colonial buildings as neat and well painted as the houses in a new suburb, while buildings of jarring modern design look weathered and lived in.

The authentic colonial buildings may never be allowed to have the shabbiness that many of them must have shown in the colonial era. Still, fresh paint can be a useful warning of the unbridgeable gulf between past and present. It has the same advantage as the specially colored plaster used in restoring European remains. The fresh paint and newly applied wallpaper which discomfit the romantic visitor actually can help save Colonial Williamsburg from the tea room "quaintness" found along New England highways. To the colonials themselves, the buildings were, of course, anything but quaint. They wanted a look of orderly newness as much as we do today.

The same kind of difficulty is presented by the lack of odors which were among the most vivid sensations of any colonial town. Yet if somehow these odors could be re-created, they would probably blot out everything else. We must remember that body odors, and odors of food, sewage, and cover-up perfume, were commonplace to the age. Any large-scale effort to reproduce colonial smells would seem melodramatic, and might actually destroy verisimilitude for twentieth-century visitors. Odors were routine for Jefferson, Wythe, and their contemporaries; revived today they would seem more pungent and more offensive than they ever did to them. This is only one of the many ways in which even the most sensible and skillful restorer is doomed (by his very success as a twentieth-century interpreter) to miss the precise "aroma" of colonial life.

If Colonial Williamsburg is to serve its historical as well as its patriotic purpose, it must dramatize the uniqueness of Southern and of colonial, as much as of all American, institutions. This can best be accomplished by allowing the accurately restored community to speak for itself and to speak concretely and in detail. This purpose was best expressed by Mr. Rockefeller himself when he explained: "I wasn't trying to re-create a lovely city, nor was I interested in a collection of old houses. I was trying to re-create Williamsburg as it stood in the eighteenth century." In their very efforts to deal with these problems, the restorers of Colonial Williamsburg have told us a great deal more about America, past and present, than its founders ever imagined.

CHAPTER 13

The Perils of Unwritten Law

IN SOME SENSE OR OTHER law is a creature of society, and society is a creature of law. We generally think of a lawbreaker as a person who is antisocial. We cannot improve our laws without at the same time improving our society. On the other hand, a person can be antisocial without being a lawbreaker; and a person is not always serving his society by obeying its laws.

"Society" is in some ways a much larger term than "Law." Every society includes a system of law, yet Law is somehow more durable, more chronologically extensive. "Roman Society" calls to mind the way men lived at some particular time. But "Roman Law" suggests ways of living that extended over generations. Society extends primarily in space, Law primarily in time. The relations between Law and Society then must have something to do with the relations between the peculiar needs and habits of men in some particular place at a given time, and the persistent practices of a large group of men over generations.

I wish to focus not on the "real" relationship between a Society and its Laws, but rather on how people have thought of that relationship. My focus will be on the United States, and on the attitudes of laymen, the consumers of the law.

In taking the layman's point of view, I will use no technical or philosophical definition but rather prefer the common dictionary definition of law: "All the rules of conduct established and enforced by the authority, legislation, or custom of a given community or other group." I will explore a few of the changing ways in which thoughtful

159

laymen in America have come to look on the relation between these rules and all the rest of their social experience. How have literate, self-conscious Americans thought about the relation between their law and their society? What have they wanted to believe? I will be concerned with some examples of what William James called the Will to Believe, and with some Varieties of Legal Experience.

One of the difficulties of talking about the relation between law and society is that in law, as in all other deep human concerns, the demands we make of our world are contradictory. We wish to believe both that our laws come from a necessity beyond our reach, and that they are our own instruments shaping our community to our chosen ends. We wish to believe that our laws are both changeless and changeable, divine and secular, permanent and temporary, transcendental and pragmatic. These demands are perhaps no more contradictory than those we make of the world when we think of mortality, love, our personal choice of vocation, or our national destiny.

The progress of man, Alfred North Whitehead has shrewdly observed, depends largely on his ability to accept superficial paradoxes, to see that what at first looks like a contradiction need not always remain one. It must have seemed odd to the first man who tried a raft or a bridge that he could cross over a stream of water and not get wet. Now, in modern legal history, the paradox which modern man has learned to live with is that though he can somehow make his own laws, yet they can have an authority above and beyond him.

The discovery, or even the belief, that man could make his own laws, was burdensome. Formerly man could find authority for his laws in the mysterious sanction of ancient practice "to which the mind of man runneth not to the contrary," or in a misty divinity. When, however, men came to see that they, or some majority of them, were the sources of the law, much of the charm melted away. Many men had doubted the wisdom of their kings or their priests. But nearly every man knew in his own heart the vagueness of his own knowledge and the uncertainty of his own wisdom about his society. Scrupulous men were troubled to think that their society was governed by a wisdom no greater than their own.

"Laws that emanate from the people," Orestes A. Brownson wrote in 1873, "or that are binding only by virtue of the assent of the governed, or that emanate from any human source alone, have none of the essential characteristics of law, for they bind no conscience, and restrain, except by force, no will." Brownson had been led to this conclusion by his interpretation of American history and his views of the American scene. He had taken an active part in the "Hard Cider" presidential campaign of 1840, on the side of the losing Democratic candidate Martin Van Buren, whom he believed to be "the last first-class man that sat, or probably that ever will sit, in the presidential chair of the United States." "What I saw served to dispel my democratic illusions, to break the idol I had worshipped, and shook to its foundation my belief in the divinity of the people, or in their will as the expression of eternal justice." In search of a higher authority, Brownson took refuge in the Roman Catholic Church.

Of course, most Americans have not been so deeply disturbed by this problem. They have preferred to believe that the trouble has not been in the source of the authority, but in how the authority was exercised. That if the people were not yet able to make good laws for themselves, it was not because somebody else should make their laws for them, but because the people were not yet literate enough, or wise enough, or pure enough in their motives.

The rise of self-conscious lawmaking has remained, however, a parable of the peculiar problems of modern man. Man's growing control over nature has given him an unprecedented power to move about the earth, to reproduce the objects he needs, and to make images of nature. The Industrial Revolution in England and elsewhere in Europe, and the American mass-production system of manufacturing permitted man to surround himself with objects of his own making, to shape his environment to his own needs and desires, and even to his whims. And, incidentally, this allowed him to get in his own way or in the way of his neighbors, as he had never before imagined. In England this worried people like John Ruskin and Matthew Arnold; in America it troubled fewer, but there were still some, like Brownson and Henry David Thoreau. The sentiment ·was summed up in Benjamin Disraeli's aphorism that "Man is not the creature of circumstances. Circumstances are the creatures of men." The new sciences of sociology, psychology, and anthropology further heightened the self-consciousness of man's power to make himself.

Man's power to make his own laws was, despite everything, the most burdensome of his new responsibilities for himself and the universe. His new powers to make things and his powers over nature would have worried him much less if somehow he had felt confident that his laws were rooted outside his society. But in acquiring his mastery over nature he had acquired the guilty secret that his laws might be rooted only in his version of the needs of his time and place.

Now the two contrary beliefs which we still want to hold are (a) that our laws are immanent (or the mere symptom of an indwelling necessity) and (b) that our laws are instrumental (tools we shape to our chosen ends). These two emphases correspond roughly to the two great stages in the development of law which were described by Sir Henry Maine—the movement from customary law or divinely given codes to legislative law. I prefer to call these the successive stages of unself-conscious lawmaking and self-conscious lawmaking. But the rise of self-conscious lawmaking does not abolish the need for belief in immanence; it merely transforms that belief. It makes the need for that belief more acute. Now men are burdened not only because they make their particular laws, but because they realize that they have the power to make their very concept of law.

This leads us to the most tantalizing problem—the mystery—of law in modern society. How retain any belief in the immanence of law, in its superiority to our individual, temporary needs, after we have adopted a wholehearted modern belief in its instrumentality? How continue to believe that something about our law is changeless after we have discovered that it may be infinitely plastic? How believe that in some sense the basic laws of society are given us by God, after we have become convinced that we have given them to ourselves?

How persuade ourselves that our laws can be both ancient and up-to-date, when almost nothing else we know has these contrary virtues? Under the older (immanent) view there were no good laws or bad laws, but only laws more or less established, more or less clearly revealed; under the later (instrumental) view there can be good laws, bad laws, better laws, worse laws, laws more effective or less effective. In the United States today we still want to believe that the laws of our community are somehow an inseparable part of our being, of the laws of the universe, of the order of nature, of God's plan for us. Yet we wish also to believe that these have been shaped primarily by our will—the will of the people—and that they are well shaped to the ends which our community has freely chosen.

In modern America, the subtlest problem has been how to retain a balanced sense of legal immanence. Many modern tendencies in social science push us toward extreme dogmas of the instrumental nature of law. Before describing the peculiar problems of finding legal immanence in twentieth-century America, I would like to illustrate what I mean by belief in the immanence of law by two examples. Both are taken from American history before the middle of the nineteenth century: before the flowering of modern social science, and before the rise of pragmatism as an explicit philosophy (or substitute for philosophy).

It is hard to find a better example of belief in an indwelling law than among the Quakers of colonial Pennsylvania. For the English Quakers in the seventeenth century the law took its proper shape from the very nature of God, man, and society. This law was supposed to prevail against all the commands of the state. George Fox had exhorted, "My friends . . . going over to plant, and to make outward plantations in America, keep your own plantations in your hearts, with the spirit and power of God, that your own vines and lilies be not hurt." But William Penn, founder of Pennsylvania, was a very sensible man, a man of this world and no mean politician. His Preface to his "Frame of Government for Pennsylvania" (1682) was one of the wisest political manifestoes of the age. In it he warned against excessive faith in any form of government or of laws:

> Any government is free to the people under it (whatever be the frame) where the laws rule, and the people are a party to those laws, and more than this is tyranny, oligarchy, or confusion. But, lastly, when all is said, there is hardly one frame of government in the world so ill designed by its first founders, that, in good hands, would not do well enough. . . . Governments, like clocks, go from the motion men give them; and as governments are made and moved by men, so by them they are ruined too. Wherefore governments rather depend upon men, than men upon governments. Let men be good, and the government cannot be bad; if it be ill, they will cure it. But if men be bad, let the government be never so good, they will endeavour to warp and spoil it to their turn.

Such an emphasis on the indwelling spirit of man as the shaper of society and its laws was the keynote of the Quaker Colony. For the first half-century of its life, Quaker Pennsylvania flourished, and it remained decisively Quaker. Although sects struggled among themselves, the Quakers managed to rule.

But by the early decades of the eighteenth century, a great struggle had developed. Politically speaking, it was a struggle between the Quakers, settled mostly in Philadelphia and eastern Pennsylvania, and later immigrants who settled to the westward and were beginning to engulf the Quakers even in their Friendly City. It was also, however, a struggle between two concepts of law. On the one side was the Quaker view of an indwelling law, implanted in man and in society by God's beneficent spirit. On the other side was the view of an instrumental law, a man-shaped tool to protect the society against its enemies foreign and domestic.

The weightiest Quakers obstinately insisted on preserving the purity of the law which dwelt within them. They refused to take oaths, because the indwelling law forbade it; they refused to bear arms, or to support the purchase of arms, because their indwelling law was a law of peace; they refused to deal prudently and cautiously with the threatening Indians, because their indwelling law of love commanded that the Indians were good, and that they be treated as brothers. The result is now a familiar story. The Quakers were driven from power in the Pennsylvania Assembly in 1756 and became strangers in their own colony. The government of the colony was taken over by non-Quakers, and by the party of the shrewd Benjamin Franklin. From rulers of a society, the Quakers became prophets of a sect. Thereafter they gave most of their energy to reforming their own members, to building miscellaneous humanitarian institutions, and to stirring the larger community toward specific, seemingly utopian reforms. They agitated against slavery and the slave trade, they worked to humanize prisons and insane asylums, they built hospitals, they opposed war on principle. Although a long political struggle had been needed to displace them from power, their fate had actually been sealed a century before when a Quaker Yearly Meeting had declared: "The setting up and putting down Kings and Governments is God's peculiar prerogative, for causes best known to himself."

The Pennsylvania Quaker experience in the eighteenth century dramatized on the American colonial stage both the strengths and the weaknesses of one extreme form of belief in the immanence of law. Rigid and changeless, it was a law of self-righteousness—of the righteousness of the self. But it was a law careless of its effects, more concerned for self than for community, blind to the needs of suffering women and children in the Indian-harried backwoods. It was a law of intransigent individuals. Inevitably Quaker law became a sectarian credo rather than the foundation of a large society.

Certain features of the Quaker law must be noted. The Quakers were an untheoretical, untheological, unlegislative people. Their law was untechnical. Their law consisted in a few general tenets: love, peace, no swearing, all men are good. Paradoxically, its very unsystematic, unwritten, untechnical character made the Quakers the more fearful of bending any provisions of their law to the needs of community.

These rigid, unrealistic qualities of Quaker law were not the necessary consequences of a belief in God, or in a divine foundation for society. Less than three hundred miles away were the New England Puritans. The laws of Puritanism were highly elaborated, very much written, and not lacking in technicality. In the long run the written, technical, elaborated laws of the Bibliolatrous New England Puritans—God-based though they were—proved far more flexible than the unwritten, inarticulate, untechnical benevolent spirit which governed the Pennsylvania Quakers.

Another, and in many ways contrasting, form of belief in immanent law developed in the Southern United States in the half-century before the Civil War. It shared many of the formal features of the colonial Pennsylvanian law of the Quakers. It, too, was unwritten, inarticulate, untechnical, and unbending. But it differed in its content, its source, and its sanction.

The rise in the South of belief in immanent law must be explained by two dominant facts of Southern life in this period. The first was the institution of slavery; the second was the defensive spirit, the feeling that the whole Southern society was under attack from the outside.

The great planters ran their affairs by informal understandings, gentlemen's agreements, and pledges of honor. Surprisingly little legal paper was used in the conduct of the Southern plantation and Southern commerce in the early years of the nineteenth century. This is, of course, one of the reasons why it is hard to learn as much as we would like about the daily life of the time. The tendency to rely on unwritten rules was accentuated by the existence of slavery and by the very character of that institution. Slavery was a labor system in which the rules were local custom or the arbitrary decision of the master. Since the common law of England did not recognize the status of slavery, there was no developed body of law concerning slavery, the rights of the slave, or the duties of the master in the English slaveholding colonies. By contrast, as has often been noted, Latin America and the Caribbean areas, governed by the Roman law transmitted through Spain or Portugal, had a highly developed law of slavery with traditions and practices reaching back to ancient times.

An ironic result of the fact that English law favored liberty and refused to recognize slavery was thus that the Negro slave in the English colonies was a mere chattel, with virtually no recognizable legal personality, and few if any rights against his master. He was in many ways worse off than were slaves in a society that had inherited a long tradition of legalized slavery. The legal situation of the slave in the Southern United States was further worsened by the failure of Protestantism to take the strong religious-equalitarian stand of Catholicism, and by the indelible identification of race with the status of slavery. In Roman law, slavery was, of course, a legal status independent of race; and as the slave laws of Cuba, for example, developed, they recognized gradations of servitude and racial gradations (mulatto, quadroon, octoroon, etc.). But in the North American English colonies and in the States derived from them slavery was an all-or-nothing proposition.

Another striking fact about the institution of slavery in the Ante-Bellum South is not merely the meager or nonexistent rights of the Negro slave, but the meager amount of legal literature concerning the laws of slavery. Slave codes were sparse and did not purport to cover all possible situations. Even treatises on slavery were few and far between. The best legal treatises of the age on American Negro slavery (with the conspicuous exception only of Thomas R. R. Cobb's *Law of Negro Slavery,* 1858) did not come from the South at all, but were written in New York or Philadelphia.

When the Southerner confronted this fact of the sparseness of the formal legal rights of the Negro and the meagerness of written law, he began to claim, by the 1840s and 1850s, that these symbolized the virtues of the South's peculiar institution. Not only extremist defenders of slavery, like George Fitzhugh, but other loyal Southerners as well, argued that this distinction between the legalistic, pettifogging, literal-minded, mean-spirited North—with its eye always on written records and the cashbox—and on the other hand, the generous, chivalrous, kind-hearted, honor-governed South, expressed the whole difference between their institutions.

"Human Law," George Fitzhugh of Virginia explained in *Cannibals All! or, Slaves Without Masters* (1857), "cannot beget benevolence, affection, maternal and paternal love; nor can it supply their places; but it may, by breaking up the ordinary relations of human beings, stop and disturb the current of these finer feelings of our nature. It may abolish slavery; but it can never create between the capitalist and the laborer, between employer and employed, the kind and affectionate relations that usually exist between master and slave." The essence of slavery, Southern defenders argued, was that it did not depend on explicit, instrumental rules; and this was precisely its virtue. For, under slavery, they said, the laws of employment became one with the natural currents of social sentiment on both sides: kindness and generosity on the side of the employer, loyalty and industry on the side of the employed. "Experience and observation fully satisfy me," remarked Judge O'Neall of South Carolina in 1853, "that the first law of slavery is that of kindness from the master to the slave . . . slavery becomes a family relation, next in its attachments to that of parent and child."

To understand the Southern law of slavery, then, you could not look at the lawbooks, but instead had to observe the actual ways of the community. The defense of slavery became more and more a defense of the unwritten law, the immanent law, the ways which dwelt in the ongoing Southern society, or as it was sometimes said, in the Southern Way of Life.

The South then came to idealize the unwritten law, which was said to be the only proper law for a Christian society, an ennobling influence on all who allowed themselves to be ruled by it. Just as slavery made it possible for the relations between superior and inferior to be governed in this fashion, so, too, a code of "honor" made it possible for relations among equals to be similarly governed. And the gentlemen of the Southern ruling class spurned the letter of the law which, in the Southern States, as elsewhere, forbade the duel and punished it as homicide. They actually made resort to the duel (the Code of Honor) a symbol of their respect for the immanent as against the instrumental law of the community. In the South, in the half-century before the Civil War, there was hardly a leader in public life who had not fought a duel. Much as a war-record nowadays attests a man's high devotion to his community, and is supposed to help qualify him for public office, so in those days, having fought an "affair of honor" proved a gentleman to be a "man of honor," for it showed that he held the unwritten law of the society above its petty explicit rules.

The Southern defense of its immanent law, of the actual rules by which the South lived, against the attacks by literal-minded, casual travelers and bookish Northerners who judged all societies by their written rules—this itself became a defense of the Southern Way of Life. Southerners were increasingly holistic and mystical in their praise of their institutions. Southern Ways, they declared, fitted together so neatly and so subtly, that one dared not jar them by tinkering with the explicit rules.

Southerners became social narcissists. What were the proper virtues of any society, what were the laws by which any society should be ruled? Look at the South and you would see. Not at the rules in books, or the statutes passed by legislatures, or the decisions of judges (there were precious few of these anyway), but at the society itself, at how it actually worked. The proper laws of the South, it was said again and again, dwelt in the actual ways of the South. For the laws of its society the South came more and more to look in the mirror.

The consequences of this increasingly intransigent, increasingly narrow, increasingly inward and tautologous way of looking at law were, of course, to be far-reaching. They were tragic for the nation, and still remain tragic for the South. But we need not follow them out in detail to see that the South had developed an extreme and uncompromising belief in the immanence of law. The Southerners, we might say, had developed an odd kind of social Quakerism. The Quakers were a "peculiar people" (so they called themselves); the Southerners lived by their "peculiar institution." The Quakers lived by a law which dwelt in each individual, and against which there could be no proper appeal to statute books, legislatures, or lawcourts. The Southerners too lived by a law which dwelt in their society, and against which they believed there could be no appeal. Both societies had chosen to live by an immanent law: unwritten, inarticulate, untechnical, and unbending.

Belief in the immanence of law runs deep in our American tradition. In the story of the development of our institutions what distinguishes both the Quakers of colonial Pennsylvania and the Ante-Bellum Southerners is not their belief in some form of legal immanence, but the extreme and intransigent intensity of their belief.

A striking feature of our history is how few examples we offer of individuals or communities embracing a radically instrumental theory of law. Jeremy Bentham, therefore, is one of the most un-

American of English thinkers. Few nations have legislated more than the United States, or put more faith in legislation; few have put less faith in any explicit theory of legislation. Traditional legal learning has sometimes been overvalued here because of its scarcity, but it has generally commanded the same naïve respect accorded to all ancient lineages in raw countries.

In this New World, where men have so often boasted of their opportunity to make a New Beginning, movements to codify or new-fashion laws have made surprisingly little headway. In the early nineteenth century, which was an age of codes and radical legislation in Western Europe, we were making constitutions and elaborating an American common law. Even in England, much of the legal history of the nineteenth century can be written around movements self-consciously to change society by using law as a tool; in the twentieth century there have been triumphs of intricate and subtle codification, like the Real Property Act of 1928. But in the United States, while we have codified some of our procedure and made some headway toward Uniform State Laws, even in this century our distinctive contributions have been our modest efforts to draw the private law together and to make it accessible rather than boldly to reshape it to serve new social needs. Perhaps our most distinctive contributions have been our extralegal devices for indexing, key-numbering, collecting, and retrieving cases. Our great twentieth-century effort to reformulate the law has produced informal "Restatements" rather than revisions or codifications.

We have been a nation, then, of many laws, but of few law reforms. The circumstances of our American Revolution had encouraged belief that the laws of our nation were not malleable instruments to attain specific social purposes, but were part of our very being. We inherited a legal system which was brought here in the very minds of the settlers. We had no self-conscious "reception" of the common law comparable to that which agitated the European Continent over the "reception" of Roman Law. Our legal theory could thus remain impressively inarticulate, while Continental legal thinkers asked again and again how laws could be used to serve social ends. What, they asked, was the proper relation between law and society? What were the healthiest roots of laws?

The leading German legal thinkers, Friedrich Karl von Savigny and Rudolf von Jhering, remained even more exotic than Bentham; to this day they are hardly known among American lawyers. Here there was no widespread open battle between legal systems. Our battle was only among jurisdictions. Our common law had come with us. Since no conscious act of adoption or acceptance was ever needed, we continued to see a certain inevitability about our whole system of law. The common law and its tradition of constitutionalism seemed part of the very fiber of our social being. We embraced the Blackstonian view (which in England even by the time of our Revolution was coming to seem obsolete) that the common law was a providential embodiment of Reason and Nature. We inherited a great legal literature, which summed up the general rules without our ever having been required to make those rules, or even to make the effort of "discovering" them.

One symptom of the relatively minor role we have given legislation as an instrument for social change is the extraordinary importance we have given to constitutions. What Willard Hurst has called our tradition of constitution worship has embodied the still deeper tradition that our laws must somehow be the expressers rather than the shapers of our society.

American tradition has, of course, given a mystic role to the framers of the Federal Constitution. They have been adored for what we suppose to have been a declaratory rather than a creative act. Again and again we have held that they surely revealed the innermost spirit of the new American nation, and embodied it in words.

"The system is no invention of man," a nineteenth-century writer observed, "is no creation of the [Constitutional] convention, but is given us by Providence in the living constitution of the American people. The merit of the statesmen of 1787 is that they did not destroy or deface the work of Providence, but accepted it and organized the government in harmony with the real order, the real elements given them. They suffered themselves in all their positive substantial work to be governed by reality, not by theories and speculations."

When Justice Samuel F. Miller of the Supreme Court spoke in 1887 at the centennial celebration of the framing of the Federal Constitution, he recalled George Bancroft's description of the last hours of the Convention: "The members were awestruck at the results of their councils, the Constitution was a nobler work than anyone of them had believed possible to achieve." Justice Miller himself expressed his satisfaction that the Constitution had originally been intended to establish a truly national government.

For us, the idea of a constitution—a fundamental law which in some strange way is less changeable than the ordinary instruments of legislation—has had a peculiar therapeutic attraction. Since 1776, there have been over two hundred state conventions to adopt or revise constitutions. Yet we have seldom amended our Federal Constitution and it remains the oldest working written constitution in the Western world. We retain an incurable belief that constitutions are born but not made, and this despite the carelessness, prolixity, crudity, and proven ineptitude of many of our State constitutions.

The two great armed conflicts on our soil, the American Revolution and the Civil War, were both victories for legal orthodoxy, for traditional legal doctrines—at least according to the victors. We have a remarkable continuity in our political and legal history. Any decisive innovations in our institutions (for example, those induced by the Depression of 1929) have sooner or later been hallowed by the Supreme Court. The Court certifies that the laws required by newly emerging problems somehow were implied and authorized in the very charter of our national existence. The continuous power and dignity of the Supreme Court make the Court a distinctive American embodiment of belief in the immanence of our laws. Despite everything, we insist on believing that what the Court does is not to make the law but to declare it: not *jus dare* but *jus dicere*.

Never yet have we experienced a forcible deflection of our national institutions by arms, by coup d'état, or the seizure of power by one party or one class. Thus we have never really been jolted into seeing laws as the mere instruments of power. But in this as in so many other ways, the South has been an exception.

Since the early years of the twentieth century events on the international scene have pushed us as a nation toward an increasing belief in legal immanence. More and more we have come to believe that a nation's laws are not mere instruments toward ends, but are themselves essential to the character of the society, inseparable from the society, an indwelling expression of a nation's purposes.

This movement toward a wider belief in the oneness of a society's laws with its ends is illustrated by the contrast between our stated national objectives in World War I and in World War II. There is a striking contrast between the kind of objectives stated by President Woodrow Wilson in his "Fourteen Points" (Annual Address to Congress, January 8, 1918) and those stated by President Franklin Delano Roosevelt in his "Four Freedoms" (Annual Address to Congress,

January 6, 1941). President Wilson itemized a number of objectives on the international scene. These were quite specific political and economic readjustments, for example: reduction of armaments, the impartial settlement of colonial claims, the evacuation of Russia, the restoration of Belgium, the freeing of invaded portions of France, the adjustment of the frontiers of Italy, the autonomy of the peoples of Austria-Hungary, etc. etc. Such objectives required laws for their accomplishment, but the objectives were plainly separate from the laws.

President Roosevelt's "Four Freedoms" Speech, on the other hand, described perils to "the democratic way of life" which was "assailed in every part of the world." His "Four essential human freedoms"—freedom of speech and expression; freedom of every person to worship God in his own way; freedom from want; and freedom from fear—were called way-of-life objectives. They were not political aims to be attained by legal tools. Rather the aims themselves were as much legal as political. A nation's laws now were the touchstone. Laws were assumed to be not a mere instrument but the primary expression of its way of life. From the American point of view the conflict was between law-loving, law-fearing societies, and others.

In the three decades after our entry into World War I, leading Americans had ceased to believe that on the international scene the United States was concerned merely with the preservation of a political system. What had to be defended, it was said again and again, was a Way of Life. The terrors of totalitarian democracies—of dictatorships which actually could claim to express the will of the majority of their people—revealed that the mere fact that a government represented a current majority was no guarantee of decency or of respect for human rights. Only slowly did Americans abandon the political fallacy. They hung on to their belief, which many have not yet abandoned, that if a government outraged decency then, ex hypothesi, it could not express the will of the majority of its people. But it has lately dawned on more and more of us that political democracy is only one element and not enough in itself to insure decent institutions. Way of life means much more. It includes a society's laws, and its attitude toward its laws. The traditional American distrust of legal instrumentalism has been expressed anew in a popular antipathy to "isms": fear of any concept of society that would abstract and dogmatize national objectives, and then use its laws as mere tools to those ends.

We have seen that the kind of immanence which people find in the law, and which can satisfy their belief that the law is not arbitrary or purely instrumental, varies a great deal. It is far too narrow to identify this belief exclusively with natural law or with a belief in God. In the Soviet Union, and perhaps in other Communist countries, it seems possible for people to have this satisfaction of a belief in legal immanence by seeing their laws as a manifestation of rules indwelling in history, as expounded in the Gospel according to Marx, Lenin, Stalin, and their followers. In Nazi Germany people secured it by belief in a racial destiny, an indwelling "law of the folk"— expounded in the Gospel according to Hitler, Rosenberg, and Goebbels. We are too ready from our provincial point of view to view totalitarianism as a barefaced unhallowed instrumentalism, in which rulers use the law for their own ends. But this is not how such systems look to their supporters, from the inside. These peoples have not given up the need to find some immanence—some transcendental indwelling validity in their laws. Rather they find forms of immanence unfamiliar to us. We have yet to see a government that has ruled a society effectively without providing its people with some persuasive way of believing that their laws come from some higher, deeper, indwelling source.

In the United States the kind of belief in immanence which has been growing in the last half-century, bears, superficially at least, some discomfiting similarities to that which I have described in the Southern States before the Civil War. Although the content is very different, the formal character of the beliefs and some of the surrounding circumstances are quite comparable. Our belief in legal immanence has arisen out of a dominant—one might almost say a fetishistic—belief in the peculiar virtue and perfection of political democracy as we know it, and as it is practiced in the United States. And *our* belief, too, has been a kind of response to outside attack. In order to strengthen ourselves against the threat of Communist conspiracy and totalitarian subversion we take a holistic view. While Southerners came to see the institution of slavery as the lifeblood of all social good, nourishing the peculiar virtues of political, social, economic, and cultural life in the South, so we see our institution of political democracy informing our political, social, economic, and cultural life. Just as the Southerners saw a peril, not only to their political system and their economy, but to their whole Way of Life, so with us. With the increase of Northern threats the intransigence of Southerners' belief in themselves and their peculiar institution hardened. Their belief in immanence was expressed in their faith in a law which was unwritten, untechnical, and unbending. And so is ours.

I have characterized the Ante-Bellum Southern belief in immanence as a tendency toward Social Narcissism. The society came to worship itself. Reform movements virtually disappeared. Southern thinkers came to confuse sociology with social morality. They looked into the mirror to see what they should be. Certain tendencies in American life today suggest that we too are in danger of finding our immanence in the mirror.

In the last half-century, the predominant fact of intellectual history shaping our thinking about law and society has been the rise of the social sciences, and the idea of social science. Only a few decades ago courses in sociology in the better colleges were still entitled "The Prevention of Poverty." They were primarily concerned with such topics as crime, delinquency, and "the social evil." But nowadays sociology is concerned with "techniques of social control," the structure of society, the functions of cities, ethnicity, and the roles of social classes and races. The study of government has become "political science"; political economy has become the science of economics. Even history has become more and more social-scientific. *An American Dilemma: the Negro Problem and Modern Democracy,* a collaborative work in social sciences by Gunnar Myrdal and many others, was published in 1944. The unanimous Supreme Court decision declaring racial segregation in the public schools unconstitutional came exactly ten years later, in 1954. The "future" which Justice Holmes in his "Path of the Law" (1897) predicted would belong to "the man of statistics and the master of economics"—that future has now arrived.

The conviction grows—and is expressed in the curricula of our best law schools—that the lawyer must not only know law. He must know the facts of life, the facts of our society, the laws of social behavior inherent in society itself. Only recently have we begun to act on the truism that one cannot know a society's laws without knowing the society. There are obviously many advantages, for the lawyer, and for the society.

But with this belief comes the tendency to find the immanence of the law in the supposedly inevitable tendencies of the society itself. It has often been remarked that Justice Holmes's classic description of the object of legal study as "prediction, the prediction of the incidence of the public force through the instrumentality of the courts," while helpful to the practicing lawyer, is not very useful to the legislator, the citizen, or the social scientist trying to decide how legal development should be directed. The great danger of the social-science emphasis in the training of lawyers, the great danger of finding the immanence of our law in the very processes of our society, is that we should make law into tautology. The predictive theory of law could lead us to make all our society's laws nothing but self-fulfilling prophecies. Obviously, our laws cannot ignore the facts of our social life, but they must do more than merely reflect them. Intelligent citizens cannot be guided by what their opinion polls tell them is their opinion.

We suffer ever-stronger temptations to social narcissism. In a beleaguered world we are ever more tempted to be satisfied that our laws should reflect a society which we define as ex hypothesi good. But to do so is to deprive our laws of the normative role which, in the common law tradition, has made them a bulwark for each generation against the specious urgencies of its own age.

One of the most difficult problems in our society today is to get a message in from the outside. We believe in our power to make ourselves. The more we see our laws as a reflection of norms indwelling in current social practice, pressures, and disorders, the more we deprive ourselves of an opportunity to make law a means of communication between the past and the present. For this purpose the preservation of a tradition of professionalism, of technicality, is essential. Here we must more than ever rely on what Sir Edward Coke—against the arbitrary James I, the amateur lawyer who said he knew all he needed to know of the law—said was not natural reason but "the artificial reason and judgment of the law, which law is an art which requires long study and experience, before that a man can attain to the cognizance of it."

PART IV

UNSUNG EXPERIMENTS

I learn more from your doubts than from
all that the divine Aristotle, the wise
Plato, and the incomparable Descartes have
affirmed so lightly.

FREDERICK THE GREAT TO VOLTAIRE
Sept. 21, 1737

CHAPTER 14

The Courage to Doubt

I<small>N LATE WINTER</small> of February 1790, Benjamin Franklin at the age of eighty-four was gravely and painfully ill and suspected that he did not have much longer to live. He received a letter from his old friend the Reverend Ezra Stiles, then president of Yale, asking him for the specifics of his religion. It was a serious matter for Stiles. He had spent some years experimenting with electricity at Franklin's suggestion, and then spent many more years reflecting on whether he really believed in the Christian doctrine when he accepted ordination.

Franklin's reply was laced with Franklin wit. He said, "I believe in one God, Creator of the universe. That He governs it by His providence. That He ought to be worshiped. That the most acceptable service we render Him is doing good to His other children." But Stiles had also asked him what he thought of the divinity of Jesus. To which Franklin replied, "I think the system of morals and his religion as he left them to us, the best the world ever saw or is likely to see; but I have, with most of the present Dissenters in England, some doubts as to his divinity; though it is a question that I do not dogmatize upon, having never studied it, and think it needless to busy myself with it now, when I expect soon an opportunity of knowing the truth with less trouble."

With his usual political concern, Franklin added the request that Stiles should not make his letter public because, Franklin said, "I've ever let others enjoy their religious sentiments, without reflecting on them for those that appeared to me unsupportable and even absurd. All sects here, and we have a great variety, have experienced my good will in assisting them with subscriptions for building their new places of worship; and, as I never opposed any of their doctrines, I hope to go out of the world in peace with them all."

This parable represents the beliefs of many of the Founding Fathers and the spirit that formed their making of much of the Constitution. From the vantage point of Franklin's skepticism, I would like to try to offer a larger historical perspective.

The United States was the first modern nation founded on purpose in the bright light of history. The mere existence of the nation was itself a kind of Declaration of Independence from the folk gods and religious and semireligious myths that had always and everywhere surrounded governments and their rulers. Kings and queens were customarily crowned and hallowed by priests, bishops, cardinals, and popes. And they had good reason to want the odor of sanctity. Queen Elizabeth I, for example, made trouble for an author who wrote too freely describing the dethroning of her predecessor Richard II. Prudent divine-right sovereigns saw that their protection lay in controlling the prying research of inquiring historians. They preferred simply to legitimize themselves by descent from the Trojans or from the gods.

Some would say that religious liberty is probably the most distinctive and certainly one of the greatest contributions of the American experience to all human progress. Religious liberty in the United States is the product not only of the courageous personal humility of the Founding Fathers. It is a by-product of some happy facts of American history. But because these facts appear obvious, we are inclined to ignore them.

First, since the founding of the nation—by an act of revolution and by the framing of a Constitution—was accomplished in a relatively brief time, living men and women could see that it was a product of their struggles, discussion, and handiwork, not the fiat of some sanctified, myth-enshrouded past.

Second, the nation was created from areas with diverse sects. Oddly enough, the fact that the colonies already had their several and various established churches contributed to this necessity. A federal nation was plainly not founded on an orthodox religious base. The Protestant Reformation came as a disruptive force into the relatively monolithic world of the medieval church. In England, for example, Protestant orthodoxy became indelibly identified with national identity. But in the American colonies, religious variety preceded political unity and had to be accommodated within it.

Third, the diffusion of American colonial settlements with no one capital, the great distance of colonial urban centers from one another, and the oceanic separation from London or Rome, all made religious independence a fact of geography as well as of theology. So much of the population was at the edges and out beyond the range of the churches. One of the consequences of this was a different line of historical development of the relation between church and state, one which is so grand and so unique that we are perhaps inclined to ignore it. Over there, the development was generally from religious orthodoxy enforced by the state, to toleration—and only later to religious liberty. Historically speaking, of course, religious toleration is to be sharply contrasted to religious liberty. Toleration implies the existence of an established church, and toleration is always a revocable concession rather than a defensible right. In the United States, for the first time in modern Western history, the nation leaped from the provincial religious preference of its regions into religious liberty for the whole nation. The Founding Fathers despised the condescension that was implied in the very concept of toleration. That was a stage necessary for Old World nations, but not for our New World nation.

Religious persecution, that is to say, the punishment, torture, execution, or civil disability of individuals for their refusal to embrace a particular religious doctrine, is a modern Western and especially a Christian invention. It was virtually unknown in Greek and Roman antiquity. Socrates was condemned to death for an essentially political crime. In Rome, where religion seems to have been more in the nature of a patriotic ritual than an affirmation of doctrinal orthodoxy, the execution of Christians in the first three centuries was less because of governmental opposition to their theology than for their refusal to participate in the imperial rites. It is well known, of course, that as the Roman empire expanded the Romans simply incorporated the local deities into the Roman pantheon.

Judaism, monotheistic and theocratic, did offer more basis for intolerance. While the Jews detested and opposed idolatry, their religion remained in many respects national or perhaps even tribal. Of the Eastern religions, Buddhism was notoriously free from intolerance. The only apparent example of Buddhism becoming the basis for persecution—in seventeenth-century Japan—turns out to have been for political and not for theological purposes and was stirred by

the fear of Christian missionaries. Hinduism, with its wealth of pan-
theistic lore, was not a persecuting religion and did not encounter
problems of religious warfare and genocide until it encountered
Islam, which was of course a successor to Christianity.

Christianity then, along with its benefits, brought also the spirit
of intolerance and persecution. The Protestant Reformation did not
help much against these particular evils. It brought a new version of
religious (now Protestant) persecution, and it was a long time before
the Reformation brought political liberalism and religious liberty.
Some of the most bitter religious wars in Western history (the Thirty
Years War, for example, between 1616 and 1648, which killed about
one tenth of the population of Germany), were fought mainly for
religious doctrinal reasons. Their horrors were taking place at the
very time when the New England Puritans were settling in the New
World in quest of their own religious liberty, and incidentally, their
freedom to persecute in their own way.

But after the American Revolution, Washington, Jefferson, and
others could see what the New England Puritans could not see, that
their government was not described and foremodeled in the Bible
but was the prudential product of human struggle, compromise, and
the pursuit of decency.

From the force of circumstances, as well as from long and deep
reflection, our Founding Fathers brought forth this nation in the
wholesome atmosphere of the courage to doubt. Federalism in politics meant pluralism in religion, which incidentally meant a faith in
the wisdom of mankind but a doubt of the wisdom of orthodox man.
Their spirituality, their God, was a God of common human quest and
not the God of anybody's dogma.

There is no more eloquent apostle of the courage to doubt than
Jefferson. Belief in the happy diversity of mankind and human
thought was probably his first religious axiom after belief in God.
"Rebellion to Tyrants Is Obedience to God" was the motto that
Jefferson chose for his seal in 1776. Jefferson's God was a God not of
orthodoxy, but of diversity. "As the creator has made no two faces
alike," Jefferson said, "so no two minds, and probably no two creeds,"
and he substantiated this view with the latest psychology and medicine of his day. He believed that the study of the variety of the
creation was itself an act of worship.

In 1811, when Jefferson was about to resume cordial relations
with his old friend John Adams, he asked, "Why should we be disso-

cialized by mere differences of opinion in politics, in religion, in philosophy, or anything else? His opinions are as honestly formed as my own. Our different views of the same subject are the result of a difference in our organization and experience." So it is not surprising that Jefferson refused to accept the dogma of any religious sect. He made his own humanist anthology of the teachings of Jesus and we reap a rich harvest of his differences with John Adams from his treasure trove of correspondence in his last years.

An eloquent and reverent expression of the implications of this courage to doubt—a belief in religious liberty and the creator's delight in the multiformity of men's minds—was offered by Thomas Paine, who was a prophet and publicist of the American Revolution. But he was hardly a favorite of dogmatic theologians and in later generations was widely stigmatized as an atheist. This is what Paine wrote in *The Rights of Man* in 1792:

> If we suppose a large family of children who . . . made it their custom to present to their parents some token of their affection and gratitude, each of them would make a different offering, and most probably in a different manner. Some would pay their congratulations in themes of verse and prose, by some little devices as their genius dictated, or according to what they thought would please, and, perhaps the least of all, not being able to do any of those things, would ramble into the garden or the field and gather what it thought the prettiest flower it could find, though, perhaps it might be but a simple weed. The parent would be more gratified by such a variety. . . . But of all unwelcome things, nothing could more afflict the parent than to know that the whole of them had afterward gotten together by the ears, boys and girls, fighting, scratching, reviling, and abusing each other about which was the best or the worst present.

The courage to doubt, on which American pluralism, federalism, and religious liberty are founded, is a special brand of courage, a more selfless brand of courage than the courage of orthodoxy. A brand that has been rarer and more precious in the history of the West than the courage of the crusader.

CHAPTER 15

Political Technology

WHEN WE LOOK BACK on the series of events between 1776 and 1789 which brought forth the United States of America, we must first be struck that the leaders were interested less in the ideology than in the technology of politics. They were testing well-known principles by applying them to their specific problems. Their special concern was "to organize the means for satisfying needs and desires"—which is a dictionary definition of technology. There are a number of clues to this open, experimental, *technological* spirit of our North American revolutionaries.

Our first and most obvious clues are in the basic and enduring documents of the Revolution. The most important of these, of course, was the Declaration of Independence, which bore the date of July 4, 1776. The most-quoted and best-known passage, the Preamble, was actually the least characteristic. The colonists' principles were first described as "self-evident." Then "a decent Respect to the Opinions of Mankind" (as well as the undeclared exigencies of diplomacy) required a cogent summary of the causes of the particular act which they declared—the separation of thirteen British colonies. When Jefferson was accused of writing a document that had not one new idea in it, he recalled his clear, simple, practical purpose: "Not to find out new principles, or new arguments, never before thought of, not merely to say things which had never been said before; but to place before mankind the common sense of the subject, and to justify ourselves in the independent stand we are compelled to take."

The body of the Declaration applied these well-known principles—not the dogma of a particular sect, but accepted tenets of British political life during the previous century—to the conduct of the British King who had asserted unlimited sovereignty over certain American colonists. The heart of the document was a list not of principles but of grievances. Some twenty-six items indicted the King for specific crimes. These ranged from the King's wanton refusal to assent to needed legislation, to interference with the courts, the imposition of standing armies without the consent of the colonial legislatures, the quartering of troops on unwilling inhabitants, the protection of murderers, the obstruction of seaports, and the cutting off of trade.

Our nation's birth certificate thus unwittingly but obviously certified a congenital concern for everyday consequences. The document was not primarily a declaration of principles or a proclamation of the rights of man, it was a declaration of *independence*.

How did the Founders describe this new nation that had declared its independence so urgently? The open, empirical spirit was apparent in the very name they chose. Familiarity has dulled the meaning of the words—or rather has given them a precision they never possessed at the hour of christening. In the various documents directed to the King and Parliament during the struggle for independence this new cluster of political entities referred to itself first as "the colonies," then as "the united Colonies," and eventually as "The United Colonies of America," or "of North America." Commissions in the newly raised army were actually written in these last two forms. The colonists' deliberative revolutionary body, when it first met in Philadelphia (September 5 to October 26, 1774), adopted for its official title nothing more explicit than "the Congress." In common usage at the time the word "Continental" was added to make "the Continental Congress," and so distinguish this one from the numerous other provincial congresses. Of course the so-called Continental Congress, representing only Atlantic seaboard colonies, was anything but continentwide.

After the act of independence, the new nation required a name. But it was by no means clear what the country should call itself. The heading of the text of the Declaration of Independence described the enacting body as "the thirteen united states [sic] of America." The uncertainties of the situation were expressed in the fact that the word "united" (written with a lower-case *u*) was treated as a mere adjective rather than as part of the proper noun. The colonists were still so dubious of their future that they dared not make "united" an indissoluble part of their nation's name.

The name finally adopted—United States of America (even later the definite article was not capitalized)—connoted all the openness that we future constituents could possibly have wished. As German Arciniegas, the brilliant Colombian man of letters, has recently observed, the United States was to be the only country in the world that did not really have a name of its own. "To say *United States* is like saying *federation, republic,* or *monarchy.* Those of the north are not the only United States of America, because there exist the United States of Mexico, the United States of Venezuela, and the United States of Brazil." If Mexico is Mexico, he rightly noted, Venezuela is Venezuela, and Brazil is Brazil, they are all just as much a part of America as this particular North American republic. In their self-description when our North American revolutionaries chose the word "States," they chose a name as indeterminate as any name that could be found for a new political entity. Incidentally, "America," the word they used to locate their States, was an entity whose dimensions were only vaguely known at the time, and whose terrain, especially in North America, had barely begun to be explored. It would have been hard then to find a more imprecise geographic term. "America" was still a near-synonym for *terrae incognitae.*

Their final choice—United States of America—is all the more remarkable and their calculating ambiguity is all the more significant when we remember the literary talents of that generation. Believing eloquence and a feeling for poetry essential for the great statesman, in their documents and their speeches they left us many mellifluous phrases. But they gave to their greatest work, the new nation, a name that was unpoetic and even awkward, unyielding of appealing adjectives. Ambiguity acquired the look of arrogance. Now, when we citizens merely of the United States of North America arrogate to ourselves the encompassing title "Americans," we still bear witness to the open and undogmatic hopes of our Founding Fathers.

While, of course, independence was what made the new nation possible, confederation was what made it durable. Despite its eloquence, the Declaration of Independence might have remained buried in colonial archives along with the early state papers of Bermuda, the Bahamas, and Jamaica if it had not been followed within a dozen years by the Constitution of the United States of America. The longevity and vitality of the Constitution came from the fact that the Framers aimed to guide the future but not fence it in. The best evidence of their self-denying intention was that their document was so brief. The Constitution of the United States, which anyone can read in an hour, is a scant twenty-five pages long. By contrast the constitution of my home state of Oklahoma is 158 pages, not counting amendments. Because the Framers of the federal constitution were scrupulous to say no more than necessary, they provided a document uncannily open to the future.

With wholesome brevity came a pregnant vagueness, revealed in the very first words. The Preamble reads:

> We the People of the United States, in Order to form a more perfect Union, establish Justice, insure domestic Tranquillity, provide for the common defence, promote the general Welfare, and secure the Blessings of Liberty to ourselves and our Posterity, do ordain and establish this Constitution for the United States of America.

The three opening words "We the People" would prove troublesome. In their ambiguity was rooted the bloody Civil War of 1861–1865. For the leaders of the Southern States, preferring to imagine that these words really meant "We the States," argued that the States which had made the Union could also dissolve it.

The Constitution was not to take effect until the people had adopted it. "This expression [We the People]," explained Henry ("Light-Horse Harry") Lee, "was introduced . . . with great propriety. This system is submitted to the people for their consideration, because on them it is to operate, if adopted. It is not binding on the people until it becomes their act." The Framers had the wisdom, in preparing a Constitution for posterity, not to try to elaborate or make more explicit the meaning of "the People." They did not say "we the property owners" or "we the qualified voters." Their words, an adequate working definition in their time, would be a providential receptacle for new meanings—as civil and political rights were extended to nonproperty owners, to former slaves, to women, to persons above the age of eighteen, and possibly to other categories now still beyond our imagining.

All the listed purposes of the Constitution grew out of the urgencies of the Framers' recent experience. The tribulations of the loose confederation during the late war signaled the need for "a more perfect Union," the oppressive interference of the British government with the courts indicated the need to "establish Justice," recent civil disorders (Shays' Rebellion in western Massachusetts, and others elsewhere) made obvious the need to "insure domestic tranquillity." The war itself and the later designs of European powers on the new nation showed the need to "provide for the common defence"—and so it went. This antidoctrinaire empirical spirit would keep the document openly responsive to later needs.

If we turn from style to institutions, again we find a wholesome deference to the future. The power to amend the Constitution (Article V) was no casual item but the result of extended debate. A few members of the Constitutional Convention, led by Charles Pinckney of South Carolina, feared such a provision, for they questioned the wisdom of permitting posterity to undo their work. But George Mason countered: "The plan now to be formed will certainly be defective, as the Confederation has been found on trial to be. Amendments therefore will be necessary, and it will be better to provide for them, in an easy, regular and Constitutional way than to trust to chance and violence."

James Madison reminded the convention of the lesson to be learned from Virginia, whose "state government was the first which was made, and though its defects are evident to every person, we cannot get it amended." He drew, too, on European experience. "The Dutch have made four several attempts to amend their system without success. The few alterations made in it were by tumult and faction, and for the worse." Without some orderly means of amending the Constitution, Madison cautioned, "The fear of Innovation, and the Hue & Cry in favor of the Liberty of the people will prevent the necessary Reforms."

Finally, then, the Constitution described the means for its own amendment. The pathway that the Founders marked out for amendment would be neither facile nor impossible. With the exception of the 18th Amendment and its repealing 21st Amendment concerning intoxicating beverages, the amendments have all had a constitutional dignity. Meanwhile, the very difficulty of amendment has encouraged us to exercise our ingenuity to make the original form of the Constitution workable. Our Supreme Court, filling the breach, has become a kind of continuing Constitutional Convention, reinterpreting words as circumstances require. Most important, our peaceful amending process has encouraged a continuing national debate over the needs for amendment, and has discouraged the use of violence to accomplish what is so explicitly covered by law.

The Founding Fathers not only provided (in Article V) a means to amend the Constitution, they actually provided (in Article IV) the means to amend the nation. Some doubted the wisdom of allowing the nation to expand so far that the original States might be overpowered by the new. Gouverneur Morris of New York was against allowing an unlimited number of new States to be admitted on an equality with the original thirteen. He hoped for all time "to secure to the Atlantic States a prevalence in the National Councils." Against this provincialism the open spirit once again prevailed. James Madison and George Mason, among others, saw the promise in the unfathomed West. "The Western States," Madison insisted, "neither would nor ought to submit to a Union which degraded them from an equal rank with the other States." "If it were possible by just means to prevent emigrations to the Western Country," George Mason added, "it might be good policy. But go the people will as they find it for their interest, and the best policy is to treat them with that equality which will make them friends not enemies."

They made the process of amending the nation, by contrast with that of amending the Constitution, remarkably easy. A new State could be admitted by a simple majority vote in the Congress. The young States would in all respects be equal to their elders. Along with this came the important provision that the United States would guarantee to every State a "republican" form of government. But, after debate, the Founders wisely refused to cast this into a guarantee of any State's "existing laws." For, as William Houstoun of Georgia noted, some laws of his own State were defective, and he did not want a new federal constitution that might become an obstacle to change. In later years, when, from time to time, the Congress tried to attach specific conditions, prohibitions, and requirements to the admission of particular States (such, for example, as were attached to the admission of Louisiana), the Supreme Court again and again declared them unconstitutional. It was this equality of States that opened the way for the United States to become a fully continental, even a transoceanic, federal republic.

In these and countless other ways the Founding Fathers declared themselves custodians of an expanding future. Federalism was their grand device for holding together experimenting communities. Each State's experiments were limited only when they violated the rights of individuals, threatened the experiments of others or weakened the whole national community. The ingenious Add-a-State Plan allowed a national laboratory to grow by installments.

"We may safely trust to the wisdom of our successors the remedies of evils to arise," Jefferson wrote to Adams less than a decade after the Constitutional Convention.

> Never was a finer canvas presented to work on than our countrymen. All of them engaged in agriculture or the pursuits of honest industry, independent in their circumstances, enlightened as to their rights, and firm in their habits of order and obedience to the laws. This I hope will be the age of experiments in government, and that their basis will be founded on principles of honesty, not of mere force. We have seen no instance of this since the days of the Roman republic, nor do we read of any before that. Either force or corruption has been the principle of every modern government.

The new nation was to be not a citadel but a laboratory.

The best symbol of the Founders' experimental spirit was the federal system itself, the very framework of the new nation. In retrospect, their inspiring tentativeness stands out against the new absolute, the empyrean abstraction which others at that time imagined to be embodied in every really modern state. That abstraction was "sovereignty." It haunted governments, inflating them with an ill-founded sense of omnipotence. The feudal world of medieval Europe saw political powers, rights, and duties diffused across the land in myriad, variegated clusters. As new national states emerged after the sixteenth century, each tried to homogenize its piece of the political landscape. Each tried to build a pyramid of power, which, of course, could have only one apex.

By the later eighteenth century, British lawyers and political thinkers had imagined sovereignty to be the elixir of modern nationhood. They defined "sovereignty" as one and indivisible. "It is impossible," Governor Thomas Hutchinson of Massachusetts insisted in 1773, "there should be two independent Legislatures in the one and the same state." "In Sovereignty," Dr. Samuel Johnson wrote in *Taxation No Tyranny* (1774), "there are no gradations." For the American colonies the British saw only two alternatives, "absolute dependence" or "absolute independence."

Yet between the British government and the American colonial governments a working federalism had already emerged unannounced. While certain questions were decided in London, others were left to the capitals of the thirteen colonies. Sovereignty was diffused and divided. American federalism—a product of Atlantic distances, American space, and the slowness of communication—existed in fact long before there was an American theory. Those who ruled the British Empire remained ideologues, but American colonial leaders were glad to learn lessons from their new situation. Divided sovereignty, grown up in violation of legal metaphysics, was a leading fact of the Anglo-American experience, and a key to the American political future.

The Founding Fathers prepared the way to extend their laboratory of diffused and divided sovereignties into the full westward extent of the continent. What would happen if a growing people of varied origins and on varied landscapes went on trying federal experiments? The United States became a nation in quest of itself.

This experimental spirit, which had made the new nation politically possible, would explain much that would distinguish the nation's life in the following two centuries. The American limbo—a borderland between experience and idea, where old absolutes were dissolved and new opportunities discovered—would puzzle thinkers from abroad. With their time-honored distinction between fact and idea, between materialism and idealism, they labeled a people who had so little respect for absolutes as vulgar "materialists." In the gloriously filigreed cultures of the Old World it was not easy to think of life as experiment. But American life *was* experiment, and experiment was a technique for testing and revising ideas. In this American limbo all sorts of novelties might emerge. What to men of the Old World seemed a no-man's-land was the Americans' native land.

The experimentalism which had worked on the land, and would test the varied possibilities of fifty States, had found new arenas in the course of the nineteenth century. What federalism was in the world of politics, technology would be in the minutiae of everyday life. While ideology fenced in, federalism and technology reached out. Just as federalism would test still-unexplored possibilities in government, so technology would test unimagined possibilities in the modes of common experience.

It was not surprising that the United States would become noted, some would say notorious, as a land of technology. The Swiss writer Max Frisch once described technology as "the knack of so arranging the world that we don't have to experience it." But in American history technology could equally well be described as "the knack of so arranging the world as to produce new experiences." In America the time-honored antithesis between materialism and idealism would become as obsolete as that old petrified absolute of "sovereignty," which had made the British Empire come apart, and then made the American Revolution necessary. Experiment—in its older political form of American federalism and in its more modern generalized form of American technology—would become the leitmotif of American civilization.

CHAPTER 16

From Charity to Philanthropy

IF YOU ARE an American interested in education and public institutions and you travel about France today, you find something strangely missing from the landscape. In Paris, of course, you find a host of sites and buildings serving public purposes—from the Champs Élysées, the Place de la Concorde, the Louvre, the Tuileries, the Petit Palais, the Grand Palais, and the Invalides, to the Collège de France, the Académie, and the Sorbonne. All over the country, of course, you see mairies and parish churches and cathedrals. Along the Loire, on the Côte d'Azur, or scattered elsewhere, splendid châteaux and country estates are monuments to private grandeur, past and present.

You are apt to feel puzzled, a bit lost and disoriented, simply because what you see there, like much else in Europe, is classifiable with an unfamiliar neatness. The sites and buildings are, with few exceptions, either public or private. They are monuments of the wealth and power, *either* of individuals *or* of the state. The University of Paris is an organ of the Ministry of Education; the Louvre and the Bibliothèque Nationale are the responsibility of the minister of culture; the schools are run by the national government. Even the most imposing religious monuments—Notre-Dame, Chartres, and Mont-Saint-Michel, for example—are essentially public, for they have been supported by taxation. The French church has enjoyed privileges which, despite the freedom of religion, have amounted to making it an organ of the state. If you are not in a private building, you are in an institution created and supported and controlled by the government.

In a great American city, by contrast, many—even most—of the prominent public buildings and institutions are of a quite different character. They do not fall into either of these sharply separated classes. Strictly speaking, they are not private, nor are they run by the government. They are a third species, which in many important respects is peculiarly American. They have many unique characteristics and a spirit all their own. They are monuments to what in the Old World was familiar neither as private charity nor as governmental munificence. They are monuments to community. They originate in the community, depend on the community, are developed by the community, serve the community, and rise or fall with the community.

They are such familiar features of our American landscape that we can easily forget, if we have ever noticed, that they are in many ways a peculiar American growth—peculiar both in their character and in their luxuriance, in what has made them grow and in what keeps them alive and flourishing. Prominent features of life in Chicago, where I spent many happy years, are the Art Institute, the Chicago Museum of Natural History (sometimes called the Field Museum), the Shedd Aquarium, the Adler Planetarium, the Museum of Science and Industry (commonly called the Rosenwald Museum), and the University of Chicago (founded by John D. Rockefeller). Each of these—in fact, nearly all the major philanthropic, educational, and public-serving institutions of the city (with only a few conspicuous exceptions)—was founded and is sustained voluntarily by members of the community. One finds comparable institutions in every other American city.

Of course, there are numerous hospitals, universities, and other enterprises supported by our government; but these are far more often the creatures of local or state than of the national government. Scattered examples of community institutions of this type are not unique to the United States. Something like them—some of the Oxford and Cambridge colleges, for example—existed even before the New World was settled by Europeans. In one form or another a few such institutions are found today probably in every country in the world, except in Communist countries, where the autonomous public spirit is prohibited. But in extent, power, influence, and vitality our community institutions are a peculiarly American phenomenon.

Here in the United States, even some of our institutions ostensibly run by one or another of our governments are in fact community institutions in a sense in which they are not elsewhere in the world. Take, for example, our "public" schools. In the great nations of Western Europe, the schools which are supported by the general citizenry and which anyone can attend free of charge are run not by separate communities through school boards but from the center by the national government headquartered in Paris or in Rome. It was once a familiar boast of the French Minister of Education that he could look at his watch and tell you exactly what was being taught in every classroom in the country. Our European friends are surprised to learn that in the United States we have no official with similar authority and that, except for a few constitutional safeguards like those of freedom of religion and free entry to public facilities, the control of our public instruction is decentralized. It is in local community hands.

This notion of community is one of the most characteristic, one of the most important, yet one of the least noticed American contributions to modern life. From one point of view it is simply another example of how the time-honored distinctions and sharp antitheses of European life became blurred, befogged, and softened in America. The familiar theme of recent European politics is the antithesis The Man versus The State, which had already begun to dominate Old World thought even before Herbert Spencer published his book under that title in 1884. Other expressions of this way of thinking were the antitheses Individualism versus Socialism and Laissez Faire versus Collectivism, and there have been many others. This set of polar contrasts has framed much of European public debate. Even in England, where the brittle oppositions of Continental politics tend to be softened by good humor and common sense, they have dominated the political vocabulary. The best general history of English legislation in the nineteenth century—A. V. Dicey's *Law and Opinion*—tells the whole story as a movement from "individualism" to "collectivism."

Meanwhile, in the United States the political vocabulary—by which I mean the vocabulary of debate and not of vituperation—has been different. Despite the extravagant optimism expressed by Marx and Engels that the so-called working masses would be more resentful in the United States than elsewhere, that they would be more revolutionary and more socialistic, still American socialism as an organized articulate movement has made very little headway. The fact is pretty obvious. Socialist parties here have had even less success than our other minor political parties. For example, even during what some textbooks call the Golden Age of American Socialism, in the first decade of this century, the Socialists were not able to elect more than two Congressional representatives. The interesting question about socialism in the United States was put by the German economist Werner Sombart in the title of his book, *Why Is There No Socialism in the United States?* The most popular explanation is summed up in Sombart's own observation that "on the reefs of roast beef and apple pie socialistic Utopias of every sort are sent to their doom."

There is another, or rather, additional, explanation, which so far as I know has not yet been seriously proposed but which may help us understand much that is distinctive about our political life and about our whole culture, including the forms given to the philanthropic spirit in America. Yet it is very simple and obvious: the American idea and institution of community.

We have been misled into thinking that the terms of the European debate force us too into a choice between the two terms "individualism" and "socialism." This false choice inevitably leads us to put ourselves, or to think we can put ourselves, in the camp of "individualism." It is significant that the first use of "individualism" in the English language recorded by the *Oxford English Dictionary* is in Henry Reeve's translation (1840) of Tocqueville's *Democracy in America.* Reeve apologizes for taking the word directly from the French. Tocqueville used the word to describe what he thought was an American way of feeling, but here his misunderstanding of American life was peculiarly French, or, rather, Old Worldly. For he used "individualism" as a term of half-reproach, describing it as "of democratic origin, and it threatens to spread in the same ratio as the equality of conditions." With the eye of a perceptive but short-term traveler, he was understandably baffled by the attitude of Americans toward the activities of their governments.

After Tocqueville, the term "individualism," like "socialism," had very little vogue in America for most of the nineteenth century. Walt Whitman vaunted the "individual," but he was no man of doctrine. The best known use of the word "individualism" in recent American history was by Herbert Hoover in a campaign speech in New York (October 22, 1928), when he offered it as half of the familiar European antithesis: "We were challenged with a peacetime choice between the American system of rugged individualism and a European philosophy of diametrically opposed doctrines—doctrines of paternalism and state socialism."

Just as the antitheses Man versus the State and Individualism versus Socialism had little relevance in America, so too the word "individualism" would be a misleading slogan if identified with an American Way of Life. Of course Americans had an unprecedented opportunity to discover their individuality, and of course many Americans have been preoccupied with their own private interests even in conflict with those of the community. But egotism, in the sense of unalloyed selfishness, has probably played no greater role in American history than elsewhere. To emphasize this aspect of American life is simply to try to import one of the Siamese twins of modern European politics. Yet to us the one is no more relevant than the other. What is instead peculiar to our way of thinking and feeling is the idea of community.

In Western Europe, with insignificant exceptions, men found themselves wherever they were in the nineteenth century because they were born there. The act of choice, of consciously choosing their particular community, had been made, if ever, only by remote ancestors—the contemporaries of Beowulf, William the Conqueror, Siegfried, or Aeneas. On the other hand, because we were an immigrant nation, everybody here, except the Indians and the Negroes and those others who had been forcibly transported, was here because he or a recent ancestor (a father, grandfather, or great-grandfather) had chosen this place. The sense of community was inevitably more vivid and more personal because, for so many in the community, living here had been an act of choice.

In crowded, preempted Europe, with its no-trespassing signs all over the place, by the nineteenth century or even before, governments covered the map. The decisive contrasting fact, not sufficiently noticed, is that in America, even in modern times, *communities* existed before governments were here to care for public needs. There were many groups of people with a common sense of purpose and a feeling of duty to one another before there were political institutions forcing them to perform their duties. A classic example is the Pilgrims, who landed at Plymouth in November 1620. Of course, they were held together by a strong sense of common purpose. But since they were landing in an unexpected place—they had intended to land in Virginia and not in New England—they were a community without a government. While still on board the *Mayflower,* they were frightened by the boast of their few unruly members who threatened to take advantage of this fact as soon as they touched land. So by the Mayflower Compact they set up a new government. The Pilgrim community thus had preceded the government of Plymouth.

This order of events was repeated again and again in American history. Groups moving westward from New England and other parts of the Atlantic seaboard organized themselves into communities in order to conquer the great distances, to help one another drag their wagons uphill, to protect one another from Indians, and for a hundred other cooperative purposes. They knew they were moving into open spaces where jurisdiction was uncertain or nonexistent. Or take the remote mining towns, founded here and there in what is now Colorado, California, Montana, or Nevada—places where men knew that their silver or gold could not be secured unless they managed to stay alive and preserve their property. In all these places men who were already a community formed do-it-yourself governments. Communities preceded governments.

Not least important was this phenomenon in the new Western cities. Chicago was to be the greatest, but there were others, like Cincinnati, Kansas City, Omaha, and Denver, which had become flourishing communities before they had well-established, elaborate governments.

This simple American order of experience was to have deep and widespread effects on American thinking about society, government, and the responsibilities of the individual. While Europe was everywhere cluttered with obsolete political machinery, in America *purposes* usually preceded machinery. In Europe it was more usual for the voluntary activities of groups to grow up in the interstices of ancient government agencies. In America more often the voluntary collaborative activities of members of the community were there first, and it was government that came into the interstices. Thus, while Americans acquired a wholesome respect for the force of the community organized into governments, they tended to feel toward it neither awe nor reverence nor terror. The scrupulous faithfulness with which most Americans pay most of their taxes (even their income taxes!) continually astonishes continental Europeans. This is only another vivid reminder that Americans tend to think of government as their servant and not their master.

Seldom have a people been more anxious than Americans have

been to share their common purposes. We are desperately earnest to make our community include as much as possible of our daily life. This has sometimes been ridiculed in such phrases as "Babbittry" or "the organization man," but it goes deeper than has been suspected and reaches far back in our history. In our country, unlike France, for example, if you are somebody's business associate, you are more than likely expected also to be his golf partner, his friend, and to share his general religious beliefs, his political ideals, and his standard of living.

In the seventeenth century the American Puritans began with an encompassing, we might say a "totalitarian," concept of community. Nowadays, fortunately, we only seldom require people to subscribe formally to explicit beliefs; but we still expect people to act and feel as if they believed the same thing. To pass for a religious person in the United States, it is less important that you be able to define sharply what you believe than that you be able, however vaguely, to share the equally vague religiosity of others. Our political faith is much the same. It is less important for an American public man to have clearly defined political principles than for him to share the vague political beliefs of as many as possible of his fellow citizens. Thus, although we proclaim ourselves to be a religious nation by the word "God" on our coins and (by Act of Congress) in our Pledge of Allegiance, it is unlawful to express or avow in our public schools any specific religious sentiments to which everybody else could not agree. Our political parties must have platforms; but no party would get far unless its platform was as much as possible like that of the other party.

A sometimes discomfiting aspect of our ideal of maximal community is the proverbial American lack of privacy. We insist that public servants—or even public figures—share their private lives with us. Not the walled garden, but the front porch, the open lawn, the golf course, and the football stadium are the scenes of the so-called private lives of our public men.

In nineteenth-century England a number of cities like London, Birmingham, and Manchester grew with unprecedented rapidity. But this speed was slow compared to the contemporary growth of many American cities, which became metropolises almost before geographers had located them on their maps. The population of Illinois, for example, more than quadrupled between 1810 and 1820, more than trebled between 1820 and 1830, and again between 1830 and 1840. The city of Chicago (then Fort Dearborn) counted a hundred people in 1830 and by 1890 it had passed the million mark. Though it had taken a million years for mankind to produce its first city of a million inhabitants, Americans—or perhaps we should say Chicagoans—accomplished this gargantuan feat within a single lifetime. Similar phenomena occurred not only in Chicago but in dozens of other places—in Omaha, Cincinnati, Denver, Kansas City, St. Louis, and Dallas, to mention only a few.

Such fantastic growth itself fostered a naive pride in community, for men literally grew up with their towns. From this simple fact came a much maligned but peculiarly American product: the Booster Spirit. The spirit which had grown in the nineteenth century was pretty conscious of itself by about 1900 when the word "booster" was invented. In cities of explosive growth, group needs were urgent and rapidly changing. Sewage disposal, water supply, sidewalks, parks, harbor facilities, and a thousand other common needs at first depended on the desires, the willingness, and the goodwill of individuals. Could people who had very little governmental machinery do these things for themselves and their neighbors? Could they rapidly change the scale and the ends of their thinking about their town? Were they willing? By saying "Yes," they proved that they were a community.

Hardly less remarkable than this sudden intensity of community feeling in upstart cities was the fluidity of the population and the readiness with which people came and went. During a single day in the summer of 1857, 3,400 immigrants arrived in Chicago on the Michigan Central Railroad alone. People came not only from the eastern and southern United States but from Ireland, Germany, and Scandinavia, and, very soon, too, from Poland, Italy, China, and other remote places. People who came so readily sometimes also left soon and in large numbers. Such cities flourished partly because they were distribution points—spigots from which people poured into the spongelike hinterland.

Thus was nourished the Booster Spirit, distinctively American not only in intensity and volubleness but in the readiness with which it could be detached from one community and attached to another. Booster loyalties grew rapidly; yet while they lasted, they seemed to have an oaklike solidity. Here today and there tomorrow. Chicago today; tomorrow Omaha, Denver, or Tulsa. "But while I'm here, I'm with you 150 percent." "We'll outgrow and outshine all the rest!"

Never was a loyalty more fervent, more enthusiastic, more noisy—or more transferable. This was the voluntary, competitive spirit. It was illustrated in people like Dr. Daniel Drake (1785–1852), who was born in New Jersey, migrated to Kentucky, and became an early booster of Cincinnati, publishing in 1815 the first influential promotional tract for the city. But he spent much of his later life in Lexington and Louisville, where the prospects for his profession looked better.

How natural that we should become a nation of "joiners" when—provided one was not a Negro or a member of certain other marked minorities—one could join or leave his community at will. And much of the time one was likely to be considering moving to other still more attractive communities.

Everywhere personal and community prosperity were intermixed in many obvious ways. Community meant common*wealth*. Each person who came into town was one more customer, one more client, one more patient—in short, another potential booster. His mere presence increased the value of real estate and the business possibilities for everyone. To build Chicago, then, was to build my own fortune. By building my fortune, I built Chicago. We could detect this same interfusion of ideas in midtwentieth century when Charles Wilson said, "What's good for General Motors is good for the country" and when Walter Reuther replied by saying, "What's good for America is good for the Labor Movement."

The keynote of all this was *community*. American history had helped empty the word of its connotations of selflessness. Notice how irrelevant were the antitheses of Individualism versus Socialism, The Man versus The State. Governments here were not the transformed instruments of hereditary power. American businessmen were eager and ingenious at finding ways for federal, state, or local government to serve their enterprises—whether they were New England shippers, Western lumbermen, transcontinental railroad builders, manufacturers, or simple farmers or merchants. Of course, this was not because they were socialists but rather because, starting from the fact of community, they could not help seeing all agencies of government as additional forms through which specific community purposes could be served.

There are few better illustrations of this central concept—perhaps it might better be called a sentiment—in American life than the history of American philanthropy. And there has been no more effective exponent of the community spirit in philanthropy than Julius Rosenwald (1862–1932). I will not try to tell the story of Rosenwald's philanthropies. I will, rather, describe some of the distinctiveness of certain American developments and show how Julius Rosenwald participated in them.

Philanthropy or charity throughout much of European history has been a predominantly private virtue. In most of Western Europe the nation states and their organs were elaborated before the needs of modern industrial society came into being. The state and its organs had therefore preempted most of the areas of public benevolence, improvement, education, and progress even before the appearance of the great fortunes which modern industry made possible. The creators of the modern state—for example, Queen Elizabeth I in England, Napoleon in France, and Bismarck in Germany—developed arms of the state to do more and more jobs of public service, public enrichment, public enlightenment, and cultural and scientific progress. The charitable spirit was a kind of residuum; it inevitably tended to become the spirit of almsgiving. Of course, everybody was required to contribute by taxes or gifts to state or church institutions. But because the state—and its ancient partner, the church—had taken over the business of wholesale philanthropy, the independent charities of wealthy men were generally left to alleviating the distress of the particular individuals whom they noticed.

By the nineteenth century in France or Italy and even in England, it was by no means easy, though one had the means and the desire, to found a new university (the legislature might not charter it; it might confuse or compete against the state-organized system; it might become a center of "revolutionary" or of "reactionary" ideology, etc.), a new museum, or a new research institute. The right to establish new institutions, like the right to bear arms, was jealously guarded by the sovereign, which, of course, usually meant the single national government at the center.

Meanwhile Christian teachings had long exalted the spirit of charity and the practice of almsgiving. "If thou wilt be perfect, go and sell that thou hast, and give to the poor, and thou shalt have treasure in heaven: and come and follow me. . . . Verily I say unto you, That a rich man shall hardly enter into the kingdom of heaven" (Matthew 19:21–23). "Knowledge puffeth up, but charity edifieth" (I Corinthians 8:1). "And now abideth faith, hope, charity, these three; but the greatest of these is charity" (I Corinthians 13:13). Charity ennobled the giver; it was more blessed to give than to receive.

The first characteristic of the traditional charitable spirit, then, was that it was *private* and *personal*. This fact has made difficulties for scholars trying to chronicle philanthropy, especially outside the United States. Donors have often been reluctant to make known the size (whether because of the smallness or the largeness) of their donations. They have sometimes feared that signs of their wealth might bring down on them a host of the poor, confiscatory demands from the tax farmer, or jealousy from the sovereign. For more reasons than one, therefore, charity, which was a salve for the conscience, became an innermost corner of consciousness, a sanctum of privacy. A man's charities were a matter between him and his God. Church and conscience might be intermediaries, but the community did not belong in the picture.

Second, the traditional charitable spirit was perpetual, unchanging, and, even in a certain sense, rigid. "The poor," said Jesus, "ye always have with you" (John 12:8). The almsgiver was less likely to be trying to solve a problem of this world than to be earning his right to enter into the next. There hardly seemed to be any problem of means or of purpose. Since it was always a greater virtue to give than to receive, the goodness of charity came more from the motive of the giver than from the effect of the gift. Only a hypocrite, a proud man, or one impure of heart would hesitate while he chose among the objects of the gift.

The philanthropic spirit, as it has developed, changed, flourished, and become peculiarly institutionalized in America, has been very different. In some respects it has even been opposed to these two characteristics of the time-honored virtue. Here, again, the dominant note, the pervading spirit, the peculiar characteristic, has been a preoccupation with community. This transformation of the charitable spirit has been expressed in at least three peculiarly American emphases.

The focus of American philanthropy has shifted from the giver to the receiver, from the salving of souls to the solving of problems, from conscience to community. No one better expressed this spirit than Julius Rosenwald, when he said:

In the first place "philanthropy" is a sickening word. It is generally looked upon as helping a man who hasn't a cent in the world. That sort of thing hardly interests me. I do not like the "sob stuff" philanthropy.

What I want to do is to try to cure the things that seem to be wrong. I do not underestimate the value of helping the underdog. That, however, is not my chief concern but rather the operation of cause and effect. I try to do the thing that will aid groups and masses rather than individuals.

This view, which we should probably call (in William James's phrase) "tough-minded" rather than hardhearted, has long dominated what has been the peculiarly American charitable spirit.

The patron saint of American philanthropy is not Dorothea Dix or any other saintly person but rather Benjamin Franklin, the man with a business sense and an eye on his community. For Franklin, doing good was not a private act between bountiful giver and grateful receiver; it was a prudent social act. A wise act of philanthropy would sooner or later benefit the giver along with all other members of the community. While living in Philadelphia, Franklin developed philanthropic enterprises which included projects for establishing a city police, for the paving and the better cleaning and lighting of city streets, for a circulating library, for the American Philosophical Society for Useful Knowledge, for an Academy for the Education of Youth (origin of the University of Pennsylvania), for a debating society, and for a volunteer fire department.

Like Julius Rosenwald, Franklin did not go in for "sob stuff" philanthropy. Few, if any, of his enterprises were primarily for the immediate relief of distress or misfortune. Notice, also, that in Franklin's mind and in his activities the line between public and private hardly existed. If an activity was required and was not yet performed by a government—by city, state, or nation—he thought it perfectly reasonable that individuals club together to do the job, not only to fill the gap, but also to prod or shame governments into doing their part. A large number, but by no means all, of his activities have been taken over by the municipality of Philadelphia, the state of Pennsylvania, or the federal government. From his point of view the important thing was not whether the job was done by government or by individuals: Both governments and individuals were agencies of community. The community was the thing. Notice also that Franklin's opportunity to step into the breach with community enterprises arose in large part because the community was relatively new, because state activities were still sparse—in a word, because the community existed before the government.

Julius Rosenwald was sometimes unable to resist his impulse to help the individual, and he did occasionally obey the almsgiving impulse—most notably during the stock market crash of October 1929. He was himself no speculator, yet at the time of the crash he promptly and unhesitatingly supported the initiative of his son, Lessing Rosenwald, and guaranteed the personal stock market accounts of about three hundred of his employees, thus saving many of these families from financial collapse. His greatest contributions were to the Negro—not so much to the direct relief of destitution among Negroes as to the cause of Negro education. He did this in part by the wise expenditure of over $22 million through the Rosenwald Fund alone. He was not the largest philanthropist of this century, but there was none who gave more thought to the purposes and community effect of his gifts. "Viewing the matter in retrospect," Rosenwald observed in 1929, "I can testify that it is nearly always easier to make one million dollars honestly than to dispose of it wisely."

While publicly generous, he was not personally extravagant. The story is told that, when Rosenwald was traveling by Pullman train one night between Chicago and New York, another Pullman porter asked the porter of the car in which Rosenwald was sleeping whether he had any interesting passengers. The porter glowed with excitement as he boasted, "I've got Julius Rosenwald!"

After the train arrived in New York, the first porter asked the second again, "How did you make out?"

To which he received the reply, "All right, but I guess Mr. Rosenwald is really more for the race than for the individual."

While, as we have just observed, the focus of American philanthropy has shifted from giver to receiver, there has occurred another equally important shift in point of view. The clear lines between the roles of the giver and the receiver, which in the traditional European situation were so distinct, in America became blurred. In an American equalitarian, enterprising, fluid society the ancient contrasts between the bountiful rich and the grateful poor, the benefactor and the beneficiary, on which the almsgiving situation had depended, became obsolete. In America a community—the ultimate beneficiary—was increasingly expected to be its own benefactor. The recipient here (who became more difficult to identify as a member of a fixed social class) was now viewed less as a target of individual generosity than as an integral part of the social capital, an item of community investment.

It is not surprising, then, that the time-honored notion that it is more blessed to give than to receive, like some other ancient fixed axioms of charity, began to be dissolved. When you no longer believe the ancient axiom that "the poor are always with you," a recipient is no longer a member of a permanent social class. So far did we move from the old notion; now the ideal recipient of philanthropy was himself viewed as a potential donor. Just as the value of a charitable gift tended to be judged less by the motive of the giver than by the social effect of the gift, so the suitability of a recipient was judged less by his emotional response—his gratitude or his personal loyalty to a benefactor—than by his own potential contribution to the community. A free citizen who receives assistance is no mere receptacle of benevolence; he prepares himself to become a fountain of benevolence.

By a twist of New World circumstances, by the transformation of the charitable spirit, in the United States it often happened that those who received most from an act of philanthropy were also those who gave most. Julius Rosenwald, and some other characteristically American philanthropists, have viewed this as the ideal philanthropic situation. Take, for example, a scene in Boligee, Alabama, in the winter of 1916–17. This was one of the so-called arousement meetings to raise money from the local Negro community to meet Julius Rosenwald's offer of a matching sum to build a simple schoolhouse. We are fortunate to have an eyewitness account:

> When the speaking was over we arranged for the silver offering, and to tell the truth I thought we would do well to collect ten dollars from the audience; but when the Master of Ceremonies, Rev. M. D. Wallace, who had ridden a small mule over the county through the cold and through the rain, organizing the people, began to call the collection the people began to respond. You would have been over-awed with emotion if you could have seen those poor people walking up to the table, emptying their pockets for a school. . . . One old man, who had seen slavery days, with all of his life's earnings in an old greasy sack, slowly drew it from his pocket, and emptied it on the table. I have never seen such a pile of nickels, pennies, dimes, and dollars, etc., in my life. He put thirty-eight dollars on the table, which was his entire savings.

These were the people who would benefit most from the Rosenwald gift, yet they were the people who in proportion to their means were giving most.

Someone with less faith in his fellowmen might simply have given the sums outright without asking any matching funds, for the Negroes of Alabama were surely depressed and underprivileged. In a recent previous year, when the state of Alabama had appropriated $2,865,254 for public education, only $357,585, or less than 15 percent, went to Negro schools. This despite the fact that Negroes made up about half the population of the state. Rosenwald had faith in the Negroes of Alabama—not only in their potentiality but, still more important, in their present determination and their ability to help themselves.

By the time of his death in 1932, Rosenwald had contributed to the construction of 5,357 public schools, shops, and teachers' homes in 883 counties of fifteen Southern states at a total cost of $28,408,-520. Julius Rosenwald's personal contribution of $4,366,519 was monumental for those times. But a fact of which he would have been still prouder was that his contribution had induced others to contribute still more. While his contribution amounted to 15 percent of the whole, the Negroes themselves had given $4,725,871, or 17 percent. Local white friends had contributed $1,211,975, or 4 percent. And tax funds in these communities had contributed $18,104,115, or 64 percent.

In his attitude Rosenwald was not alone. Leading American philanthropists of his day shared his view. Andrew Carnegie would not give a library building without assurance that the community would invest heavily in its support. An obvious but most important common characteristic of the greatest American philanthropic enterprises of the nineteenth and early twentieth centuries in this country—of Carnegie's libraries, museums, and music halls, of the universities endowed by Vanderbilt, Cornell, Stanford, and Rockefeller, of the art galleries and institutes aided by Cooper, Peabody, and Mellon— was that they were voluntary organizations. No one would be helped by them unless the person was willing to make an effort to help himself. For this effort no place was better than a library. The passive beneficiary had no place in this scheme. "The best means of benefiting the community," said Carnegie, "is to place within its reach the ladders upon which the aspiring can rise." Thus the struggle for equal educational opportunities for everybody everywhere is the most characteristically American and the most fruitful form of philanthropy.

When philanthropy ceases to be a matter only between a man and his God, when the community enters, then anonymity loses much of its blessedness. For the community has a right to know, and can profit from knowing. Although Julius Rosenwald again and again refused his permission to let institutions be named after him (for example, the Museum of Science and Industry in Chicago), and repeatedly refused incidental honors like honorary degrees, he was opposed to anonymous giving. Simply because he believed that one of the purposes of giving was to stimulate others to give, Rosenwald believed that secrecy and inactivity were likely to go together and to explain each other.

Faith, hope, and charity were as changeless as God or human nature, but philanthropy must change with its community. American philanthropists were citizens of fast-growing cities with shifting populations, novel enterprises, and a speedy obsolescence of social problems as of everything else. To do their job, they had to keep their eyes open and their feet on the ground. They had to be alert to new needs which required new investments by everybody in a progressive community.

Julius Rosenwald, who had grown up with the West and with Chicago, was well aware of all this. He warned vain men against seeking immortality by attaching their names to institutions; he reminded them of Nesselrode, "who lived a diplomat, but is immortal as a pudding."

Rosenwald never tired of pointing to the dangers of rigid philanthropy, of gifts in perpetuity for unchanging purposes, which might become a burden rather than a blessing. He recalled the case of the Brian Mullanphy Fund, established in 1851 for "worthy and distressed travelers and emigrants passing through St. Louis to settle for a home in the West"—a fund which, for lack of beneficiaries even before Rosenwald's time, totaled a million dollars. Or the fund established by John Edgar Thompson, once president of the Pennsylvania Railroad, who gave $2 million for the benefit of daughters of railroad workers whose lives were accidentally lost in the service of the company. Because of the decline in railway accidents, the fund was virtually without a purpose in 1930; and the decline of railways would make it even more difficult for Mr. Thompson's purpose to be served in later years. Or there was the benefactor of Bryn Mawr College who, in days before the weight-losing fad, left a fund to provide a baked potato for each young lady there at every meal.

His favorite example, and one still very relevant, was the orphan asylum. "Orphan asylums," Rosenwald remarked in 1929, "began to disappear about the time the old-fashioned wall telephone went out." Yet millions had been accumulating for orphan asylums; at that date the Hershey endowment for these purposes alone totaled over $40 million. But ideas had changed. Already in 1929, it was generally believed that other ways of helping orphans—for example, placing them in foster homes—were far preferable.

Julius Rosenwald's long experience as a trustee of the University of Chicago further convinced him, as he observed on numerous occasions, of the unwisdom of philanthropic gifts narrowly limited. It takes courage for a man to crusade for his ideas and to stake his life and fortune on them; it takes still greater courage for a man to stake his life and fortune on a belief that his ideas will become obsolete.

Perhaps Julius Rosenwald's leading contribution to our thinking about philanthropy was his insistence on the need for flexibility and self-liquidation in American philanthropic institutions. In his widely read article, "Principles of Public Giving" (*Atlantic Monthly,* May 1929), and its sequel, "The Trend Away from Perpetuities" (*Atlantic Monthly,* December 1930), he championed lifetime, rather than testamentary, giving and urged other ways of allowing each generation to face its own problems. The Rosenwald Fund, which was probably one of the most successful philanthropic enterprises of this or any other century, was set up with the express provision, which Rosenwald wrote into the gift, that both the income and all the principal be spent within twenty-five years of Rosenwald's death. Rosenwald died in 1932, and the Fund, under able direction, lived up to this requirement, terminating its work in 1948. He believed in applying to charity the Jeffersonian axiom that the earth belongs to the living.

CHAPTER 17

A Laboratory of the Arts

IN THE CENTURY after 1876, the United States became a laboratory and a symbol of the flowing together of world cultures. This convergence was a product of the daemonic energy, the focused genius, and the ambitions of numerous talented individual men and women. It was also an American by-product of the miseries bred by political totalitarianism, megalomania, and mass hysteria in far parts of the world. The United States became a museum, a workshop, and a marketplace for talents which were not tolerated elsewhere. America bore witness to the power of art and ideas to overrule legislative fiat and to overflow political boundaries.

In the perspective of American history there is an instructive irony in the impressive product of immigrant Americans during the last century. This was when, for the first time, immigration to the United States was quantitatively limited. Yet these years showed the forces of immigrant innovation to be more potent than ever before.

The product of immigrant artists in the United States demonstrated the long-run futility of the use of force to stultify or confine the acts of creation. For art obeys the opposite of Gresham's Law: Quality drives out quantity. Governments may encourage population growth or birth control, they may execute, imprison, or deport individual artists or thinkers. But there is no known device for artistic contraception. The brutal tyrannies of our age have dulled and diluted the cultures of their own nations. But the *world* of culture is beyond their jurisdiction. The artists whom they discourage, punish, or expel—when these manage to escape with their lives—

reappear on distant American landscapes. Here, to the freshness of their native talents they add another new dimension—their immigrants' vision.

Within this last century, such escapees and expellees helped us produce a new kind of American renaissance—a New World rebirth of Old World art and thought. Their message is peculiarly poignant because it came along with, and in spite of, a drastic change in the American spirit. In these years, despite the efforts of some of the most respectable, most "cultured" Americans, immigrant artists vindicated the American tradition of cosmopolitanism against unfriendly new American provincialisms.

The appropriate symbol of our attitude toward newcomers for the whole first century of our nation's life was the Statue of Liberty. Planned for Bedloe's Island in New York Harbor to commemorate the Centennial of the American Revolution in 1876, it was finally unveiled by President Cleveland on October 28, 1886. On its base were inscribed Emma Lazarus' now familiar (often parodied) lines:

> . . . Give me your tired, your poor,
> Your huddled masses yearning to breathe free,
> The wretched refuse of your teeming shore.
> Send these, the homeless, tempest-tost, to me,
> I lift my lamp beside the golden door!

Emma Lazarus spoke for the century of the Open Door.

When the Pilgrim Fathers had arrived some 250 years before, they carried no passports (except their Bibles!) and it is doubtful how many of them could have passed an immigrant inspector's scrutiny for physical fitness and mental balance. Their opinions had a dangerously totalitarian taint. All but a small number of the forty-odd millions who followed them after Independence also arrived passportless and without "papers." They were not required to satisfy any government official of their qualifications to become Americans.

The historic American Open Door policy was, of course, a by-product of continental vastness and emptiness and remoteness. But it was not merely a historical accident. It expressed a novel principle—the American belief in the right of voluntary expatriation, the right to leave one's country and settle elsewhere. The Declaration of Independence asserted that right. It was repeated in 1868 when European governments were claiming jurisdiction over their nationals who had fled to the United States without their permission, and the Congress declared the right of voluntary expatriation to be "a natural and inherent right of all people." A century later Americans were still asserting this right in their sense of outrage at the Soviet refusal to allow their nationals to emigrate at will. The English common law had held that a subject could not change his allegiance without the permission of his government. Old World custom, reinforced by feudal institutions, had given rulers a kind of property in their peoples. Our nation, then, grew as a haven for runaways—for people who refused to endure persecution or tyranny simply because they were born under it.

But the right of voluntary expatriation was two-sided. The right to emigrate from any place would save no one unless he also had the right elsewhere to immigrate. For the whole first century after Independence, the United States preserved both these rights substantially inviolate. The tired, the poor, the "huddled masses yearning to breathe free" not only had the right to leave the Old World, but they also were assured the right to enter the New. They poured into the United States, fully justifying Walt Whitman's boast in 1855 that we were "not merely a nation but a teeming nation of nations."

The United States adjusted itself to its immigrants and the immigrants adjusted themselves to their new country by one of two means: segregation or assimilation. Many formed their alien islands, and even hoped to preserve their isolation. The New England Puritans came here in the early seventeenth century partly because their young people had been corrupted by the laxness and heterodoxy of England or the Netherlands. Two centuries later, many who fled here from the European Revolutions of 1848 sought ways to segregate themselves. The most influential of these Forty-Eighters were Germans, and a considerable number of them seemed less anxious to take root in American soil than to transplant German culture. They kept the German language in their schools, they read their American German-language newspapers, they introduced Kindergartens and joined their own singing societies and orchestras. They came, as one contemporary put it, not to become Americanized, but to help America become Germanized.

These peculiarly American alien islands were not always formed voluntarily. Sometimes they appeared because the newcomers were socially ostracized or legally segregated. Among them were Jews, Catholics, Chinese, Africans, Mexicans, American Indians, and many others—isolated because of their "race" or supposed race, because of their unfamiliar, colorful, aggressive or passive, phlegmatic or strident ways. They fortified and solaced themselves in ethnic, racial, or religious ghettos, in neighborhoods on the wrong side of the railroad tracks, in ethnic churches and parochial schools, in lodges and brotherhoods and historical societies, in celebrations of special holidays and festivals, in spicy culinary islands of pizza parlors, kosher delicatessens, and their myriad counterparts, in defense societies and anti-defamation leagues. Their political symbol was the Balanced Ticket.

The most important alternative to segregation was assimilation. Millions of newcomers were dissolved into the mainstream. They changed their names (or their names were changed into more pronounceable alternatives by immigration officers), they went to public schools, they intermarried with Americanized earlier immigrants, they took on the protective coloration of American speech and American clothing and an American standard of living, they joined American lodges, they converted to more "American" churches or more American sects of their Old World denomination, they became boosters for their neighborhoods, their cities and their States, they entered politics. In short, they became the justification, as they were sometimes the specific product, of movements to "Americanize" the immigrant.

At the end of the first century of our Independence, the official American attitude toward immigration was transformed. The Open Door was slammed shut—or at best left slightly ajar. The warm humanitarianism of Emma Lazarus' welcome was replaced by a wary exclusionism. The new spirit was well expressed by Thomas Bailey Aldrich's warning to the nation, in the prim *Atlantic Monthly* in 1892, to set watchmen over "The Unguarded Gates":

> Wide open and unguarded stand our gates,
> And through them presses a wild motley throng—
> Men from the Volga and the Tartar steppes,
> Featureless figures from the Hoang-Ho,
> Malayan, Scythian, Teuton, Kelt, and Slav,
> Flying the Old World's poverty and scorn;
> These bringing with them unknown gods and rites,
> Those, tiger passions, here to stretch their claws.
> In street and alley what strange tongues are these,
> Accents of menace alien to our air,
> Voices that once the Tower of Babel knew!

Though the tired immigrant's first shipboard glimpse of the promised land might still be Liberty's welcoming torch, on landing he was greeted by an unwelcoming immigration inspector.

Intellectual and social forces abroad in the land had worked this transformation. During the 1880s many ambitious young American historians and political scientists streamed to German universities. When they came back, they brought with them (along with their Ph.D.s, which became their union cards and the prototype of American graduate education) an interpretation of history which traced all good institutions—parliaments, congresses, constitutions, courts, and even the very love of liberty—to the primeval Anglo-Saxons. At the same time, the Census of 1890 reported that there was no longer a "frontier line" in the American West. This supposed "closing" of the American frontier was translated by Wisconsin historian Frederick Jackson Turner in 1893 into a frontier interpretation of American democracy. Turner's disciples nostalgically traced the American virtues to the disappearing backwoods and to the countryside, and sounded an alarm against the crowding of American cities. President Theodore Roosevelt appointed a Commission on Country Life in 1908 to find new ways to preserve old rural values. When, in 1893, the nation suffered its worst depression till that time, the newly unionized skilled laborers blamed their unemployment on the influx of "cheap labor" from abroad.

By 1900 these and other forces converged into the movement that closed the immigrant gates. The need to do so was rationalized by ingenious and sometimes desperate efforts to describe the prototypical American. Small groups came up with facile definitions of "Americanism."

The most potent and most respectable of these efforts was the Immigration Restriction League, founded in 1894 by three young New England blue bloods, Charles Warren, Robert DeCourcy Ward, and Prescott Farnsworth Hall. They had been persuaded in Harvard Professor Albert Bushnell Hart's History 13 that, just as Negroes had supposedly disintegrated Southern culture, so the "new" immigrants had ruined American cities. The founders of the League were joined by an impressive list of social scientists, historians, political scientists, literati, and politicians. Among them were economists Francis A. Walker, William Z. Ripley, John R. Commons, Thomas Nixon Carver, and Richard T. Ely, sociologists Franklin H. Giddings, Richard Mayo Smith, Edward A. Ross, and Robert A. Woods, and historians John Fiske, Albert Bushnell Hart, and Herbert Baxter Adams. The League's academic galaxy included, among others, A. Lawrence

Lowell, president of Harvard University, William DeWitt Hyde, president of Bowdoin College, James T. Young, director of the Wharton School of Finance, Charles F. Thwing, president of Western Reserve University, Leon C. Marshall, dean of the University of Chicago, R. E. Blackwell, president of Randolph-Macon College, K. G. Matheson, president of Georgia School of Technology, and David Starr Jordan, president of Stanford University. Their political spokesman was Henry Cabot Lodge.

Insisting on a crucial difference between the "old" immigration and the "new," the Immigration Restriction League and their cohorts idealized the "old" immigration into people like themselves. The Good Immigrants, whom they traced to Northern and Western Europe, were said to be wholesome, literate, and enterprising—eager to become Good Americans. At the same time the League caricatured the "new" immigration into a movement from Eastern and Southern Europe of the unskilled and the illiterate, of potential prostitutes and criminals (with an inevitable admixture of "lunatics"). These "new" immigrants, who came only because they had no alternative, would obstinately perpetuate Old World customs and values. They would never be anything but unwilling Americans.

Both the idealization and the caricature were reinforced by the conclusions of the Dillingham Commission set up by Congress in 1907 to investigate the whole problem of immigration. The commission's ponderous forty-one-volume report (1911), which included testimony and evidence of social scientists, eugenicists, economists, community leaders, and politicians, purported to mark off a historical watershed between the "old" and the "new" immigration. According to the report, those who immigrated after about 1883 had mostly come "involuntarily" (seduced by steamship and railroad advertising, and by the schemes of American employers to bring in cheap labor). The older immigrants, it was said, had helped cultivate the land, but instead the newer immigrants flooded into the cities, where they had "congregated together in sections apart from native Americans and the older immigrants to such an extent that assimilation [had] been slow."

These ill-founded fears were being fed by news of labor troubles. The early 1870s saw the Molly Maguire riots in the Pennsylvania coal fields; the Haymarket bombing rocked Chicago in 1886; the Pullman strike, which paralyzed the railroads and brought out the federal troops, came in 1894. The radical Industrial Workers of the World (better known as the IWW or the Wobblies) was organized in 1904 to fight the conservative and exclusionist policies of the American Federation of Labor.

Labor troubles and other "social disorders" were attributed to recently arrived immigrant "agitators." When the United States entered World War I, it was said that pacifists and "slackers" had come mainly from this same "foreign element," not real Americans but "hyphenated" Americans. The Bolshevik Revolution of 1917 came along to give nativists a new handle on their prejudices. "These alien Socialists, Radicals, IWW's and Bolshevists," a restrictionist spokesman wrote in the *New York Times* in 1919, "served a very useful purpose in rousing Americans to the peril of an increase in their numbers."

Postwar prosperity in the 1920s somehow did not allay nativist fears or restrictionist passions. The Ku Klux Klan flourished anew and became a potent force in the politics of Southern and Midwestern States. In 1922, President A. Lawrence Lowell of Harvard (a national vice-president of the Immigration Restriction League since 1912) undertook a study of the "race distribution" within Harvard College. Professor Albert Bushnell Hart reported with alarm that 52 percent of the students in one course in government were "outside the element" from which the college had been "chiefly recruited for three hundred years." Then, with his proposed quota for Jews, President Lowell aimed to prevent the "abnormal unbalancing of races" in American colleges.

The travail of the "new" immigrant was dramatized in the trial of Sacco and Vanzetti. Recent immigrants from Italy, these were gentle men, philosophical anarchists and pacifists, and they had avoided the draft in World War I. After they were convicted of killings at a shoe factory in Braintree, Massachusetts, Governor Alvin Fuller expressed the spirit of the times when he appointed President A. Lawrence Lowell to head the committee to review the fairness of the trial. Lowell insisted, of course, that there had been no influence of "racial feeling" on their trial. Sacco and Vanzetti were executed in 1927, and entered the folklore of American martyrdom, alongside Nathan Hale, John Brown, and Barbara Fritchie.

It was, of course, the descendants of earlier immigrants (in New England and the South they preferred to call their ancestors "colonists," old "settlers," or First Families) who led the nation into a legislative program to restrict immigration. Restrictionists showed the same kind of legalistic ingenuity that white Southern legislators had employed to disfranchise the Negro. Still, the strength of the American tradition of asylum was revealed in the deviousness of the devices to which the racial restrictionists felt themselves driven.

As early as 1897 the Immigration Restriction League, still reluctant to apply an explicitly "racial" standard, tried the device of a literacy test. Hoping in this way to keep out "the undesirable classes," Senator Henry Cabot Lodge of Massachusetts sponsored a literacy bill which excluded any immigrant unable to read forty words in any language. It passed both houses of Congress, but was vetoed by President Cleveland, who declared that it violated the American tradition. Repeated attempts to enact a literacy bill failed. The bill which passed in 1913 was vetoed by President Taft; that which passed in 1915 was vetoed by President Wilson.

In February 1917, on the rising wave of patriotism which preceded our entry into World War I, Congress adopted a comprehensive new Immigration Law. This incorporated a literacy test, added new classes of exclusions (chronic alcoholics, vagrants, and "persons of constitutional psychopathic inferiority"), and established a "barred zone" in the Southwest Pacific which excluded Asiatic immigrants not already kept out by the Chinese Exclusion Act of 1882 and the Gentlemen's Agreement of 1907–1908. This bill was passed over President Wilson's veto.

The next gambit of the restrictionists was a series of laws—in 1921, 1924, and 1952—which fixed an absolute number (which remained around 150,000) for total annual immigration. That number was distributed by a quota for each national group based on the proportion of people of that origin in the United States Census of some particular year (variously, 1910, 1890, or 1920). The crudity of such a device soon appeared. It was well-nigh impossible to concoct any precise definition of "national origins" for the fluid and intermixing American population. Nevertheless the facts of sociology yielded to the urgencies of politics and prejudice.

The early decades of the twentieth century were an era when the nation's new policy of restrictive immigration was in full force. Only a few came from respectable "Anglo-Saxon" stock. Many, if not most, of the immigrant artists and intellectuals would have had to be classified in the supposedly disrespectable "new" immigration that accelerated after the 1880s. They came from Southern and Eastern Europe, from Italy, Russia, Lithuania, Hungary, and Armenia—from the exotic precincts that so frightened Thomas Bailey Aldrich and his New England colleagues. Many were Jews. Most, for one reason or another, fell within classes which the restrictionists wished to exclude—and which their laws aimed to exclude.

Artists driven by the Polish and Russian pogroms, by the rise of Communism in Russia and Eastern Europe, and by the rise of Fascism in Italy and Nazism in Germany lacked that "spontaneous" motivation which the restrictionists had idealized in their own ancestors. This was the era, par excellence, of "involuntary" immigration. People came, as D. H. Lawrence observed, not toward something, but mainly "to get away." The catastrophes they escaped were not earthquake, famine, or natural disaster. They were escaping man-made earthquakes. American civilization directly—and human civilization indirectly—would reap unpredicted benefits from Old World malevolence. And *because* these artists were displacees and refugees from new orthodoxies, from new inquisitions, from new-style pogroms, and from twentieth-century racisms, they had something special to offer.

The galaxy of artists, architects, writers, social scientists, and scientists who came in the 1930s and 1940s to escape the Nazi holocaust were the most prominent group. But they were not unique. And their characteristics typified thousands of other escapees from other holocausts. In a new sense, these were *"new* immigrants." When these men and women arrived, they had already been educated in their homeland, and so came at the height of their achievement. They had actually been expelled because of their vigor, originality, and distinction. The United States received them full-grown, without the social cost of nurturing and training. But the economic advantage was trivial compared to another special benefit.

Those who were already fully formed and equipped—and there were thousands—could add something special to civilization here and through America to the world. They brought the most advanced and most original European modes of making and thinking for a new encounter with the American scene. Not in the minds of tourists or casual travelers—but in the person of newly committed Americans. Each of them was a unique laboratory of the experimental spirit. They brought the immigrants' vision.

Not only in art, but in the sciences and the social sciences, the immigrant galaxy during these years was impressive. The arriving scientists and mathematicians included Albert Einstein, Max Delbrück, Leo Szilard, Enrico Fermi, and John von Neumann. Among the social scientists and psychologists were Florian Znaniecki, Hannah Arendt, Hans J. Morgenthau, Franz Alexander, Felix and Helene Deutsch, Herbert Marcuse, Karl Wittfogel, Theodor Adorno, Paul Lazarsfeld, Wolfgang Köhler, and Kurt Lewin. And these are only a sample. The catalog of composers and musicians, of art historians and publishers would show the same eminence.

Because of what they had seen, because they had been personally disavowed by their native lands, these new "new immigrants" had no desire to transplant Old World institutions or to Europeanize America. They enriched America, not merely like earlier immigrants with their hope and their promise, but as people who had already found their own promise, had proved their capacity for fulfillment, and welcomed new opportunities to experiment.

In no period in American history were our thought and art and culture more deeply stirred or more grandly shaped by currents from abroad. Nor had American civilization in any comparable period been more enriched by new currents. Although most of these immigrants would become Americanized with astonishing speed, they kept firm the remarkable individualities they had brought with them and which might not have been bred on American soil. During these very years when the United States had officially undertaken to reduce immigrant *numbers,* the catalytic influence of immigrants on American culture became more powerful than ever before.

While this bore witness to the indomitable hospitality of America, which could not easily be legislated out of existence, it also bore witness to the transnational character of art and thought, to the fertility of the American soil for rebirth. Once again it proved America's capacity to be a forum and a free marketplace for the world— not merely "A Nation of Nations" but an International Nation.

CHAPTER 18

The Amateur Spirit and Its Enemies

ONE OF THE LEADERS who shaped our nation's Air Force was the bold and imaginative Gen. Emmett "Rosy" O'Donnell. When people asked him what he meant by leadership, he was ready with an anecdote of his early years in the service. One day when he was a young lieutenant aide at the air base outside Denver, his general gave him an order. He dissented mildly, offering a different procedure. The general retorted, "O'Donnell, are you proposing to countermand an order?" To which the brash O'Donnell replied, "General, sir, I'm sure you didn't reach your present rank by being a yes man." "No," the general explained, "but that's how I made colonel!"

The general was describing some strong currents in American life, which have gathered force in recent decades and are likely to increase in momentum in the years ahead. Some come inevitably in a popular democracy—the familiar temptations of the demagogue. But other forces, too, stifle the spirit of the true leader. These forces, like the temptations of the democratic demagogue, have been organized into flourishing American institutions. And they too nourish the timidities of the yes man.

The great leader must, of course, have a tinge of the transcendental. He must have the clairvoyance to imagine and to believe that things can be otherwise. Gen. George Marshall, who knew a thing or two about leadership, described a leader as "a person who exerts an influence and makes you want to do better than you could."

The true leader is an amateur in the proper, original sense of the word. The amateur (from Latin *amator,* "lover"; from *amare,* "to love") does something for the love of it. He pursues his enterprise not for money, not to please the crowd, not for professional prestige or for assured promotion and retirement at the end—but because he loves it. If he can't help doing it, it's not because of the forces pushing from behind but because of his fresh, amateur's vision of what lies ahead.

Aristocracies are governed by people born to govern, totalitarian societies by people who make ruling their profession. But our representative government must be led by people never born to govern, temporarily drawn from the community, and sooner or later sent back home. Democracy is government by amateurs. The progress—perhaps even the survival—of our society depends on the vitality of the amateur spirit in the United States today and tomorrow.

The two new breeds whose power and prestige menace the amateur spirit are the *professionals* and the *bureaucrats*. Both are by-products of American wealth, American progress. But they can stifle the amateur spirit on which the special quality and vision of our American leaders must depend.

First, the professionals. Professions, as we know them, are a modern phenomenon. The word "profession," when it first came into the English language, meant the vows taken by members of the clergy. By the sixteenth century professions included other vocations in which "a professed knowledge of some department of learning or science is used in its application to the affairs of others."

For some centuries professions included, besides the clergy, only law and medicine—and gradually, too, the military. Each of these professions in England became a tight monopoly with its own schools, its own standards of admission, its own ethic and its own rules for fees and honoraria. By 1820 an outspoken Englishman could complain, "Of the professions it may be said that the soldiers are becoming too popular, parsons too lazy, physicians too mercenary and lawyers too powerful."

Then the words "scientist" and "artist" entered the English language about 1840. All over Europe the professions acquired an aura of respectability. Karl Marx and Friedrich Engels in their *Communist Manifesto* (1848) actually counted among the evils of capitalism that it disintegrated that reverence. "The bourgeoisie," they said, "has stripped of its halo every occupation hitherto honored and looked up to with reverent awe. It has converted the physician, the lawyer, the priest, the poet, the man of science into its paid wage laborers."

The American democratic magic has crowned an increasing number of occupations with the professional halo. American colleges, universities and training programs run for profit have spawned professions without precedent.

Today the list of our professions is endless. We have a clue to their number in the miscellaneous specialized degrees awarded in education, journalism, communications, business, public relations, counseling, advertising and domestic science—to name a few. Each of the professional associations—now numbering in the hundreds—has its own national and regional meetings, encouraged by our speedy, inexpensive transportation and by a growing network of hotels and convention centers. The result is the professionalization of almost everybody.

The ubiquitous professions set standards, discipline charlatans, and enforce their ethics. They also lobby for their special interests and labor to raise the prestige of their practitioners—from accountants and actuaries, through morticians and obstetricians, to women engineers and zoologists.

An ominous sign is the accelerating movement that has made business into a profession. In the eighteenth century to say someone was a man of business meant he was engaged in public affairs. David Hume in 1752 described Pericles as a "man of business."

Then, on this side of the ocean, the "businessman" became a characteristic American institution. He was not an American version of the European banker or merchant or manufacturer, and certainly not a New World Fugger or Medici. In the burgeoning American West he was a New World type of community maker and community leader—a William B. Ogden, who built Chicago; a Dr. Daniel Drake, who developed Cincinnati; or a Gen. William Larimer, who chose the site for Denver. They never could have learned their techniques for success in a school of business administration.

Today the increasing vogue of the M.B.A. signals the fall of a bastion of the amateur spirit. Who can be trained to be a seeker of opportunity, an unspecialized man of enterprise? What professional curriculum will teach men to be self-made?

The spread of professions brings with it *the professional fallacy*. George Bernard Shaw may have gone too far when he called *every* profession "a conspiracy against the laity." But latent in the organization of every profession, unspoken in every professional creed is an article of faith: The profession really exists for the sake of the professionals. Specifically this means that law exists for the sake of lawyers, medicine for the convenience, maintenance, and enlightenment of doctors, universities for the sake of professors, etc. The professional temptation goes everywhere.

In Vietnam, some historians of the press suggest, the reporting of the war was shaped by the desire of newsmen to win the accolades of their fellow journalists. Some of us, too, know what it means to live in a house designed to provide plans and photographs that will adorn an architectural journal—but with no place to put out the garbage or to park bicycles or the baby carriage.

Beneath the professional fallacy lies the confident axiom that the customer is not competent to judge. Any professional—whether a brain surgeon or plumber—must command our faith in his expertise.

Yet the books are full of episodes that shake our faith. One of the more dramatic occurred in the midnineteenth century, when the enterprising dentist William T. G. Morton introduced ether as an anesthetic. Surgeons had long performed amputations by wielding their saws on screaming patients. When Dr. Morton's new idea came on the scene, some surgeons objected, insisting that pain (besides being a necessary part of the human—especially the female—condition) was itself a kind of medication. Somehow it would prevent postsurgical infection.

The second breed of enemies of the amateur spirit are the *bureaucrats*. These, too, are a characteristically modern phenomenon. Just as professions are a by-product of the specializing of knowledge and technology, bureaucracy has come from the increasing size of enterprises and the proliferating activities of government.

The word "bureaucrat" derives from the French word *bureau*, which first meant the woolen material—green baize—used to cover writing desks in the eighteenth century. Originally it simply described people who worked on these *bureau*-covered desks in royal households.

Only with the rise of liberalism was the word "bureaucrat" used to put down the highhanded, routine procedures of government officials. By 1848 John Stuart Mill was warning against "a dominant bureaucracy." Thomas Carlyle, too, despised "the Continental nuisance called 'Bureaucracy.'" One wit soon called bureaucrats "the people who put in their place the people who put them in their places."

Early in this century the German sociologist Max Weber described bureaucracy as a pervasive and distinctive feature of modern civilization. Webster's New World Dictionary now defines bureaucracy as "the administration of government through departments and subdivisions managed by sets of appointed officials following an inflexible routine . . . see *red tape.*"

The enlarged scale of all modern enterprises has made bureaucracy pandemic. Every new technology—for roads, steamships, mines, railroads, air travel, electricity, postal service, telegraph, telephone, radio, television, etc.—has created a new bureaucracy. And bureaucracies proliferated with government supervision of the conditions of labor, energy use, consumer safety, enforcement of social equality and civil rights. More and more nongovernmental activities—businesses, schools, colleges, museums, libraries, and even our churches—have become increasingly bureaucratic. In the United States today there is hardly an institution or a daily activity where we are not ruled by the bureaucratic frame of mind—caution, concern for regularity of procedures, avoidance of the need for decision. The bureaucrats' aim is to keep things on track, to keep themselves on the ladder of promotion, on the clear road to fully pensioned retirement. Bureaucrats who rule us are themselves ruled by *the bureaucratic fallacy.* This was never better announced than on a sign over the desk of a French civil servant: "Never Do Anything for the First Time."

In my own vocation of historian I am impressed by the leadership of the great amateurs. These people tried what the professionals would not dare. Some did their great work even before there was an organized profession for historians. Among the great English amateurs are Edward Gibbon, Thomas Babington Macaulay, and Winston Churchill; among the Americans are George Bancroft, Francis Parkman, William H. Prescott, and Henry Adams.

Historical writing has recently been afflicted by both the professional fallacy (historians writing for one another) and the bureaucratic fallacy (historians writing monographs that fit into the expected pattern and will insure academic tenure). Among historians, too, it is only since the rise of the profession that "amateur" has become a disparaging word—to describe work that is "unprofessional," crude or "amateurish." Today our most widely read, most durable historians continue to be amateurs.

In our government, too, the great work depends on the ability to keep the amateur spirit—in its original sense—alive. How?

The framers of our Constitution gave us a clue when they made the President the Commander in Chief of our armed forces. Civilian control takes the top command out of the hands of military professionals. When Jefferson insisted that none of our diplomatic corps should serve abroad for longer than seven years before returning home, he was alert to the professional fallacy. He feared that the ambassador might become so attached to his prescribed procedures and to the land of his assignment that he would cease to speak for the citizens back home.

Our Congress, like our armed forces and our foreign service, needs men and women of experience who are adept at parliamentary procedure and familiar with the executive machinery. But laws that prevent members from keeping open their avenues to their former—alternative—occupations remove the best insurance of their independence.

Back in the eighteenth century the Tory Sir William Blackstone argued that no one should be paid for sitting in Parliament. He plausibly explained that, unlike men who needed the job, those who served without fee would be gentlemen of substance, not easily corrupted. Even if his assumption of the identity of wealth and virtue was naive, his objective—the nonprofessional representative—was good.

In our democracy it is of course essential to keep representative posts accessible to people who are not gentlemen of leisure. We can and must find ways to help our representatives preserve their amateur spirit.

We do that, for example, when we allow and even encourage them to keep their ways open to other means of earning a living if their constituents will no longer support them. It is a sorry sign of the decline of the amateur spirit when the main employment for former congressmen is as lobbyists—a by-product of their defunct political career.

The representative of the people, however frequently reelected, must be wary of becoming a *professional* politician. The more complex and gigantic our government, the more essential that the layman's point of view have eloquent voices.

The amateur spirit is a distinctive virtue of democracy. Every year, as professions and bureaucracies increase in power, it becomes more difficult—yet more urgent—to keep that spirit alive. In a word, we need leaders with the customers' point of view—which is another name for the citizens' slant on government.

Can we continue to breed leaders who draw on the expertise of professionals without suffering the contagion of the professional fallacy, who enlist the loyalty and industry of bureaucrats without being paralyzed by their caution? Only leaders informed by this amateur spirit can prepare us for the one certainty in history—which is the unexpected.

PART V

THE MOMENTUM OF TECHNOLOGY

Admiring Friend:
    "My, that's a beautiful baby you have there!"
Mother:
    "Oh, that's nothing—you should see his photograph!"

CHAPTER 19

Two Kinds of Revolutions

FOR ONLY A TINY fragment of human history has man been aware even that he had a history. During nearly all the years since man first developed writing and civilization began, he thought of himself and of his community in ways quite different from those familiar to us today. He tended to see the passage of time, not as a series of unique, irreversible moments of change, but rather as a recurrence of *familiar* moments. The cycle of the seasons—spring, summer, fall, winter, spring—was his most vivid, most intimate signal of passing time. When men sought other useful signposts in the cycle, at first they naturally chose the phases of the moon, because the reassuring regularity of the lunar cycle, being relatively short, was easily noted. It was some time before recognition of the solar cycle (a much more sophisticated notion), with its accompanying notion of a yearly cycle, became widespread.

And, in that age of cyclical time, before the discovery of history, the repetition of the familiar provided the framework for all the most significant and dramatic occasions in human experience. Religious rituals were re-creations or recapitulations of ancient original events, often the events which were supposed to have created the world. The spring was a time not only of new crops, but of a re-created earth. Just as the moon was reborn in every lunar cycle, so the year was reborn through the solar cycle.

Just as the sacred year always repeated the Creation, so every human marriage reproduced the hierogamy—the sacred union of heaven and earth. Every hero relived the career and recaptured the spirit of an earlier mythic prototype. A familiar surviving example of the age of cyclical time before the rise of historical consciousness is the Judaeo-Christian Sabbath. Our week has seven days, and by resting on the seventh day, we reenact the primordial gesture of the Lord God when on the seventh day of the Creation He "rested . . . from all his work which he had made" (Genesis 2:2).

The archaic man, as Mircea Eliade puts it, lived in a "continual present" where nothing is really new, because of his "refusal to accept himself as a historical being."

Perhaps the greatest of all historical revolutions was man's discovery, or his invention, of the idea of history. Obviously it did not occur in Western Europe on any particular day, in any particular year, or perhaps even in a particular century, but slowly and painfully. If we stop to think for a moment, we will begin to see how difficult it must have been for people whose whole world had consisted of a universe of seasons and cycles, of archetypes and resurrections, of myths relived, of heroes reincarnate, to think in a way so different.

This was nothing less than man's discovery of the new. Not of any particular sort of novelty, but of the very possibility of novelty. Men were moving from the relived-familiar, from the always-meaningful reenactment of the archetype, out into a world of unimagined, chaotic, and possibly treacherous novelty.

When did this first crucial revolution in human thought occur? In Western European civilization it seems to have come at the end of the Middle Ages, probably around the fourteenth century. The power of older ways of thinking, the dominance of cycles and rebirths, was revealed in the very name "Renaissance," which actually did not come into use till the nineteenth century, for the age when novelty and man's power for breaking out of the cycles were discovered.

Symptoms of this new way of thinking (as Peter Burke has chronicled in his *Renaissance Sense of the Past*) are found in the writings of Petrarch (1304–1374), who himself took an interest in history, in the changing fashions in coins, clothing, words, and laws. He saw the ruins of Rome not as the work of mythic giants, which was a conventional explanation until then, but as relics of a different age. Lorenzo Valla (c. 1407–1457) pioneered historical scholarship when he proved the so-called Donation of Constantine to be a forgery, and he also laid a basis for historical linguistics when, in *De elegantia linguae latinae,* he showed the relationship between the decline of the

Roman Empire and the decline of Latin. Paintings by Piero della Francesca (c. 1420–1492) and by Andrea Mantegna (1431–1506) began to abandon the reckless anachronism of earlier artists and made new efforts at historical accuracy in armor and in costume.

Roman law, which would continue to dominate continental Europe, ceased to be a suprahistorical, transcendental phenomenon. And other legal systems began to be seen as capable of change. In England, for example, where the common law was imagined to be the rules "to which the mind of man runneth not to the contrary," the fiction of antiquity began to dissolve, and by the seventeenth century innovation by legislation was thought to be possible. The Protestant Reformation, too, brought a new interest in historical sources and opened the way for a new kind of scrutiny of the past.

The awakening sense of history, which opened new worlds and unimagined worlds of the new, brought its own problems. Names had to be found, or made, for the novelties which knowledge of history would bring. The new inquiring spirit, the newly quizzical mood for viewing the passing current of events, stirred scholars to look beneath the surface for latent causes and unconfessed motives. Early efforts to describe and explain historical change still leaned heavily on the old notion of cycles. A late version of this was offered in about 1635 in a rich baroque metaphor by Sir Thomas Browne:

> As though there were a Metempsychosis, and the soul of one man passed into another, opinions do find, after certain revolutions, men and minds like those that first begat them . . . men are lived over again, the world is now as it was in ages past . . . because the glory of one state depends upon the ruin of another, there is a revolution and vicissitude of their greatness, and must obey the swing of that wheel, not moved by intelligences [such as the souls that moved the planets] but by the hand of God, whereby all estates arise to their zenith and vertical parts according to their predestined periods. For the lives, not only of men, but of Commonwealths, and of the whole world, run not upon a helix that still enlargeth, but on a circle, where, according to their meridian, they decline on obscurity, and fall under the horizon again.

But as the historical consciousness became more lively, the historical imagination became both more sensitive and bolder. There were more artists and scholars and lawyers and chroniclers who saw the passage of time as history.

Several words which once had a specific physical denotation

began to be borrowed and given extended meanings, to describe processes in history. The word "revolution" had described the movement of celestial bodies in an orbit or circular course and had also come to mean the time required to complete such a full circuit. By the early seventeenth century (as the *Oxford English Dictionary* reveals) "revolution" came to be used figuratively to denote any great change. In a century shaken by "commotions" which overthrew established governments, "revolution" came to mean what we still think of it as meaning.

At about the same time, the word "progress" also acquired a new meaning. Until then, it had been used almost exclusively in the simple physical sense of an onward movement in space or the onward movement of a story. Originally neither of these senses was eulogistic. By the early eighteenth century "progress" had come to mean advancement to a higher stage, to better conditions, continuous improvement. That was the age of the English Enlightenment, which encompassed John Locke, Sir Isaac Newton, Robert Boyle, David Hume, and Joseph Priestley. Hardly surprising that it needed a name for progress! Similarly, by the midnineteenth century, as a philologist explained in 1871, the word "decadence" (derived from *de* + *cadere,* which meant "to fall down") "came into fashion, apparently to *denote* decline and *connote* a scientific and enlightened view of that decline on the part of the user."

The century after 1776 was not only a period of great revolutions, it was also a period of great historians. In England that century produced the works of Edward Gibbon, Thomas Babington Macaulay, Henry Thomas Buckle, and W. E. H. Lecky. In the United States it was the century of Francis Parkman, William Hickling Prescott, George Bancroft, and Henry Adams. Western culture was energetically, even frantically, seeking a vocabulary to describe the new world of novelty. Historians willingly grasped at metaphors, adapted technical terms, stretched analogies, and extended the jargon of other disciplines in their quest for handles on the historical processes.

Two giants came on this scene. And partly from the desperate need for a vocabulary, partly from their vigorous style, partly from their own towering talents for generalizing, these two have dominated much of Western writing and thinking about history into our own day. The first, of course, was Charles Darwin. In 1859 his *Origin of Species* offered with eloquent and persuasive rhetoric some strikingly new ways of describing the history of plants and animals. And he providentially satisfied the needs of man's new historical consciousness. For unlike earlier biologists he offered a way of describing and explaining the continuous emergence of novelty. Darwin brought the whole animate world into the new realm of historical consciousness. He showed that every living thing had a history. The jargon that grew out of his work, or was grafted onto his work—"evolution," "natural selection," "struggle for survival," "survival of the fittest," among other expressions—proved wonderfully attractive to historians of the human species.

There were many reasons why Darwin's vocabulary was attractive. But one of the most potent was the simplest. He provided a way of talking about change, of making plausible the emergence of novelty in experience, and of showing how the sloughing off of the old inevitably produces the new.

In Europe the nineteenth century, like the seventeenth, was an age of "commotions." After the American Revolution of 1776 and the French Revolution of 1789, revolution was in the air. And the man who translated biology into sociology, who translated the origin of species into the origin of revolutions, was Karl Marx. He freely admitted his debt to Darwin. When the first English translation of the first volume of *Das Kapital* was about to appear, Marx wrote to Darwin asking permission to dedicate the volume to him. Darwin's surprising reply was that, while he was deeply honored, he preferred that Marx not dedicate the book to him, because his family would be disturbed to have dedicated to a Darwin a book that was so Godless!

Darwin and Marx together provided the vocabulary which has dominated the writing and thinking of historians—Marxist and anti-Marxist, communist and anti-communist—into our own time.

Since Marx, every sort of social change has been christened a revolution. So we have the Industrial Revolution, the Sexual Revolution, and even the so-called Paperback Revolution. The word "revolution" has become a shorthand to amplify or dignify any subject. Revolution has become the very prototype, even the stereotype, of social change.

All this reminds us that mankind has generally been more successful in describing the persisting features of experience—warfare, state, church, school, university, corporation, community, city, family—than in describing the processes of change. Just as man has found it far simpler, when he surveys the phenomena of nature, to describe or characterize the objects—land, sea, air, lakes, oceans, mountains, deserts, valleys, bays, islands—that surround him than to describe the modes of their alteration or their motion, just as man's knowledge of anatomy has preceded his understanding of physiology, so it has been with social process.

Political changes, including the overthrow of rulers, have tended to be both more conspicuous and speedier than technological changes. Those limited numbers of people who could read and write and who kept the records have tended to be attached to the rulers and hence most aware of the changing fortunes of princes and kings.

Rapid technological change, the sort of change that can be measured in decades and that occurs within the span of a lifetime, is a characteristic of modern times. There was really no need for a name for rapid technological change until after the wave of revolutions that shook Europe beginning in midseventeenth century. It is during this period that men have developed their historical consciousness. The writing of history, a task of the new social sciences, only recently has become a self-conscious profession. The Regius chairs of history at Oxford and Cambridge were not established till the eighteenth century. At Harvard, the McLean professorship of history was not established till 1838, and American history did not enter the picture till much later.

What is most significant, then, about technology in modern times (the eras of most of the widely advertised "revolutions") is not so much any particular change, but rather the dramatic and newly explosive phenomenon of change itself. American history, more perhaps than that of any other modern nation, has been marked by changes in the human condition—by novel political arrangements, novel products, novel forms of manufacturing, distribution, and consumption, novel ways of transporting and communicating. To understand ourselves and our nation we must grasp these processes of change and reflect on our peculiarly American ways of viewing these processes.

In certain obvious but crucial ways, the process of technological change differs from the process of political change. I will now briefly explore these differences and suggest some of the consequences of our temptation to overlook them.

The Why. People are moved to political revolutions by their grievances, real or imagined, and by their desire for a change. Stirred by disgust with old policies and old regimes, they are awakened by visions of redress, of reforms, or of utopia. "Prudence, indeed, will dictate," Jefferson wrote in the Declaration of Independence,

> that Governments long established should not be changed for light and transient causes; and accordingly all experience hath shewn, that mankind are more disposed to suffer, while evils are sufferable, than to right themselves by abolishing the forms to which they are accustomed. But when a long train of abuses and usurpations, pursuing invariably the same Object, evinces a design to reduce them under absolute Despotism, it is their right, it is their duty, to throw off such Government, and to provide new Guards for their future security. Such has been the patient sufferance of these Colonies; and such is now the necessity which constrains them to alter their former Systems of Government.

This was a characteristically frank and clear declaration which could be a preface to most political revolutions. The Glorious Revolution of 1689 had its Declaration of Rights, the French Revolution of 1789 had its Declaration of the Rights of Man, the revolutions of 1848 had their Communist Manifesto, among others, and so it goes. The people who have initiated and controlled far-reaching political changes have seen declarations as somehow giving the Why of their revolution.

But, in this sense, the great technological changes do not have a *Why*. The telegraph was not invented because men felt aggrieved by the need to carry messages over roads, by hand and on horseback. The wireless did not appear because men would no longer tolerate the stringing of wires to carry their messages. Television was not produced because Americans would no longer suffer the inconvenience of going to a theater to see a motion picture, or to a stadium to see a ball game. All this is obvious, but some of its significance may have escaped us. Although in retrospect we can always see large social, economic, and geographic forces at work, still technological revolutions, by contrast with political revolutions, really have no *Why*. While political revolutions tend to be conscious and purposeful, technological revolutions are quite otherwise.

Each political revolution has its ancien régime, and so inevitably looks backward to what must be redressed and revised. Even if the hopes are utopian, the blueprint for utopia is made from the raw materials of the recent past. "Peace, Bread, and Land!" the slogan of the Russian Revolution of 1917, succinctly proclaimed what Russian peasants and workers had felt to be lacking. It was the obverse of

"War, Starvation, and Servitude," which was taken to be a description of the ancien régime.

Technological revolutions generally do not take their bearings by any ancien régime. They more often arise not from resentful staring at the past, but from casual glimpses of what might be in the future: not so much from the pangs of empty stomachs as from the light-hearted imagining of eating quick-frozen strawberries in winter. True enough, political revolutions usually do get out of hand, and so go beyond the motives of their makers. But there usually is somebody trying to guide events to fulfill the motives of the revolutionaries, and trying to prevent events from going astray. By contrast even with the most reckless and ill-guided political revolutions, technological revolutions are still more reckless.

An example comes from World War II. From one point of view, the war in Europe was a kind of revolution, an international uprising against the Nazis, which concluded in their overthrow and removal from power. That movement had a specific objective and ran its course: surrender by the Nazis, replacement of the Nazi regime by another, War Crimes trials, etc. After that revolution took place, a Germany was left which, from a political point of view, was not radically different from pre-Nazi Germany. This was an intended result of the efforts of politicians inside and outside the country.

Now, contrast the course of what is sometimes called the Atomic Revolution, which took place during these same years. The well-documented chronicle of United States' success in achieving controlled nuclear fission leaves no doubt that a dominant motive was to develop a decisive weapon against the Nazis. But the connection between Hitler and atomic fission was quite accidental. Atomic fission finally was a result of long uncoordinated efforts of scientists in Germany, Denmark, Italy, the United States, and elsewhere. And, in turn, the success in producing controlled nuclear fission and in designing a bomb, spawned consequences which proved uncontrollable. Although, after the war, efforts at international agreement to control atomic weapons have not been entirely unsuccessful, the atom remains a vagrant force in the world.

The overwhelming and most conspicuous result of this great advance in human technology—controlled atomic fission—was not a set of neat desired consequences. In fact, the Nazis had surrendered before the bomb was ready. But the atomic bomb was to produce unpredictable and terrifying consequences. It would give a new

power to small nations and introduce strange new strategic consider-
ations in the relations of large nations. The Atomic Revolution has
proved reckless, with extensive consequences which make the reck-
lessness of Hitler look like caution. Even when men think they have
a *Why* for their technological revolution, as indeed Albert Einstein,
Harold Urey, Leo Szilard, Enrico Fermi, and James Franck felt they
had, they are deceived.

A tantalizing, exhilarating fact about great technological changes
is that each of them, like the invention of controlled atomic fission,
seems to be a law unto itself. Each grand change brings into being
a whole new world. But we cannot forecast the rules of any particular
new world until after it has been discovered. It can spawn all sorts
of outlandish monsters. Who, for example, could have predicted that
the internal-combustion engine and the automobile would breed a
new world of installment buying, credit cards, franchises, and annual
models—that they would revise the meaning of cities, and even
transform notions of crime and morality with no-fault insurance?

In the world of technology we discover to our horror that we are
not so much masters as victims. This is due, in part, to the wonderfully unpredictable course of human knowledge. But it is also simply
due (as the history of electricity, radio, radar, the transistor, and the
computer suggests) to all the undiscovered characteristics of the
physical world. These will re-create our world and populate it with
creatures we never imagined.

The How. It is not impossible to put together some helpful generalizations about how political revolutions are made. Some of the
more familiar in modern times are those offered by Francis Bacon,
Machiavelli, Montesquieu, Jefferson, John Adams, Marx, Lenin, and
Mao Tse-tung. Political revolutions in modern times are the final
result of long and careful planning toward specific ends, of countless
clandestine meetings and numerous public rallies, of collaborative
shaping toward a declared goal. Organized purposefulness, focus,
clarity, and limitation of objectives are crucial.

The general techniques for bringing about a political revolution—
including propaganda, organization, the element of surprise, the
enlistment of foreign allies, the seizure of centers of communication—have changed very little over the centuries. Of course the
means by which these have been accomplished have changed. John
Adams, who knew a thing or two about how political revolutions

were made, after the American Revolution lamented how little man had increased knowledge of his own political processes. "In so general a refinement, or more properly a reformation of manners and improvement in science," Adams observed in 1786, "is it not unaccountable that the knowledge of the principles and construction of free governments, in which the happiness of life, and even the further progress of improvement in education and society, in knowledge and virtue, are so deeply interested, should have remained at full stand for two or three thousand years?" The principles of political science "were as well understood at the time of the neighing of the horse of Darius as they are at this hour." Sadly he noted that the ancient wisdom on these matters was still applicable.

Much of the satisfaction of reading *political* history, and especially the history of political revolutions, comes from seeing men declare their large objectives, use familiar techniques, and then succeed or fail in their grand enterprise. These are the elements of frustrated ambitions and disappointed hopes, of epic and of high tragedy. But the stories of the great technological revolutions are quite different. More often than not, it is hard to know whether an effort at technological innovation is tragedy, comedy, or bluster, whether success spells good fortune or bad. How, for example, are we to assess the invention, elaboration, and universal diffusion of the airplane? Of atomic fission? Or of television?

The patterns of political history remain in the familiar mode of Shakespeare's tragedies and historical plays. Changes of political regime can still be seen in the mold of Coriolanus, King Lear, Richard II, Richard III, and Macbeth. But is there any classic mode for technological history? Much of the excitement in this story comes from the surprising coincidence, the inconceivable, and the trivial—from the boy Marconi playing with his toy, from the chance observation by Madame Curie, from the lucky accident which befell Sir Alexander Fleming, and from myriad other occasions equally odd and unpredictable.

The midtwentieth-century American Research and Development Laboratory is perhaps mankind's most highly organized, best-focused effort to promote technological change. Yet it is a place of vagrant questing. "Research directing," explained Willis R. Whitney, the pioneer founder of the General Electric Laboratories, "is following the openings of acceptable new ideas. It is watching the growth of thought in the minds and hands of careful investigators. Even the lonely mental pioneer, being grub-staked, so to speak, advances so far into the generally unknown that a so-called director merely happily follows the new ways provided. All new paths both multiply and divide as they proceed." A modern research laboratory, then, as Irving Langmuir observed, is not so much a place where men fulfill assignments as a place where men exercise "the art of profiting from unexpected occurrences." Of course, the most adept managers of political revolutions—the Sam Adams, the Robespierre, and the Lenin—also had to know how to profit by the unexpected. But they always used it to help them reach a prefixed destination.

The brilliant technological innovator, on the other hand, is in search of a destination. He is on the lookout for new questions. While he hopes to find new solutions, he remains alert to discover that what he thought were solutions were really new problems. Political revolutions are made by men who urge known remedies for known evils, technological revolutions by men finding unexpected answers to unimagined questions. While political change starts from problems, technological change starts from the search for problems. And, as our most adventuring scientists and technologists provide us with solutions, our society is faced with ways of preventing the solutions (for example, asbestos or saccharin or "disposable" containers) from themselves becoming new problems.

Of course, there are some conspicuous examples, such as the building of the first atomic bomb or the effort to land a man on the moon, where the purpose is specific, and where the organization resembles that of political enterprises. But here too we are plagued by momentum from the size of the enterprise, the size of the investment, and the unpredictability of knowledge.

If we look back, then, on the great political revolutions and the great technological revolutions, we see a striking contrast. Political revolutions, generally speaking, have revealed man's organized purposefulness, his social conscience, his sense of justice—the aggressive, assertive side of his nature. Technological change, invention, and innovation have tended, rather, to reveal his play instinct, his desire and his ability to go where he has never gone, to do what he has never done. The one shows his willingness to sacrifice in order to fulfill his plans, the other his willingness to sacrifice in order to pursue his quest. Many of the peculiar successes and special problems of our time come from our efforts to assimilate these two kinds of activities. We have tried to make government more experimental and at the same time to make technological change more purposive than ever before.

The What of It? By this I mean the special character of their consequences. Political revolutions tend, with certain obvious exceptions, to be *displacive.* The Weimar Republic displaced the regime of Imperial Germany; the Nazis displaced the Weimar Republic; and after World War II, a new republic displaced the Nazis. Normally this is what we mean by a political revolution. Moreover, to a surprising extent, political revolutions are *reversible.* In the political world, you *can* go home again. It is possible, and even common, for a new regime to go back to the ideas and institutions of an earlier regime. Many so-called revolutions are really the revivals of anciens régimes. The familiar phenomenon of the counterrevolution is the effort to reverse the course of change. And it is even arguable that counter-revolutions generally tend to be more successful than revolutions. The reactionary, whose objective is always more recognizable and easier to describe, thus is more apt to be successful than the revolutionary. It is the possibility of such reversals that has lent credibility to the largely fallacious pendulum theory of history.

Technological changes, however, thrive in a different sort of world. Momentous technological changes commonly are neither displacive nor reversible. Technological innovations, instead of displacing earlier devices, actually tend to create new roles for the devices which they might at first seem to displace. When the telephone was introduced in the later nineteenth century, some people assumed that it would make the postman obsolete. Few dared predict that the United States Post Office might become decrepit before it was fully mature. Similarly when wireless and then radio appeared, some wise people thought that these would spell the end of the telephone. When television came in, many were the voices lamenting the death of radio. And we still hear Cassandras solemnly telling us that television spells the death of the book. In our own time we have had an opportunity to observe how and why such forecasts are ill founded. We have seen television, together with the automobile, provide new roles for the radio. By preempting the supply of spot news, radio and television have encouraged the newspaper press to resume its older role of investigative journalism. And all these have created newly urgent roles for the book.

The great technological changes tend *not* to be reversible. There is no technological counterpart for the political restoration or the counterrevolution. Of course there are changes in style, and the antique, the obsolete, and the camp have a perennial charm. There will, I hope, always be individual devotees of "voluntary simplicity" who go in search of their own Waldens. But their quixotry simply reminds us that the march of modernity is ruthless and can never retreat. In France, for example, the century following the Revolution of 1789 was an oscillation of revolutions and anciens régimes; aristocrats were decapitated, parties were voted out of power, old ideologies were abandoned. But during the same years the trend of technological change was unmistakable and irreversible. Unlike the French Revolution, the Industrial Revolution, despite an occasional William Morris, produced no powerful counterrevolution.

The Difference Between Our Ability to Imagine Future Political Revolutions and to Imagine Future Technological Revolutions. This is perhaps the most important, if least observed, distinction between the political and the technological worlds. Our failure to note this distinction could be called the Gamut Fallacy. "Gamut," an English word rooted in the Greek "gamma" for the lowest note in an old musical scale, means the complete range of anything. When we think of the future of our political life, we can have in mind substantially the whole range of possibilities. It is this, of course, which authenticates the traditional wisdom of political theory. It illustrates "John Adams' Law," namely, that political wisdom does not substantially progress. No wonder the astronomical analogy of "revolving," the primary meaning of "revolution," was so tempting!

Again the history of technology is quite another story. We cannot envisage, or even imagine, the range of alternatives from which future technological history will be made. One of the wisest—and, surprisingly enough, one of the most cautious—of our prophets in this area is Arthur C. Clarke, the author of *2001* and other speculations. Clarke provides us with a valuable rule-of-thumb for evaluating prophecies. In his *Profiles of the Future* he reminds us of the prophecies by experts who proved that the atom could not be split, that supersonic transportation was physically impossible, that man could never escape from the earth's gravitational field and could certainly never reach the moon. He then offers us Arthur Clarke's Law: "When a distinguished but elderly scientist states that something is possible, he is almost certainly right. When he states that something is impossible, he is very probably wrong."

This is Clarke's way of warning us against the Gamut Fallacy. If *any*thing is possible, then we really cannot know what is possible, simply because we cannot imagine *every*thing. Where, as in the political world, we make the possibilities ourselves, the limitations of the human imagination are reflected in the limitations of actual possibilities themselves. But the physical world is not of our making, and hence its full range of possibilities is beyond our imagining.

Even in this later twentieth century, when much of mankind has begun to acquire historical consciousness, we are still plagued by the ancient problem of how to come to terms with change. The same old problem, of how to name what we so imperfectly understand, how to describe the limits of our knowledge while those very limits disqualify us from the task, still befuddles us.

Much of mankind, as we have seen, has tended to reason from the political and social to the technical, and has drawn its analogies in that direction. Faced from time immemorial with the ultimately insoluble problems of man in society, most of mankind has tended to assume that other kinds of problems might be equally insoluble. The wise prophets of the great religions have found various ways to say that, on this earth, there is no solution to the human condition. In our Western society, the parable of man's personal and social problem is the Fall of Man. "Original Sin" is another way of saying that perfection must be sought in another world, perhaps with the aid of a savior. We have been taught that in human society there are only more or less *in*soluble problems, and ultimately no solutions. The problem of politics, then, is essentially the problem of man coming to terms with his *problems.*

But our problem in the United States, and, generally speaking, the central problem of technology, is how to come to terms with *solutions.* Our misplaced hopes, our frustrations, and many of our irritations with one another and with other nations come from our unwillingness to believe in the "insoluble" problem, an unwillingness rooted in our New World belief in solutions. Inevitably, then, we overestimate the role of purpose in human change; we overvalue the power of wealth and the power of power.

One way of explaining, historically, how we have been tempted into this adventurous but perilous way of thinking is that we Americans have tended to take the technological problem, the soluble problem, as the prototype of the problems of our nation, and then, too, of all mankind. Among the novelties of American experience, none have been more striking than our innovations in technology, in standard of living, in the machinery of everyday life. And, as I have suggested, one of the obvious characteristics of a problem in technology is that it may really be soluble. Do you seek a way to split the atom and produce a controlled chain reaction? You have found it. *That* problem is solved. And so it has been with many problems, large and small, in our whole world of technology. Do you want an adhesive that will not require moistening to hold the flaps of envelopes? Do you want a highway surface that will not crack under given variations in temperature? Do you want a pen that will write under water? Do you want a camera that will produce an image in twenty seconds? Do you want that image in full color? We can provide you all these things. These are specific problems with specific solutions.

Taking this kind of problem as our prototype, we have too readily assumed that all other problems may be like them. Much of the rest of mankind has reasoned from the political and social to the technological, and therefore, often prematurely, drawn mistaken and discouraging conclusions. But we Americans have drawn our analogies in the other direction. By reasoning from the technological to the political and the social, we have been seduced into our own kind of mistaken, if prematurely encouraging, conclusions. It may be within our power to provide a new kind of grain and so cure starvation in some particular place. But it may not be in our power to cure injustice anywhere, even in our own country, much less in distant places.

Without being arrogant, or playing God, who alone has all solutions, we may still perhaps learn how to come to terms with our problems. We must learn, at the same time, to accept John Adams' Law (that political wisdom does not significantly progress and hence the wisdom of the social past is never obsolete), while we also accept Arthur Clarke's Law (that all technological problems are substantially soluble and hence the technological past is always becoming obsolete).

We must be willing to believe both that politics is the Art of the Possible and that technology is the Art of the Impossible. Then we must embrace and cultivate both arts. Our unprecedented American achievements both in politics and in technology therefore pose us a test, and test us with a tension, unlike that posed to any people before us in history. Never before has a people been so tempted, and with such good reason, to believe that anything is *technologically* possible. And a consequence has been that perhaps no people before us has found it so difficult to continue unabashed in search of the prudent limits of the politically possible. In this American limbo, our new world of hope and terror, we have a rare opportunity to profit from man's recent discovery that he has a history.

CHAPTER 20

From the Land to the Machine

W HEN THE SEAFARING Pilgrim Fathers disembarked from the *Mayflower* on November 21, 1620, and stepped out on their new home country, "they fell upon their knees and blessed the God of Heaven who had brought them over the vast and furious ocean, and delivered them from all the periles and miseries thereof, againe to set their feete on the firme and stable earth, their proper elemente." They were on their way to discovering, and inventing, a New World. They had committed themselves to a country that their fellow Europeans had not even imagined scarcely a century before. This might have been called the Impossible Land, for the American Continent had no place in the European's tradition. In the later Middle Ages the best authorities on the shape and extent of the known world had described a three-part planet of Europe-Asia-Africa. Their *mappae mundi* placed Jerusalem at the center and filled the rest with settled lands, real or imagined. There was no room on their map—and hardly any in their thinking, or in their history or travel literature—for a fourth continent.

By the time the Pilgrim Fathers landed, Europeans were painfully and reluctantly discovering that these shores were not part of Asia, that the Great Khan would probably not be encountered, and that the Emperor of Japan would not be met on the next island. Much of what explorers had learned in the century before the Pilgrims arrived was negative. The bold settlers knew they were coming to a New World unspoiled and mostly uninhabited. But they did not yet know how new their New World might be. Despite the strenuous

nostalgic efforts of several generations of colonials and "New Englanders," America would not become a New Europe.

The American experience would be different. Here men would
discover new possibilities in the land, man's "proper elemente." In
Europe man had shaped his notions of himself—of what he could and
could not do—by his experience on familiar lands. Grandchildren
and great-grandchildren usually relived their traditional experience
on a friendly landscape. America offered a landscape strange and not
always friendly.

There had been migrations before: the ancestors of American
Indians across the Bering land bridge from Asia; the Normans into
Britain, Sicily, and the Middle East; the Crusaders and their followers
toward the Holy Land; the Mongols and the Turks into Eastern
Europe. But most such migrations had been crusades or invasions.
The ebb and flow of soldiers, nomads, bedouins, and traders had
touched many lands without occupying them. The Great Atlantic
Migration—in only the century and a half between 1820 and 1970—
would bring some 36 million Europeans to the United States.

The American settlers came to take and shape the land. The first
occupants of the land—the "Indians" whom the European migrants
encountered—would not be treated, in the pattern of the Romans,
as people to be incorporated into an empire. Instead, they were
treated as part of the landscape. Most of them were simply cleared
away, like the forests, or pushed back, like the wilderness.

By an oddity of history one large portion of the temperate regions
of the planet, the heart of North America, had remained sparsely
settled. When the Europeans came in the late fifteenth and sixteenth
centuries, there were perhaps 2 or 3 million Indians scattered over
an area about twice the size of Europe—which then had a population
estimated at about 100 million. The pre-Columbian Americans had
spread so thinly across North America that they had made little
impression upon the land—cliff-cut pueblos in the Southwest, the tipi
encampment, the occasional village. So the continent which the English and French settlers saw was almost untouched by human hand.
An explorer could walk for miles through the American wilderness,
or float for days down one of the broad rivers, without once seeing
a sign of humankind.

Just as the Indians lacked the technology to drive off the European settlers, they also lacked the technology to change the face of
the land. The land was virginal too because people elsewhere, espe-

cially Europeans, had remained so long ignorant of this part of the world. The common phrase "the Discovery of America" tells volumes about how Europeans thought—their unashamed provincialism, their isolation, the self-imprisonment of the Old World imagination.

The European encounter with the land was shaped not only by what had not happened to America but also by what had been happening in Europe. The Renaissance in Europe was an Age of Discoveries, of which the discovery of America was only one. The foundations of modern science were being laid while the Pilgrims landed at Plymouth. Francis Bacon's *Novum Organum* persuaded men to turn from the authority of Aristotle to the evidence of their senses. Settlers who came during the seventeenth and eighteenth centuries not only possessed firearms and the knowledge to navigate thousands of miles at sea but lived in an age that was beginning to chart the flow of blood through the human body and that was tracing the planets in their orbits around the sun.

When these European settlers came to North America, there was a new kind of encounter, one that could not have happened before and which would never happen again. "Civilized" people—possessing the accumulated cultures of Western Europe, the inheritance of much of Arabic learning, the traditions and literatures of the classical world, the institutions, theologies, and philosophies of Judaism and Christianity, and the experience of a passage across a perilous ocean—seeking their God and their fortunes in a raw and savage land. A rare opportunity!

The Puritans, who were adept at finding God's purpose in everything, explained that Divine Providence had for centuries kept this New World secret from mankind. New England, they believed, had thus been held in reserve until, at last, these English Protestants could fill it with their Puritanized religion. The Indians, then, were God's Custodians, unwittingly assigned to hold the land until the Puritans arrived.

The discovery of America did not end with the arrival of the Pilgrims. Settlers from Europe and elsewhere continued their collaborative voyages of discovery in and around and across a continent. American history, for at least a full century after the Declaration of Independence, could be summed up as a continuing discovery of America—a discovery at great cost and with great rewards—of what the land held, what people could make of the land, and how its resources could remake people's lives. This strangely American encounter with the raw land left birthmarks on American civilization at least into the later twentieth century.

The mystery-laden faith in the future was, for much of American history, a faith in the land. The gradual unfolding of the wonders of the continent, of what could be grown on it, of what might be found under it, of how one could move up and down and across it, reinforced faith that this country was a treasure house of the unexpected. An early surprise came in the Old Northwest, the still-unmapped regions around the Great Lakes between the Ohio and the Mississippi rivers, ceded to the United States by the Treaty of Paris in 1783. This was not, as many imagined, a land of swamps and deserts but a domain of well-watered plains and fertile valleys.

And the surprises multiplied. Who could have guessed that in 1848 the streams in northern California's foothills would prove to be gold mines? Or that eleven years later there would be found in the mountains of western Nevada silver deposits rich beyond the dreams of avarice? Or that the "folly" of Edwin Drake, a vagrant ex-railroad conductor, would turn out to be a treasure of flowing black mineral underneath the soil of western Pennsylvania? Who could imagine where there might be copper, coal, iron—or uranium? Who could predict where a farmer could grow sugar beets, soybeans, oranges, peanuts? Where a rancher could raise cattle for beef, sheep for wool—even alligators for luggage? Such surprising qualities of the land were not the only shaping facts of the first American centuries. But they did dominate the lives and open and define the opportunities for millions of Americans.

As the unexpected treasures of the continent-nation were revealed, as every generation uncovered some astonishing new resource, Americans quite naturally created the legend that this was a Golden Land. This legend—perhaps an overstatement but never a lie—brought more and more settlers. And Americans naturally enough believed that a God who had provided such riches for the people of His New World nation must surely have assigned them some special mission. All these once-hidden resources somehow helped persuade Americans that they had a destiny which was "manifest." Their destiny was clear, obvious, even "self-evident"— like the rights enumerated in the Declaration of Independence. Americans, then, had the further duty of discovering for all mankind the promises still hidden in the New World.

Much of the special character of American life and American civilization, at least until the Centennial of the American Revolution in 1876, came from the continuing encounter of post-Renaissance Europeans with pre–Iron Age America. Here was the first surprising promise of the New World, a promise that would be fulfilled in many ways. Americans would find new ways to work the land. They would build new kinds of cities—cities in a wilderness—and new kinds of schools and colleges, a new democratic world of learning. They would bring together from all over the world people with an immigrant's vision—who saw, and created, new possibilities in politics, in society, in art, in literature, in science, in technology. The promise— that civilization could transform the raw land—would explain why so many Americans were on the move, why they were so energetic at building canals, so precocious at laying railroads and at making their own kind of steamboats and locomotives. It explained the special opportunities for Americans to better their lot and rise in the world.

The rich variety of the land also helped explain why there would be a Civil War. Out of this variety would emerge problems, tragedies, and a new sense of nationhood. The Civil War, which stained with blood the first century of national life, was a conflict between opposing views of freedom, contrasting ways of life, and contrasting regions.

In the second century of national life, the land remained, and the landscapes of the continent-nation still inspired wonder. But the special qualities of American civilization were no longer the result of the encounter of sophisticated men and women with a raw continent. Now there was another, no less dramatic and no less characteristic: the encounter of Man and the Machine.

Like the other, this encounter was remarkable for its anachronism, its scale, and its speed. The new nation somehow compressed the history that Europe had experienced through two thousand years into a compact century or two. Here appeared some of the relics— slavery in the South, trial by personal combat in the West—of earlier stages of European civilization. America, though, could skip some of those stages on its way to becoming a modern nation. Moving along with unprecedented haste, America did not have to go through feudalism—with its fragmentation of loyalties, its creation of aristocracies. History here, compared to the history of Western Europe, was like a fast-motion movie, speeded up to be shown at five times the normal rate. And, in the American version, many of the episodes in the original European story were left out.

The United States never had a Middle Ages. The nation's great commercial cities—Boston, Philadelphia, Chicago, Pittsburgh—had no "city companies" or powerful, monopolizing craft guilds of the kind that had grown up over the centuries in London. In the nineteenth century this nation, by contrast with England, France, or Germany, had unexpected industrial advantages, similar to those of the bombed-out nations after World War II. The Americans could build an industrial plant from scratch. The United States, for example, astonished the world by the pace and style of its railroad building. Railways were laid more speedily—and often more flimsily—than elsewhere, and the young United States fast outdistanced the world in railroad mileage. In Great Britain the railways grew in laborious competition with ancient roads. Foreign visitors, especially the British, marveled at how American railroads stretched "from Nowhere-in-Particular to Nowhere-at-All." This was accomplished not in spite of, but because of, the "primitiveness" of the land. In half-wild America, today's technology did not have to compete with yesterday's technology.

The United States was still only half explored when it entered the Machine Age. Even before the nation had ceased its encounter with the land, the special qualities of the machine began to put their lasting mark on American civilization. The tone and rhythm of American life—no longer the humble refrain of "Only God can make a Tree"—became "Only Man can make a Machine." Americans lived in a world that every year became more man-made.

While the Machine made man feel himself master of his world, it also changed the feeling of the world that he had mastered. The Machine was a homogenizing device. The Machine tended to make everything—products, times, places, people—more alike. In the pre-Machine Age, man's life had been controlled by the weather, the landscape, the distances between places. His diet was confined by the season. In winter his house was cold; in summer it was hot. Much of what he bought was made in his neighborhood and by his neighbors. His ability to witness events was limited by the narrow range of his own eyesight. Visits to distant parts of the nation required weeks or even months, and travel was uncertain or dangerous.

The Machine changed all this. Central heating became so widespread by the midtwentieth century that most middle-class Americans never even thought of it as an American peculiarity. Nor did they realize that central heating was a way of mastering the weather, of transforming the indoor climate from winter into summer. By the later twentieth century air-conditioning completed man's mastery of the indoor climate.

Before the end of the nineteenth century the American diet had begun to be shaped by the Machine. The railroad refrigerator car brought fresh meat and milk to the cities. Canning, then refrigeration in the home, and finally quick-freezing and dehydration, made winter and summer diets more alike. By the midtwentieth century the TV dinners that Americans ate were as unregional and as homogeneous as the network programs they watched in their living rooms. Continental distances had a new meaninglessness. The automobile had brought the city to the farmer; the airplane projected the Chicago businessman into easy reach of New York City or San Francisco. Thousands of Americans now visited Paris or Tokyo during their two-week vacations.

While this machine-mastery of the world simplified and enriched the lives of Americans in many ways, there was always a price. The golf carts that carried sedentary Americans around the courses deprived them of the pleasure of walking—and made golf a hurried, automotive sport. The snowmobile that took hordes of unskiworthy Americans across the virgin snow polluted the mountain air and shattered the mountain silence. Perhaps the special appeal of baseball, basketball, and football was their inability to be mechanized. Even the National Parks were not immune. This characteristic American institution became frustrated by its success. Despite the efforts of the National Park Service, some of the nation's most beautiful camping grounds were made into rural slums as cars and motorcycles brought millions to the "wilderness."

The very wonders of American democracy, which aimed to bring everything to everybody, brought new complications and confusions. The vast majority had more things, ate better, had an opportunity for more education, the chance for a better life. But were these benefits less enjoyed? Less appreciated?

The relations of Americans to their elected officials and to their governments had somehow changed. When President Thomas Jefferson received a letter, it was placed on his desk. He very likely would have opened it himself. If it merited his attention, he would have written his reply. By the middle of the twentieth century, letters directed to the President of the United States were being "processed" in the White House Mail Room, opened by an electric letter opener, and routed to one of the hundreds of workers "in the White House." The few letters that reached the President's attention would get dictated replies, probably by one of the President's assistants. The letter might appear to be signed by the President. But a signature machine affixed the President's signature—or, rather, a facsimile thereof—not only to that letter but also to most of the documents that he appeared to have signed.

The fictitious and the real overlapped. Not only in the White House was there a merging of the artificial and the authentic. Americans watching television were often puzzled about when and where the visible events had occurred. They wondered whether what they saw in "living color" was indeed happening then at all, whether it was "simulated" or real, fact or fiction, history or fantasy.

The Machine brought endless novelty into the world. There was hardly an activity of daily life that some device could not make more interesting—or at least more complicated. The carving knife and the toothbrush were simple tools long in use. But American inventiveness and American love of novelty would produce in time the electric knife and the electric toothbrush. And what would come next?

In the early twentieth century a philosophical American humorist, Rube Goldberg, had entertained Americans by caricaturing their love of the Machine. He also gave them an ironic motto for modern times: "Do it the hard way!" When he first began illustrating the motto in cartoons of impossible mechanisms, Americans had become newly infatuated with complicated ways of simplifying everyday life. Why walk if you could ride? Why use a wooden pencil if you could use a metal pencil with retractable lead—including many colored leads that you did not need? Or why not a ballpoint pen that could write underwater? Why write with a pencil or pen if you could use a typewriter? And why use a simple hand-operated typewriter when you could use a much more complicated electric machine or, better yet, a word processor? Why write it yourself at all if you could first dictate it into a machine that recorded your voice on tape, which could be put into another machine to be played back to a person who would transcribe the words on another machine? And so it went.

Just as the American's love affair with his land produced pioneering adventures and unceasing excitement in the conquest of the continent, so too his latter-day romance with the Machine produced pioneering adventures—of a new kind. There seemed to have been an end to the exploration of the landed continent—and an end to the traversing of uncharted deserts, the climbing of unscaled mountains. But there were no boundaries to a machine-made world. The New World of Machines was of man's own making. No one could predict where the boundaries might be or what his technology might make possible. To keep the Machine going, the American advanced from horse power to steam power to electrical power to internal-combustion power to nuclear power—to who could guess what.

The challenge of the Machine was as open-ended as the human spirit. Americans in the latter part of the twentieth century, in defiance of some fashionable woe-sayers, had more chance than ever before to do the unprecedented. Their problem was not the lack of opportunity for adventure but the shallowness of their human satisfaction and human fulfillment. The American challenge was how to keep alive the sense of quest which had brought the nation into being. How to discover the endless novelties of the Machine, how to make a plastic heart, devise television in three dimensions, explore the moon and planets. How to do a thousand still-unimagined works of machine magic without becoming the servant of the Machine or allowing the sense of novelty to pall or the quest for the new to lose its charm.

CHAPTER 21

A Flood of Pseudo-Events

THE SIMPLEST of our extravagant expectations concerns the amount of novelty in the world. There was a time when the reader of an unexciting newspaper would remark, "How dull is the world today!" Nowadays he says, "What a dull newspaper!" When the first American newspaper, Benjamin Harris' *Publick Occurrences Both Forreign and Domestick,* appeared in Boston on September 25, 1690, it promised to furnish news regularly once a month. But, the editor explained, it might appear oftener "if any Glut of Occurrences happen." The responsibility for making news was entirely God's—or the Devil's. The newsman's task was only to give "an Account of such considerable things as have arrived unto our Notice."

Although the theology behind this way of looking at events soon dissolved, this view of the news lasted longer. "The skilled and faithful journalist," James Parton observed in 1866, "recording with exactness and power the thing that has come to pass, is Providence addressing men." The story is told of a Southern Baptist clergyman before the Civil War who used to say, when a newspaper was brought in the room, "Be kind enough to let me have it a few minutes, till

---

This and the two following chapters, "From Hero to Celebrity" and "From Traveler to Tourist," are adapted and abridged from my book, *The Image: A Guide to Pseudo-Events in America.* The introduction to that book is entitled "Extravagant Expectations," and other chapters deal with the phenomenon of "digests," the relation among literary, dramatic, cinematic, and television forms, "The Search for Self-Fulfilling Prophecies" in advertising, and "The Self-Deceiving Magic of Prestige." That volume introduced some expressions which have since entered our dictionaries, including "pseudo-event" itself and "well-knownness."

I see how the Supreme Being is governing the world." Charles A. Dana, one of the great American editors of the nineteenth century, once defended his extensive reporting of crime in the New York *Sun* by saying, "I have always felt that whatever the Divine Providence permitted to occur I was not too proud to report."

Of course, this is now a very old-fashioned way of thinking. Our current point of view is better expressed in the definition by Arthur MacEwen, whom William Randolph Hearst made his first editor of the San Francisco *Examiner:* "News is anything that makes a reader say, 'Gee whiz!' " Or, put more soberly, "News is whatever a good editor chooses to print."

We need not be theologians to see that we have shifted responsibility for making the world interesting from God to the newspaperman. We used to believe there were only so many "events" in the world. If there were not many intriguing or startling occurrences, it was no fault of the reporter. He could not be expected to report what did not exist.

Within the last hundred years, however, and especially in the twentieth century, all this has changed. We expect the papers to be full of news. If there is no news visible to the naked eye, or to the average citizen, we still expect it to be there for the enterprising newsman. The successful reporter is one who can find a story, even if there is no earthquake or assassination or civil war. If he cannot find a story, then he must make one—by the questions he asks of public figures, by the surprising human interest he unfolds from some commonplace event, or by "the news behind the news." If all this fails, then he must give us a "think piece"—an embroidering of well-known facts, or a speculation about startling things to come.

This change in our attitude toward "news" is not merely a basic fact about the history of American newspapers. It is a symptom of a revolutionary change in our attitude toward what happens in the world, how much of it is new and surprising and important. Toward how life can be enlivened, toward our power and the power of those who inform and educate and guide us, to provide synthetic happenings to make up for the lack of spontaneous events. Demanding more than the world can give us, we require that something be fabricated to make up for the world's deficiency. This is only one example of our demand for illusions.

Many historical forces help explain how we have come to our present immoderate hopes. But there can be no doubt about what we now expect, nor that it is immoderate. Every American knows the anticipation with which he picks up his morning newspaper at breakfast or opens his evening paper before dinner, or listens to the newscasts every hour on the hour as he drives across country, or watches his favorite commentator on television interpret the events of the day. Many enterprising Americans are now at work to help us satisfy these expectations. Many might be put out of work if we should suddenly moderate our expectations. But it is we who keep them in business and demand that they fill our consciousness with novelties, that they play God for us.

The new kind of synthetic novelty which has flooded our experience I will call "pseudo-events." The common prefix "pseudo" comes from the Greek word meaning false, or intended to deceive. Before I recall the historical forces which have made these pseudo-events possible, have increased the supply of them and the demand for them, I will give a commonplace example.

The owners of a hotel, in an illustration offered by Edward L. Bernays in his pioneer *Crystallizing Public Opinion* (1923), consult a public relations counsel. They ask how to increase their hotel's prestige and so improve their business. In less sophisticated times, the answer might have been to hire a new chef, to improve the plumbing, to paint the rooms, or to install a crystal chandelier in the lobby. The public relations counsel's technique is more indirect. He proposes that the management stage a celebration of the hotel's thirtieth anniversary. A committee is formed, including a prominent banker, a leading society matron, a well-known lawyer, an influential preacher, and an "event" is planned (say a banquet) to call attention to the distinguished service the hotel has been rendering the community. The celebration is held, photographs are taken, the occasion is widely reported, and the object is accomplished. Now this occasion is a pseudo-event, and will illustrate all the essential features of pseudo-events.

This celebration, we can see at the outset, is somewhat—but not entirely—misleading. Presumably the public relations counsel would not have been able to form his committee of prominent citizens if the hotel had not actually been rendering service to the community. On the other hand, if the hotel's services had been all that important, instigation by a public relations counsel might not have been necessary. Once the celebration has been held, the celebration itself becomes evidence that the hotel really is a distinguished institution. The occasion actually gives the hotel the prestige to which it is pretending.

It is obvious, too, that the value of such a celebration to the owners depends on its being photographed and reported in newspapers, magazines, on radio, and over television. It is the report that gives the event its force in the minds of potential customers. The power to make a reportable event is thus the power to make experience. One is reminded of Napoleon's apocryphal reply to his general, who objected that circumstances were unfavorable to a proposed campaign: "Bah, I make circumstances!" The modern public relations counsel—and he is, of course, only one of many twentieth-century creators of pseudo-events—has come close to fulfilling Napoleon's idle boast. "The counsel on public relations," Mr. Bernays explains, "not only knows what news value is, but knowing it, he is in a position to *make news happen.* He is a creator of events."

The intriguing feature of the modern situation, however, comes precisely from the fact that the modern news makers are not God. The news they make happen, the events they create, are somehow not quite real. There remains a tantalizing difference between man-made and God-made events.

A pseudo-event, then, is a happening that possesses the following characteristics:

1. It is not spontaneous, but comes about because someone has planned, planted, or incited it. Typically, it is not a train wreck or an earthquake, but an interview.

2. It is planted primarily (not always exclusively) for the immediate purpose of being reported or reproduced. Therefore, its occurrence is arranged for the convenience of the reporting or reproducing media. Its success is measured by how widely it is reported. Time relations in it are commonly fictitious or factitious; the announcement is given out in advance "for future release" and written as if the event had occurred in the past. The question, "Is it real?" is less important than, "Is it newsworthy?"

3. Its relation to the underlying reality of the situation is ambiguous. Its interest arises largely from this very ambiguity. Concerning a pseudo-event the question, "What does it mean?" has a new dimension. While the news interest in a train wreck is in *what* happened and in the real consequences, the interest in an interview is always, in a sense, in *whether* it really happened and in what might have

been the motives. Did the statement really mean what it said? Without some of this ambiguity a pseudo-event cannot be very interesting.

4. Usually it is intended to be a self-fulfilling prophecy. The hotel's thirtieth-anniversary celebration, by saying that the hotel is a distinguished institution, actually helps make it one.

In the last half century a larger and larger proportion of our experience, of what we read and see and hear, has come to consist of pseudo-events. We expect more of them and we are given more of them. They flood our consciousness. Their multiplication has gone on in the United States at a faster rate than elsewhere. Even the rate of increase is increasing every day. This is true of the world of education, of consumption, and of personal relations. It is especially true of the world of public affairs.

A full explanation of the origin and rise of pseudo-events would be nothing less than a history of modern America. For our present purposes it is enough to recall a few of the more revolutionary recent developments.

The great modern increase in the supply and the demand for news began in the early nineteenth century. Until then newspapers tended to fill out their columns with lackadaisical secondhand accounts or stale reprints of items first published elsewhere at home and abroad. The laws of plagiarism and of copyright were undeveloped. Most newspapers were little more than excuses for espousing a political position, for listing the arrival and departure of ships, for familiar essays and useful advice, or for commercial or legal announcements.

Then newspapers began to disseminate up-to-date reports of matters of public interest written by eyewitnesses or professional reporters near the scene. The telegraph was perfected and applied to news reporting in the 1830s and '40s. Two newspapermen, William M. Swain of the Philadelphia *Public Ledger* and Amos Kendall of Frankfort, Kentucky, were founders of the national telegraphic network. Polk's presidential message in 1846 was the first to be transmitted by wire. When the Associated Press was founded in 1848, news began to be a salable commodity. Then appeared the rotary press, which could print on a continuous sheet and on both sides of the paper at the same time. The New York *Tribune*'s high-speed press, installed in the 1870s, could turn out 18,000 papers per hour. The Civil War, and later the Spanish-American War, offered raw materials and incentive for vivid up-to-the-minute, on-the-spot reporting. The competitive daring of giants like James Gordon Bennett, Joseph Pulitzer, and William Randolph Hearst intensified the race for news and widened newspaper circulation.

These events were part of a great, but little-noticed, revolution—what I would call the Graphic Revolution. Man's ability to make, preserve, transmit, and disseminate precise images—images of print, of men and landscapes and events, of the voices of men and mobs—now grew at a fantastic pace. The increased speed of printing was itself revolutionary. Still more revolutionary were the new techniques for making direct images of nature. Photography was destined soon to give printed matter itself a secondary role. By a giant leap Americans crossed the gulf from the daguerreotype to color television in less than a century. Dry-plate photography came in 1873; Bell patented the telephone in 1876; the phonograph was invented in 1877; the roll film appeared in 1884; Eastman's Kodak No. 1 was produced in 1888; Edison's patent on the radio came in 1891; motion pictures came in and voice was first transmitted by radio around 1900; the first national political convention widely broadcast by radio was that of 1928; television became commercially important in 1941, and color television even more recently.

Verisimilitude took on a new meaning. Not only was it now possible to give the actual voice and gestures of Franklin Delano Roosevelt unprecedented reality and intimacy for a whole nation. Vivid image came to overshadow pale reality. Sound motion pictures in color led a whole generation of pioneering American moviegoers to think of Benjamin Disraeli as an earlier imitation of George Arliss, just as television has led a later generation of television watchers to see the Western cowboy as an inferior replica of John Wayne. The Grand Canyon itself became a disappointing reproduction of the Kodachrome original.

The new power to report and portray what had happened was a new temptation leading newsmen to make probable images or to prepare reports in advance of what was expected to happen. As so often, men came to mistake their power for their necessities. Readers and viewers would soon prefer the vividness of the account, the "candidness" of the photograph, to the spontaneity of what was recounted.

Then came round-the-clock media. The news gap soon became so

narrow that in order to have additional "news" for each new edition
or each new broadcast it was necessary to plan in advance the stages
by which any available news would be unveiled. After the weekly
and the daily came the "extras" and the numerous regular editions.
The Philadelphia *Evening Bulletin* soon had seven editions a day. No
rest for the newsman. With more space to fill, he had to fill it ever
more quickly. In order to justify the numerous editions, it was increasingly necessary that the news constantly change or at least seem
to change. With radio on the air continuously during waking hours,
the reporters' problems became still more acute. News every hour
on the hour, and sometimes on the half hour. Programs interrupted
any time for special bulletins. How to avoid deadly repetition, the
appearance that nothing was happening, that news gatherers were
asleep, or that competitors were more alert? As the costs of printing
and then of broadcasting increased, it became financially necessary
to keep the presses always at work and the TV screen always busy.
Pressures toward the making of pseudo-events became ever
stronger. News gathering turned into news making.

The "interview" was a novel way of making news which had
come in with the Graphic Revolution. Later it became elaborated
into lengthy radio and television panels and quizzes of public figures,
and the three-hour-long, rambling conversation programs. Although
the interview technique might seem an obvious one—and in a primitive form was as old as Socrates—the use of the word in its modern
journalistic sense is a relatively recent Americanism. The Boston
News-Letter's account (March 2, 1719) of the death of Blackbeard the
Pirate had apparently been based on a kind of interview with a ship
captain. One of the earliest interviews of the modern type—some
writers call it the first—was by James Gordon Bennett, the flamboy-
ant editor of the New York *Herald* (April 16, 1836), in connection
with the Robinson-Jewett murder case. Ellen Jewett, inmate of a
house of prostitution, had been found murdered by an ax. Richard
P. Robinson, a young man about town, was accused of the crime.
Bennett seized the occasion to pyramid sensational stories and so to
build circulation for his *Herald;* before long he was having difficulty
turning out enough copies daily to satisfy the demand. He exploited
the story in every possible way, one of which was to plan and report
an actual interview with Rosina Townsend, the madam who kept the
house and whom he visited on her own premises.

Historians of journalism date the first full-fledged modern interview with a well-known public figure from July 13, 1859, when Horace Greeley interviewed Brigham Young in Salt Lake City, asking him questions on many matters of public interest, and then publishing the answers verbatim in his New York *Tribune* (August 20, 1859). The common use of the word "interview" in this modern American sense first came at about this time. Very early the institution acquired a reputation for being contrived. "The 'interview,'" *The Nation* complained (January 28, 1869), "as at present managed, is generally the joint product of some humbug of a hack politician and another humbug of a reporter." A few years later another magazine editor called the interview "the most perfect contrivance yet devised to make journalism an offence, a thing of ill savor in all decent nostrils." Many objected to the practice as an invasion of privacy. After the American example it was used in England and France, but in both those countries it made much slower headway.

Even before the invention of the interview, the news-making profession in America had attained a new dignity as well as a menacing power. It was in 1828 that Macaulay called the gallery where reporters sat in Parliament a "fourth estate of the realm." But Macaulay could not have imagined the prestige of journalists in the twentieth-century United States. They have long since made themselves the tribunes of the people. Their supposed detachment and lack of partisanship, their closeness to the sources of information, their articulateness, and their constant and direct access to the whole citizenry have made them also the counselors of the people. Foreign observers are now astonished by the almost constitutional—perhaps we should say supraconstitutional—powers of our Washington press corps.

Since the rise of the modern Presidential press conference, about 1933, capital correspondents have had the power regularly to question the President face-to-face, to embarrass him, to needle him, to force him into positions or into public refusal to take a position. A President may find it inconvenient to meet a group of dissident Senators or Congressmen; he seldom dares refuse the press. That refusal itself becomes news. It is only very recently, and as a result of increasing pressures by newsmen, that the phrase "No comment" has become a way of saying something important. The reputation of newsmen—who now of course include those working for radio, TV, and magazines—depends on their ability to ask hard questions, to put politicians on the spot; their very livelihood depends on the willing collaboration of public figures. By 1950 Washington had about 1,500 correspondents and about 3,000 government information officials prepared to serve them.

Not only the regular formal press conferences, but a score of other national programs—such as *Meet the Press* and *Face the Nation*—show the power of newsmen. In 1960 David Susskind's late-night conversation show, *Open End,* commanded the presence of the Russian Premier for three hours. During the so-called Great Debates that year between the candidates in the Presidential campaign, it was newsmen who called the tune.

The live television broadcasting of the President's regular news conferences, which President Kennedy began in 1961, immediately after taking office, has somewhat changed their character. Newsmen are no longer so important as intermediaries who relay the President's statements. But the new occasion acquires a new interest as a dramatic performance. Citizens who from homes or offices have seen the President at his news conference are then even more interested to hear competing interpretations by skilled commentators. News commentators can add a new appeal as dramatic critics to their traditional role as interpreters of current history. Even in the new format it is still the newsmen who put the questions. They are still tribunes of the people.

The British Constitution, shaped as it is from materials accumulated since the Middle Ages, functions, we have often been told, only because the British people are willing to live with a great number of legal fictions. The monarchy is only the most prominent. We Americans have accommodated our eighteenth-century constitution to twentieth-century technology by multiplying pseudo-events and by developing professions which both help make pseudo-events and help us interpret them. The disproportion between what an informed citizen needs to know and what he can know is ever greater. The disproportion grows with the increase of the officials' powers of concealment and contrivance. The news gatherers' need to select, invent, and plan correspondingly increases. Thus inevitably our whole system of public information produces always more "packaged" news, more pseudo-events.

A trivial but prophetic example of the American penchant for pseudo-events has long been found in our *Congressional Record.* The British and French counterparts, surprisingly enough, give a faithful report of what is said on the floor of their deliberative bodies. But ever since the establishment of the *Congressional Record* under its present title in 1873, our only ostensibly complete report of what goes on in Congress has had no more than the faintest resemblance to what is actually said there. Despite occasional feeble protests, our *Record* has remained a gargantuan miscellany in which actual proceedings are buried beneath undelivered speeches, and mountains of the unread and the unreadable. Only a national humorlessness—or sense of humor—can account for our willingness to tolerate this. Perhaps it also explains why, as a frustrated reformer of the *Record* argued on the floor of the Senate in 1884, "the American public have generally come to regard the proceedings of Congress as a sort of variety performance, where nothing is supposed to be real except the pay."

The common "news releases" which every day issue by the ream from Congressmen's offices, from the President's press secretary, from the press relations offices of businesses, charitable organizations, and universities are a kind of *Congressional Record* covering all American life. And they are only a slightly less inaccurate record of spontaneous happenings. To secure "news coverage" for an event (especially if it has little news interest) one must issue, in proper form, a "release." The very expression "news release" (apparently an American invention, it was first recorded in 1907) did not come into common use until recently. There is an appropriate perversity in calling it a release. It might more accurately be described as a "news holdback," since its purpose is to offer something that is to be held back from publication until a specified future date. The newspaperman's slightly derogatory slang term for the news release is "handout" (first recorded use, 1927) from the phrase originally used for a bundle of stale food handed out from a house to a beggar. Though this meaning of the word is now in common use in the newsgathering professions, it has only recently entered our dictionaries.

The release is news precooked and supposed to keep till needed. In the well-recognized format, it bears a date, say February 1, and also indicates, "For release to PM's February 15." The account is written in the past tense but usually describes an event that has not yet happened when the release is given out. The use and interpretation of handouts have become an essential part of the newsman's job. The National Press Club in its Washington clubrooms has provided a large rack filled with the latest releases, so the reporter did not even have to visit the offices which gave them out. By 1947 there were about twice as many government press agents engaged in preparing news releases as there were newsmen gathering them in.

The general public has become so accustomed to these procedures that a public official can sometimes "make news" merely by departing from the advance text given out in his release. When President Kennedy spoke in Chicago on the night of April 28, 1961, early editions of the next morning's newspapers (printed the night before for early-morning home delivery) merely reported his speech as it was given to newsmen in the advance text. When the President abandoned the advance text, later editions of the Chicago *Sun-Times* headlined: "Kennedy Speaks Off Cuff . . ." The article beneath emphasized that he had departed from his advance text and gave about equal space to his off-the-cuff speech and to the speech he never gave. Apparently the most newsworthy fact was that the President had not stuck to his prepared text.

We begin to be puzzled about what is really the "original" of an event. The authentic news record of what "happens" or is said comes increasingly to seem to be what is given out in advance. More and more news events become dramatic performances in which "people in the news" simply act out more or less well their prepared script. The story prepared "for future release" acquires an authenticity that competes with that of the actual occurrences on the scheduled date.

In recent years our successful politicians have been those most adept at using the press and other means to create pseudo-events. President Franklin Delano Roosevelt, whom Heywood Broun called "the best newspaperman who has ever been President of the United States," was the first modern master. While newspaper owners opposed him in editorials which few read, FDR himself, with the collaboration of a friendly corps of Washington correspondents, was using front-page headlines to make news read by everybody. He was making "facts"—pseudo-events—while editorial writers were simply expressing opinions. It is a familiar story how he employed the trial balloon, how he exploited the ethic of off-the-record remarks, how he transformed the Presidential press conference from a boring ritual into a major national institution which no later President dared disrespect, and how he developed the fireside chat. Knowing that newspapermen lived on news, he helped them manufacture it. And he knew enough about news-making techniques to help shape their stories to his own purposes.

Take, for example, these comments which President Roosevelt made at a press conference during his visit to a Civilian Conservation Corps camp in Florida on February 18, 1939, when war tensions were mounting:

> I want to get something across, only don't put it that way. In other words, it is a thing that I cannot put as direct stuff, but it is background. And the way—as you know I very often do it—if I were writing the story, the way I'd write it is this—you know the formula: When asked when he was returning [to Washington], the President intimated that it was impossible to give any date; because, while he hoped to be away until the third or fourth of March, information that continues to be received with respect to the international situation continues to be disturbing, therefore, it may be necessary for the President to return [to the capital] before the third or fourth of March. It is understood that this information relates to the possible renewal of demands by certain countries, these demands being pushed, not through normal diplomatic channels but, rather, through the more recent type of relations; in other words, the use of fear of aggression.

FDR was a man of great warmth, natural spontaneity, and simple eloquence, and his public utterances reached the citizen with a new intimacy. Yet, paradoxically, it was under his administrations that statements by the President attained a new subtlety and a new calculatedness. On his production team, in addition to newspapermen, there were poets, playwrights, and a regular corps of speech writers. Far from detracting from his effectiveness, this collaborative system for producing the impression of personal frankness and spontaneity provided an additional subject of newsworthy interest. Was it Robert Sherwood or Judge Samuel Rosenman who contributed this or that phrase? How much had the President revised the draft given him by his speech-writing team? Citizens became nearly as much interested in how a particular speech was put together as in what it said. And when the President spoke, almost everyone knew it was a long-planned group production in which FDR was only the star performer.

Of course President Roosevelt made many great decisions and lived in times which he only helped make stirring. But it is possible to build a political career almost entirely on pseudo-events. Such was that of Joseph R. McCarthy, Senator from Wisconsin from 1947 to 1957. His career might have been impossible without the elaborate, perpetually grinding machinery of "information" which I have already described. And he was a natural genius at creating reportable happenings that had an interestingly ambiguous relation to underlying reality. Richard Rovere, a reporter in Washington during McCarthy's heyday, recalls:

He knew how to get into the news even on those rare occasions when invention failed him and he had no unfacts to give out. For example, he invented the morning press conference called for the purpose of announcing an afternoon press conference. The reporters would come in—they were beginning, in this period, to respond to his summonses like Pavlov's dogs at the clang of a bell—and McCarthy would say that he just wanted to give them the word that he expected to be ready with a shattering announcement later in the day, for use in the papers the following morning. This would gain him a headline in the afternoon papers: "New McCarthy Revelations Awaited in Capital." Afternoon would come, and if McCarthy had something, he would give it out, but often enough he had nothing, and this was a matter of slight concern. He would simply say that he wasn't quite ready, that he was having difficulty in getting some of the "documents" he needed or that a "witness" was proving elusive. Morning headlines: "Delay Seen in McCarthy Case— Mystery Witness Being Sought."

He had a diabolical fascination and an almost hypnotic power over news-hungry reporters. They were somehow reluctantly grateful to him for turning out their product. They stood astonished that he could make so much news from such meager raw material. Many hated him; all helped him. They were victims of what one of them called their "indiscriminate objectivity." In other words, McCarthy and the newsmen both thrived on the same synthetic commodity.

Senator McCarthy's political fortunes were promoted almost as much by newsmen who considered themselves his enemies as by those few who were his friends. Without the active help of all of them he could never have created the pseudo-events which brought him notoriety and power. Newspaper editors, who self-righteously attacked the Senator's "collaborators," themselves proved worse than powerless to cut him down to size. Even while they attacked him on the editorial page inside, they were building him up in front-page headlines. Newspapermen were his most potent allies, for they were his co-manufacturers of pseudo-events. They were caught in their own web. Honest newsmen and the unscrupulous Senator McCarthy were in separate branches of the same business.

In the traditional vocabulary of newspapermen, there is a well-recognized distinction between "hard" and "soft" news. Hard news is supposed to be the solid report of significant matters: politics, economics, international relations, social welfare, science. Soft news reports popular interests, curiosities, and diversions. It includes sensational local reporting, scandalmongering, gossip columns, comic strips, the sexual lives of movie stars, and the latest murder. Journalist-critics attack American newspapers today for not being "serious" enough, for giving a larger and larger proportion of their space to soft rather than to hard news.

But the rising tide of pseudo-events washes away the distinction. Here is one example. On June 21, 1960, President Eisenhower was in Honolulu, en route to the Far East for a trip to meet the heads of government in Korea, the Philippines, and elsewhere. A seven-column headline in the Chicago *Daily News* brought readers the following information: "What Are Ike's Feelings About Trip? Aides Mum" "Doesn't Show Any Worry" "Members of Official Party Resent Queries by Newsmen." And the two-column story led off:

> HONOLULU—President Eisenhower's reaction to his Far Eastern trip remains as closely guarded a secret as his golf score. While the President rests at Kaneohe Marine air station on the windward side of the Pali hills, hard by the blue Pacific and an 18-hole golf course, he might be toting up the pluses and minuses of his Asian sojourn. But there is no evidence of it. Members of his official party resent any inquiry into how the White House feels about the whole experience, especially the blowup of the Japanese visit which produced a critical storm.

The story concludes: "But sooner or later the realities will intrude. The likelihood is that it will be sooner than later."

Nowadays a successful reporter must be the midwife, or more often the conceiver, of his news. By the interview technique he incites a public figure to make statements which will sound like news. During the twentieth century this technique has grown into a devious apparatus which, in skillful hands, can shape national policy.

The pressure of time and the need to produce a uniform news stream to fill the issuing media induce Washington correspondents and others to use the interview and other techniques for making pseudo-events in novel, ever more ingenious and aggressive ways. One of the main facts of life for the wire service reporter in Washington is that the early afternoon paper on the East Coast goes to press about 10 A.M., before the spontaneous news of the day has had an

opportunity to develop. "It means," one conscientious capital correspondent confides, in Douglass Cater's admirable *Fourth Branch of
Government* (1959), "the wire service reporter must engage in the
basically phony operation of writing the 'overnight'—a story composed the previous evening but giving the impression when it appears the next afternoon that it covers that day's events."

What this can mean in a particular case is illustrated by the tribulations of a certain hard-working reporter who was trying to do his
job and earn his keep at the time when the Austrian Treaty of 1955
came up for debate in the Senate. Although it was a matter of some
national and international importance, the adoption of the Treaty
was a foregone conclusion; there would be little news in it. So, in
order to make a story, this reporter went to Senator Walter George,
chairman of the Senate Foreign Relations Committee, and extracted
a statement to the effect that under the Treaty Austria would receive
no money or military aid, only long-term credits. "That became my
lead," the reporter recalled. "I had fulfilled the necessary function of
having a story that seemed to be part of the next day's news."

The next day, the Treaty came up for debate. The debate was
dull, and it was hard to squeeze out a story. Luckily, however, Senator Jenner made a nasty crack about President Eisenhower, which
the reporter (after considering what other wire service reporters
covering the story might be doing) sent off as an "insert." The Treaty
was adopted by the Senate a little after 3:30 P.M. That automatically
made a bulletin and required a new lead for the story on the debate.
But by that time the hard-pressed reporter was faced with writing
a completely new story for the next day's morning papers.

> But my job had not finished. The Treaty adoption bulletin had gone out
> too late to get into most of the East Coast afternoon papers except the
> big city ones like the Philadelphia *Evening Bulletin,* which has seven
> editions. I had to find a new angle for an overnight to be carried next day
> by those P.M.'s which failed to carry the Treaty story.
>
> They don't want to carry simply a day-old account of the debate.
> They want a "top" to the news. So, to put it quite bluntly, I went and got
> Senator Thye to say that Jenner by his actions was weakening the Presi-
> dent's authority. Actually, the Thye charge was more lively news than
> the passage of the Austrian Treaty itself. It revealed conflict among the
> Senate Republicans. But the story had developed out of my need for a
> new peg for the news. It was not spontaneous on Thye's part. I had called
> seven other Senators before I could get someone to make a statement on

Jenner. There is a fair criticism, I recognize, to be made of this practice. These Senators didn't call me. I called them. I, in a sense, generated the news. The reporter's imagination brought the Senator's thinking to bear on alternatives that he might not have thought of by himself.

This can be a very pervasive practice. One wire service reporter hounded Senator George daily on the foreign trade question until he finally got George to make the suggestion that Japan should trade with Red China as an alternative to dumping textiles on the American market. Then the reporter went straightway to Senator Knowland to get him to knock down the suggestion. It made a good story, and it also stimulated a minor policy debate that might not have got started otherwise. The "overnight" is the greatest single field for exploratory reporting for the wire services. It is what might be called "milking the news."

The reporter shrewdly adds that the task of his profession today is seldom to compose accounts of the latest events at lightning speed. Rather, it is shaped by "the problem of packaging." He says: "Our job is to report the news but it is also to keep a steady flow of news coming forward. Every Saturday morning, for example, we visit the Congressional leaders. We could write all the stories that we get out of these conferences for the Sunday A.M.'s but we don't. We learn to schedule them in order to space them out over Sunday's and Monday's papers."

An innocent observer might have expected that the rise of television and on-the-spot telecasting of the news would produce a pressure to report authentic spontaneous events exactly as they occur. But, ironically, these, like earlier improvements in the techniques of precise representation, have simply created more and better pseudo-events.

When General Douglas MacArthur returned to the United States (after President Truman relieved him of command in the Far East, on April 11, 1951, during the Korean War) he made a "triumphal" journey around the country. He was invited to help Chicago celebrate "MacArthur Day" on April 26, 1951, which had been proclaimed by resolution of the City Council. Elaborate ceremonies were arranged, including a parade. The proceedings were being televised.

A team of thirty-one University of Chicago sociologists, under the imaginative direction of Kurt Lang, took their posts at strategic points along the route of the MacArthur parade. The purpose was to note the reactions of the crowd and to compare what the spectators were seeing, or said they were seeing, with what they might have witnessed on television. This ingenious study confirmed my observation that we tend increasingly to fill our experience with contrived content. The newspapers had, of course, already prepared people for what the Chicago *Tribune* that morning predicted to be "a triumphant hero's welcome—biggest and warmest in the history of the middle west." Many of the actual spectators jammed in the crowd at the scene complained it was hard to see what was going on; in some places they waited for hours and then were lucky to have a fleeting glimpse of the General.

But the television perspective was quite different. The video viewer had the advantage of numerous cameras which were widely dispersed. Television thus ordered the events in its own way, quite different from that of the on-the-spot confusion. The cameras were carefully focused on "significant" happenings—that is, those which emphasized the drama of the occasion. For the television watcher, the General was the continuous center of attraction from his appearance during the parade at 2:21 P.M. until the sudden blackout at 3:00 P.M. Announcers continually reiterated (the scripts showed over fifteen explicit references) the unprecedented drama of the event, or that this was "the greatest ovation this city has ever turned out." On the television screen one received the impression of wildly cheering and enthusiastic crowds before, during, and after the parade. Of course the cameras were specially selecting "action" shots, which showed a noisy, waving audience; yet in many cases the cheering, waving, and shouting were really a response not so much to the General as to the aiming of the camera. Actual spectators, with sore feet, suffered long periods of boredom. Many groups were apathetic. The video viewer, his eyes fixed alternately on the General and on an enthusiastic crowd, his ears filled with a breathless narrative emphasizing the interplay of crowd and celebrity, could not fail to receive an impression of continuous dramatic pageantry.

The most important single conclusion of these sociologists was that the television presentation (as contrasted with the actual witnessing) of the events "remained true to form until the very end, interpreting the entire proceedings according to expectations. . . . The telecast was made to conform to what was interpreted as the pattern of viewers' expectations." Actual spectators at the scene were doubly disappointed, not only because they usually saw very little, and that only briefly, from where they happened to be standing, but also because they knew they were missing a much better performance with far more of the drama they expected on the television screen. "I bet my wife saw it much better over television!" and "We should have stayed home and watched it on TV" were the almost universal forms of dissatisfaction. While those at the scene were envying the viewers of the pseudo-event back home, the television viewers were, of course, being told again and again by the network commentators how great was the excitement of being "actually present."

Yet, as the Chicago sociologists noted, for many of those actually present one of the greatest thrills of the day was the opportunity to be on television. Just as everybody likes to see his name in the newspapers, so nearly everybody likes to think that he can be seen (or still better, with the aid of videotape, actually can see himself) on television. Similarly, reporters following candidates Kennedy and Nixon during their tours in the 1960 Presidential campaign noted how many of the "supporters" in the large crowds that were being televised had come out because they wanted to be seen on the television cameras.

Television reporting allows us all to be the actors we really are. One day I wandered onto the campus of the University of Chicago and happened to witness a tug of war between teams of students. It was amusing to see the women's team drench the men's team by pulling them into Botany Pond. Television cameras of the leading networks were there. The victory of the women's team seemed suspiciously easy to me. I was puzzled until told that this was not the original contest at all; the real tug of war had occurred a day or two before when telecasting conditions were not so good. This was a reenactment for television.

On December 2, 1960, during the school integration disorders in New Orleans, Mayor de Lesseps S. Morrison wrote a letter to newsmen proposing a three-day moratorium on news and television coverage of the controversy. He argued that the printed and televised reports were exaggerated and were damaging the city's reputation and its tourist trade. People were given an impression of prevailing violence, when, he said, only one tenth of 1 percent of the population had been involved in the demonstration. But he also pointed out that the mere presence of telecasting facilities was breeding disorder. "In many cases," he observed, "these people go to the area to get themselves on television and hurry home for the afternoon and evening telecasts to see the show." At least two television reporters had gone about the crowd interviewing demonstrators with inflammatory questions like "Why are you opposed to intermarriage?" Mayor Morrison said he himself had witnessed a television cameraman "setting up a scene," and then, having persuaded a group of students to respond like a "cheering section," had them yell and demonstrate on cue. The conscientious reporters indignantly rejected the mayor's proposed moratorium on news. They said that Freedom of the Press was at stake. That was once an institution preserved in the interest of the community. Now it is often a euphemism for the prerogative of reporters to produce their synthetic commodity.

In many subtle ways, the rise of pseudo-events has mixed up our roles as actors and as audience—or, the philosophers would say, as "object" and as "subject." Now we can oscillate between the two roles. "The movies are the only business," Will Rogers once remarked, "where you can go out front and applaud yourself." Nowadays one need not be a professional actor to have this satisfaction. We can appear in the mob scene and then go home and see ourselves on the television screen. No wonder we become confused about what is spontaneous, about what is really going on out there!

New forms of pseudo-events, especially in the world of politics, thus offer a new kind of bewilderment to both politician and newsman. The politician (like FDR in our example, or any holder of a press conference) himself in a sense composes the story; the journalist (like the wire service reporter we have quoted, or any newsman who incites an inflammatory statement) himself generates the event. The citizen can hardly be expected to assess the reality when the participants themselves are so often unsure who is doing the deed and who is making the report of it. Who is the history, and who is the historian?

An admirable example of this new intertwinement of subject and object, of the history and the historian, of the actor and the reporter, is the so-called news leak. By now the leak has become an important and well-established institution in American politics. It is, in fact, one of the main vehicles for communicating important information from officials to the public.

A clue to the new unreality of the citizen's world is the perverse new meaning now given to the word "leak." To leak, according to the dictionary, is to "let a fluid substance out or in accidentally: as, the ship leaks." But nowadays a news leak is one of the most elaborately planned ways of emitting information. It is, of course, a way in which a government official, with some clearly defined purpose, makes an announcement, asks a question, or puts a suggestion. A leak, even more than a direct announcement, is apt to have some definite devious purpose behind it. It might more accurately be called a "sub rosa announcement," an "indirect statement," or "cloaked news."

The news leak is a pseudo-event par excellence. But with the elaboration of news-gathering facilities in Washington—of regular, planned press conferences, of prepared statements for future release, and of countless other practices—the news protocol has hardened. Both government officials and reporters have felt the need for more flexible and more ambiguous modes of communication between them. The origins of the Presidential press conference itself can be traced to a kind of news leak when President Theodore Roosevelt allowed Lincoln Steffens to interview him as he was being shaved. Other Presidents gave favored correspondents an interview from time to time or dropped hints to friendly journalists. Similarly, the present institution of the news leak began in the irregular practice of a government official's helping a particular correspondent by confidentially giving him information not yet generally released. But today the leak is almost as well organized and as rigidly ruled by protocol as a formal press conference. Being fuller of ambiguity, with a welcome atmosphere of confidence and intrigue, it is more appealing to all concerned. The institutionalized leak puts a greater burden of contrivance and pretense on both government officials and reporters.

In Washington these days, and elsewhere on a smaller scale, the custom has grown up among important members of the government of arranging to dine with select representatives of the news corps. Such dinners are usually preceded by drinks, and beforehand there is a certain amount of restrained conviviality. Everyone knows the rules. The occasion is private, and any information given out afterward must be communicated according to rule and in the technically proper vocabulary. After dinner the undersecretary, the general, or the admiral allows himself to be questioned. He may recount "facts" behind past news, state plans, or declare policy. The reporters have confidence, if not in the ingenuousness of the official, at least in their colleagues' respect of the protocol. Everybody understands the degree of attribution permissible for every statement made: what, if anything, can be directly quoted, what is "background," what is "deep background," what must be ascribed to "a spokesman," to "an informed source," to speculation, to rumor, or to remote possibility.

Such occasions and the reports flowing from them are loaded with ambiguity. The reporter himself often is not clear whether he is being told a simple fact, a newly settled policy, an administrative hope, or whether perhaps untruths are being deliberately diffused to allay public fears that the true facts are really true. The government official himself, who is sometimes no more than a spokesman, may not be clear. The reporter's task is to find a way of weaving these threads of unreality into a fabric that the reader will not recognize as entirely unreal. Some people have criticized the institutionalized leak as a form of domestic counterintelligence inappropriate in a republic. It has become more and more important and is the source of many of the most influential reports of current politics.

One example will be enough. On March 26, 1955, the *New York Times* carried a three-column headline on the front page: "U.S. Expects Chinese Reds to Attack Isles in April; Weighs All-Out Defense." Three days later a contradictory headline in the same place read: "Eisenhower Sees No War Now Over Chinese Isles." Under each of these headlines appeared a lengthy story. Neither story named any person as a source of the ostensible facts. The then-undisclosed story (months later recorded by Douglass Cater) was this. In the first instance, Admiral Robert B. Carney, Chief of Naval Operations, had an off-the-record "background" dinner for a few reporters. There the admiral gave reporters what they and their readers took to be facts. Since the story was "not for attribution," reporters were not free to mention some very relevant facts—such as that this was the opinion only of Admiral Carney, that this was the same Admiral Carney who had long been saying that war in Asia was inevitable, and that many in Washington, even in the Joint Chiefs of Staff, did not agree with him. Under the ground rules the first story could appear in the papers only by being given an impersonal authority, an atmosphere of official unanimity which it did not merit. The second, and contradictory, statement was in fact made not by the President himself, but by the President's press secretary, James Hagerty, who, having been alarmed by what he saw in the papers, quickly called a second "background" meeting to deny the stories that had sprouted from the first. What, if anything, did it all mean? Was there any real news here at all—except that there was disagreement between Admiral Carney and James Hagerty? Yet this was the fact newsmen were not free to print.

Pseudo-events spawn other pseudo-events in geometric progression. This is partly because every kind of pseudo-event (being planned) tends to become ritualized, with a protocol and a rigidity all its own. As each type of pseudo-event acquires this rigidity, pressures arise to produce other, derivative, forms of pseudo-event which are more fluid, more tantalizing, and more interestingly ambiguous. Thus, as the press conference, itself a pseudo-event, became formalized, there grew up the institutionalized leak. As the leak becomes formalized, still other devices will appear. Of course the shrewd politician or the enterprising newsman knows this and knows how to take advantage of it. Seldom for outright deception, more often simply to make more "news," to provide more "information," or to "improve communication."

For example, a background off-the-record press conference, if it is actually a mere trial balloon or a diplomatic device (as it sometimes was for Secretary of State John Foster Dulles), becomes the basis of official "denials" and "disavowals," of speculation and interpretation by columnists and commentators, and of special interviews on and off television with Senators, Representatives, and other public officials. Any statement or nonstatement by anyone in the public eye can become the basis of counterstatements or refusals to comment by others. All these compound the ambiguity of the occasion which first brought them into being.

Nowadays the test of a Washington reporter is seldom his skill at precise dramatic reporting, but more often his adeptness at dark intimation. If he wishes to keep his news channels open, he must accumulate a vocabulary and develop a style to conceal his sources and obscure the relation of a supposed event or statement to the underlying facts of life, at the same time seeming to offer hard facts. Much of his stock in trade is his own and other people's speculation about the reality of what he reports. He lives in a penumbra between fact and fantasy. He helps create that very obscurity without which the supposed illumination of his reports would be unnecessary. A deft administrator these days must have similar skills. He must master "the technique of denying the truth without actually lying."

These pseudo-events which flood our consciousness must be distinguished from propaganda. The two do have some characteristics in common. But our peculiar problems come from the fact that pseudo-events are in some respects the opposite of the propaganda which rules totalitarian countries. Propaganda—as prescribed, say, by Hitler in *Mein Kampf*—is information intentionally biased. Its effect depends primarily on its emotional appeal. While a pseudo-event is an ambiguous truth, propaganda is an appealing falsehood. Pseudo-events thrive on our honest desire to be informed, to have "all the facts," and even to have more facts than there really are. But propaganda feeds on our willingness to be inflamed. Pseudo-events appeal to our duty to be educated, propaganda appeals to our desire to be aroused. While propaganda substitutes opinion for facts, pseudo-events are synthetic facts which move people indirectly, by providing the "factual" basis on which they are supposed to make up their minds. Propaganda moves them directly by explicitly making judgments for them.

In a totalitarian society, where people are flooded by purposeful lies, the real facts are of course misrepresented, but the representation itself is not ambiguous. The propaganda lie is asserted as if it were true. Its object is to lead people to believe that the truth is simpler, more intelligible, than it really is. "Now the purpose of propaganda," Hitler explained, "is not continually to produce interesting changes for a few blasé little masters, but to convince; that means, to convince the masses. The masses, however, with their inertia, always need a certain time before they are ready even to notice a thing, and they will lend their memories only to the thousandfold repetition of the most simple ideas." But in our society, pseudo-events make simple facts seem more subtle, more ambiguous, and more speculative than they really are. Propaganda oversimplifies experience, pseudo-events overcomplicate it.

At first it may seem strange that the rise of pseudo-events has coincided with the growth of the professional ethic which obliges newsmen to omit editorializing and personal judgments from their news accounts. But now it is in the making of pseudo-events that newsmen find ample scope for their individuality and creative imagination.

In a democratic society like ours—and more especially in a highly literate, wealthy, competitive, and technologically advanced society—the people can be flooded by pseudo-events. For us, freedom of speech and of the press and of broadcasting includes freedom to create pseudo-events. Competing politicians, competing newsmen, and competing news media contest in this creation. They vie with one another in offering attractive, "informative" accounts and images of the world. They are free to speculate on the facts, to bring new facts into being, to demand answers to their own contrived questions. Our "free marketplace of ideas" is a place where people are confronted by competing pseudo-events and are allowed to judge among them. When we speak of "informing" the people, this is what we really mean.

Until recently we have been justified in believing Abraham Lincoln's familiar maxim: "You may fool all the people some of the time; you can even fool some of the people all the time; but you can't fool all of the people all the time." This has been the foundation belief of American democracy. Lincoln's appealing slogan rests on two elementary assumptions. First, that there is a clear and visible distinction between sham and reality, between the lies a demagogue would have us believe and the truths which are there all the time. Second, that the people tend to prefer reality to sham, that if offered a choice between a simple truth and a contrived image, they will prefer the truth.

Neither of these any longer fits the facts. Not because people are less intelligent or more dishonest. Rather because great unforeseen changes—the forward strides of American civilization—have blurred the edges of reality. The pseudo-events which flood our consciousness are neither true nor false in the old familiar senses. The very same advances which have made them possible have also made the images—however planned, contrived, or distorted—more vivid, more attractive, more impressive, and more persuasive than reality itself.

We cannot say that we are being fooled. It is not entirely inaccurate to say that we are being "informed." This world of ambiguity is created by those who believe they are instructing us, by our best public servants, and with our own collaboration. Our problem is the harder to solve because it is created by people working honestly and industriously at respectable jobs. It is not created by demagogues or crooks, by conspiracy or evil purpose. The efficient mass production of pseudo-events—in all kinds of packages, in words, on film, on the television screen, and in a thousand other forms—is the work of the whole machinery of our society. It is the daily product of men of goodwill. The media must be fed! The people must be informed! Most pleas for "more information" are therefore misguided. So long as we define information as a knowledge of pseudo-events, "more information" will simply multiply the symptoms without curing the disease.

The American citizen thus lives in a world where fantasy is more real than reality, where the image has more dignity than its original. We hardly dare face our bewilderment, because our ambiguous experience is so pleasantly iridescent, and the solace of belief in contrived reality is so thoroughly real. We have become eager accessories to the great hoaxes of the age. These are the hoaxes we play on ourselves.

Pseudo-events from their very nature tend to be more interesting and more attractive than spontaneous events. Therefore in American public life today pseudo-events tend to drive all other kinds of events out of our consciousness, or at least to overshadow them. Earnest, well-informed citizens seldom notice that their experience of spontaneous events is buried by pseudo-events. Yet nowadays, the more industriously they work at "informing" themselves the more this tends to be true.

In his now-classic work, *Public Opinion,* Walter Lippmann in 1922 began by distinguishing between "the world outside and the pictures in our heads." He defined a "stereotype" as an oversimplified pattern that helps us find meaning in the world. As examples he gave the crude "stereotypes we carry about in our heads," of large and varied classes of people like "Germans," "South Europeans," "Negroes," "Harvard men," "agitators," etc. The stereotype, Lippmann explained, satisfies our needs and helps us defend our prejudices by seeming to give definiteness and consistency to our turbulent and disorderly daily experience. In one sense, of course, stereotypes—the excessively simple, but easily grasped images of racial, national, or religious groups—are only another example of pseudo-events. But, generally speaking, they are closer to propaganda. For they simplify rather than complicate. Stereotypes narrow and limit experience in an emotionally satisfying way; but pseudo-events embroider and dramatize experience in an interesting way. This itself makes pseudo-events far more seductive; intellectually they are more defensible, more intricate, and more intriguing. To discover how the stereotype is made—to unmask the sources of propaganda—is to make the stereotype less believable. Information about the staging of a pseudo-event simply adds to its fascination.

Lippmann's description of stereotypes was helpful in its day. But he wrote before pseudo-events had come in full flood. Photographic journalism was then still in its infancy. Wide World Photos had just been organized by the *New York Times* in 1919. The first wirephoto to attract wide attention was in 1924, when the American Telephone and Telegraph Company sent to the *New York Times* pictures of the Republican Convention in Cleveland which nominated Calvin Coolidge. Associated Press Picture Service was established in 1928. *Life,* the first wide-circulating weekly picture news magazine, appeared in 1936; within a year it had a circulation of 1 million, and within two years, 2 million. *Look* followed in 1937. The newsreel, originated in France by Pathé, had been introduced to the United States only in 1910. When Lippmann wrote his book in 1922, radio was not yet reporting news to the consumer; television was of course unknown.

Recent improvements in vividness and speed, the enlargement and multiplying of news-reporting media, and the public's increasing news hunger now make Lippmann's brilliant analysis of the stereotype the legacy of a simpler age. For stereotypes made experience handy to grasp. But pseudo-events would make experience newly and satisfyingly elusive. In 1911 Will Irwin, writing in *Collier's,* described the new era's growing public demand for news as "a crying primal want of the mind, like hunger of the body." The mania for news was a symptom of expectations enlarged far beyond the capacity of the natural world to satisfy. It required a synthetic product. It stirred an irrational and undiscriminating hunger for fancier, more varied items. Stereotypes there had been and always would be; but they only dulled the palate for information. They were an opiate. Pseudo-events whetted the appetite; they aroused news hunger in the very act of satisfying it.

In the age of pseudo-events it is less the artificial simplification than the artificial complication of experience that confuses us. Whenever in the public mind a pseudo-event competes for attention with a spontaneous event in the same field, the pseudo-event will tend to dominate. What happens on television will overshadow what happens off television. Of course I am concerned here not with our private worlds but with our world of public affairs.

Here are some characteristics of pseudo-events which make them overshadow spontaneous events:

1. Pseudo-events are more dramatic. A television debate between candidates can be planned to be more suspenseful (for example, by reserving questions which are then popped suddenly) than a casual encounter or consecutive formal speeches planned by each candidate separately.

2. Pseudo-events, being planned for dissemination, are easier to disseminate and to make vivid. Participants are selected for their newsworthy and dramatic interest.

3. Pseudo-events can be repeated at will, and thus their impression can be reinforced.

4. Pseudo-events cost money to create; hence somebody has an interest in disseminating, magnifying, advertising, and extolling them as events worth watching or worth believing. They are therefore advertised in advance, and rerun in order to get money's worth.

5. Pseudo-events, being planned for intelligibility, are more intelligible and hence more reassuring. Even if we cannot discuss intelligently the qualifications of the candidates or the complicated issues, we can at least judge the effectiveness of a television performance. How comforting to have some political matter we can grasp!

6. Pseudo-events are more sociable, more conversable, and more convenient to witness. Their occurrence is planned for our convenience. The Sunday newspaper appears when we have a lazy morning for it. Television programs appear when we are ready with our glass of beer. In the office the next morning, any star performer's regular late-night show at the usual hour will overshadow in conversation a casual event that suddenly came up and had to find its way into the news.

7. Knowledge of pseudo-events—of what has been reported, or what has been staged, and how—becomes the test of being "informed." News magazines provide us regularly with quiz questions concerning not what has happened but concerning "names in the news"—what has been reported in the news magazines. Pseudo-events begin to provide that "common discourse" which some of my friends have hoped to find in the Great Books.

8. Finally, pseudo-events spawn other pseudo-events in geometric progression. They dominate our consciousness simply because there are more of them, and ever more.

By this new Gresham's Law of American public life, counterfeit happenings tend to drive spontaneous happenings out of circulation. The rise in the power and prestige of the Presidency is due not only to the broadening powers of the office and the need for quick decisions, but also to the rise of centralized news gathering and broadcasting, and the increase of the Washington press corps. The

President has an ever more ready, more frequent, and more centralized access to the world of pseudo-events. A similar explanation helps account for the rising prominence in recent years of the Congressional investigating committees. In many cases these committees have virtually no legislative impulse, and sometimes no intelligible legislative assignment. But they do have an almost unprecedented power, possessed now by no one else in the Federal government except the President, to make news. Newsmen support the committees because the committees feed the newsmen and they live together in happy symbiosis. The battle for power among Washington agencies becomes a contest to dominate the citizen's information of the government. This can most easily be done by fabricating pseudo-events.

A perfect example of how pseudo-events can dominate is the popularity of the quiz show format. Its original appeal came less from the fact that such shows were tests of intelligence (or of dissimulation) than from the fact that the situations were elaborately contrived—with isolation booths, armed bank guards, and all the rest—and they purported to inform the public.

The application of the quiz show format to the first so-called Great Debates between Presidential candidates, in the election of 1960, is only another example. These four campaign programs, pompously and self-righteously advertised by the broadcasting networks, were remarkably successful in reducing great national issues to trivial dimensions. With appropriate vulgarity, they might have been called the $400,000 Question (Prize: a $100,000-a-year job for four years). They were a clinical example of the pseudo-event, of how it is made, why it appeals, and of its consequences for democracy in America.

In origin the Great Debates were confusedly collaborative between politicians and news makers. Public interest centered around the pseudo-event itself: the lighting, makeup, ground rules, whether notes would be allowed, etc. Far more interest was shown in the performance than in what was said. The pseudo-events spawned in turn by the Great Debates were numberless. People who had seen the shows read about them the more avidly, and listened eagerly for interpretations by news commentators. Representatives of both parties made "statements" on the probable effects of the debates. Numerous interviews and discussion programs were broadcast exploring their meaning. Opinion polls kept us informed on the

nuances of our own and other people's reactions. Topics of speculation multiplied. Even the question whether there should be a fifth
debate became for a while a lively "issue."

The drama of the situation was mostly specious, or at least had an
extremely ambiguous relevance to the main (but forgotten) issue:
which participant was better qualified for the Presidency. Of course,
a man's ability, while standing under klieg lights, without notes, to
answer in two and a half minutes a question kept secret until that
moment, had only the most dubious relevance—if any at all—to his
real qualifications to make deliberate Presidential decisions on long-
standing public questions after being instructed by a corps of advisers. The great Presidents in our history, with the possible exception
of FDR, would have done miserably; but our most notorious demagogues would have shone. A number of exciting pseudo-events were
created—for example, the Quemoy-Matsu issue, concerning occupation of islands in the Taiwan Straits. But that, too, was a good example
of a pseudo-event. It was created to be reported, it concerned a
then-quiescent problem, and it put into the most factitious and trivial
terms the great and real issue of our relation to Communist China.

The television medium shapes this new kind of political quiz-
show spectacular in many crucial ways. Theodore H. White proved
this with copious detail in his *The Making of the President: 1960*
(1961). All the circumstances of this particular competition for votes
were far more novel than the old word "debate" and the compari-
sons with the Lincoln-Douglas Debates suggested. Kennedy's great
strength in the critical first debate, according to White, was that he
was in fact not "debating" at all, but was seizing the opportunity to
address the whole nation; while Nixon stuck close to the issues raised
by his opponent, rebutting them one by one. Nixon, moreover, suffered a handicap that was serious only on television. He has a light,
naturally transparent skin. On an ordinary camera that takes pictures
by optical projection, this skin photographs well. But a television
camera projects electronically, by an "image-orthicon tube" which
has an x-ray effect. This camera penetrates Nixon's transparent skin
and brings out (even just after a shave) the tiniest hair growing in the
follicles beneath the surface. For the decisive first program Nixon
wore a makeup called Lazy Shave which was ineffective under these
conditions. He therefore looked haggard and heavy-bearded by contrast to Kennedy, who looked pert and clean-cut.

This greatest opportunity in American history to educate the
voters by debating the large issues of the campaign failed. The main

reason, as White points out, was the compulsions of the medium. "The nature of both TV and radio is that they abhor silence and 'dead time.' All TV and radio discussion programs are compelled to snap question and answer back and forth as if the contestants were adversaries in an intellectual tennis match. Although every experienced newspaperman and inquirer knows that the most thoughtful and responsive answers to any difficult question come after long pause, and that the longer the pause the more illuminating the thought that follows it, nonetheless the electronic media cannot bear to suffer a pause of more than five seconds; a pause of thirty seconds of dead time on air seems interminable. Thus, snapping their two-and-a-half-minute answers back and forth, both candidates could only react for the cameras and the people, they could not think." Whenever either candidate found himself touching a thought too large for two-minute exploration, he quickly retreated. Finally the television-watching voter was left to judge, not on issues explored by thoughtful men, but on the relative capacity of the two candidates to perform under television stress.

Pseudo-events thus lead to emphasis on pseudo-qualifications. Again the self-fulfilling prophecy. If we test Presidential candidates by their talents on TV quiz performances, we will, of course, choose Presidents for precisely these qualifications. In a democracy, reality tends to conform to the pseudo-event. Nature imitates art.

We are frustrated by our very efforts publicly to unmask the pseudo-event. Whenever we describe the lighting, the makeup, the studio setting, the rehearsals, etc., we simply arouse more interest. One newsman's interpretation makes us more eager to hear another's. One commentator's speculation that the debates may have little significance makes us curious to hear whether another commentator disagrees.

Pseudo-events do, of course, increase our illusion of grasp on the world, what some have called the American illusion of omnipotence. Perhaps, we come to think, the world's problems can really be settled by "statements," by "Summit" meetings, by a competition of "prestige," by overshadowing images.

Once we have tasted the charm of pseudo-events, we are tempted to believe they are the only important events. Our progress poisons the sources of our experience. And the poison tastes so sweet that it spoils our appetite for plain fact. Our seeming ability to satisfy our exaggerated expectations makes us forget that they are exaggerated.

CHAPTER 22

From Hero to Celebrity

IN THE LAST HALF century we have misled ourselves, not only about how much novelty the world contains, but about men themselves, and how much greatness can be found among them. One of the oldest of man's visions was the flash of divinity in the great man. He seemed to appear for reasons men could not understand, and the secret of his greatness was God's secret. His generation thanked God for him as for the rain, for the Grand Canyon or the Matterhorn, or for being saved from wreck at sea.

Since the Graphic Revolution, however, much of our thinking about human greatness has changed. Two centuries ago when a great man appeared, people looked for God's purpose in him; today we look for his press agent. Shakespeare, in the familiar lines, divided great men into three classes: those born great, those who achieved greatness, and those who had greatness thrust upon them. It never occurred to him to mention those who hired public relations experts and press secretaries to make themselves look great, or, as Edward L. Bernays has said, "to make large pedestals for small statues." Now it is hard even to remember the time when the "Hall of Fame" was only a metaphor, whose inhabitants were selected by the inscrutable processes of history instead of by an ad hoc committee appointed to select the best-known names from the media.

This chapter is much abridged from my book, *The Image: A Guide to Pseudo-Events in America.* Chapters 21 (page 254) and 23 (page 297) are also adapted from that book. See the Source Note to Chapter 21.

The root of our problem, the social source of these exaggerated expectations, is in our novel power to make men famous. Of course, there never was a time when "fame" was precisely the same thing as "greatness." But, until very recently, famous men and great men were pretty nearly the same group. "Fame," wrote Milton, "is the spur the clear spirit doth raise. . . . Fame is no plant that grows on mortal soil." A man's name was not apt to become a household word unless he exemplified greatness in some way or other. He might be a Napoleon, great in power, a J. P. Morgan, great in wealth, a Saint Francis, great in virtue, or a Bluebeard, great in evil. To become known to a whole people a man usually had to be something of a hero: as the dictionary tells us, a man "admired for his courage, nobility, or exploits." The war hero was the prototype, because the battle tested character and offered a stage for daring deeds.

Before the Graphic Revolution, the slow, the "natural," way of becoming well known was the usual way. Of course, there were a few men like the Pharaohs and Augustus and the Shah Jahan, who built monuments in their own day to advertise themselves to posterity. But a monument to command the admiration of a whole people was not quickly built. Thus great men, like famous men, came into a nation's consciousness only slowly. The processes by which their fame was made were as mysterious as those by which God ruled the generations. The past became the natural habitat of great men. The universal lament of aging men in all epochs, then, is that greatness has become obsolete.

So it has been commonly believed, in the words of Genesis, that "there were giants in the earth in those days"—in the days before the Flood. Each successive age has believed that heroes—great men—dwelt mostly before its own time. Thomas Carlyle, in his classic *Heroes, Hero-Worship, and the Heroic in History* (1841), lamented that Napoleon was "our last great man!" This traditional belief in the decline of greatness has expressed the simple social fact that greatness has been equated with fame, and fame could not be made overnight.

Within the last century, and especially since about 1900, we seem to have discovered the processes by which fame is manufactured. Now, at least in the United States, a man's name can become a household word overnight. The Graphic Revolution suddenly gave us, among other things, the means of fabricating well-knownness. Discovering that we (the television watchers, the moviegoers, radio listeners, and newspaper and magazine readers) and our servants (the television, movie and radio producers, newspaper and magazine editors, and ad writers) can so quickly and so effectively give a man "fame," we have willingly been misled into believing that fame—well-knownness—is still a hallmark of greatness. Our power to fill our minds with more and more "big names" has increased our demand for Big Names and our willingness to confuse the Big Name with the Big Man. Again mistaking our powers for our necessities, we have filled our world with artificial fame.

Of course we do not like to believe that our admiration is focused on a largely synthetic product. Having manufactured our celebrities, having willy-nilly made them our cynosures—the guiding stars of our interest—we are tempted to believe that they are not synthetic at all, that they are somehow still God-made heroes who now abound with a marvelous modern prodigality.

The folklore of Great Men survives. We still believe, with Sydney Smith, who wrote in the early nineteenth century, that "Great men hallow a whole people, and lift up all who live in their time." We still agree with Carlyle that "No sadder proof can be given by a man of his own littleness than disbelief in great men. . . . Does not every true man feel that he is himself made higher by doing reverence to that which is really above him?" We still are told from the pulpit, from Congress, from television screen and editorial page, that the lives of great men "all remind us, we can make our lives sublime." Even in our twentieth-century age of doubt, when morality itself has been in ill repute, we have desperately held on to our belief in human greatness. For human models are more vivid and more persuasive than explicit moral commands. Cynics and intellectuals, too, are quicker to doubt moral theories than to question the greatness of their heroes. Agnostics and atheists may deny God, but they are slow to deny divinity to the great agnostics and atheists.

While the folklore of hero-worship, the zestful search for heroes, and the pleasure in reverence for heroes remain, the heroes themselves dissolve. The household names, the famous men and women who populate our consciousness, are with few exceptions not heroes at all, but an artificial new product of the Graphic Revolution in response to our exaggerated expectations. The more readily we make them and the more numerous they become, the less are they worthy of our admiration. We can fabricate fame, we can at will, though usually at considerable expense, make a man or woman well known; but we cannot make them great. We can make a celebrity, but we can never make a hero. In a now-almost-forgotten sense, all heroes are self-made.

Celebrity-worship and hero-worship should not be confused. Yet we confuse them every day, and by doing so we come dangerously close to depriving ourselves of all real models. We lose sight of the men and women who do not simply seem great because they are famous but who are famous because they are great. We come closer and closer to degrading all fame into notoriety.

In the last half century the old heroic human mold has been broken. A new mold has been made. We have actually demanded that this mold be made, so that marketable human models—modern "heroes"—could be mass-produced, to satisfy the market, and without any hitches. The qualities which now commonly make a man or woman into a "nationally advertised brand" are in fact a new category of human emptiness. Our new mold is shaped not of the stuff of our familiar morality, nor even of the old familiar reality. How has this happened?

Our age has produced a new kind of eminence. This is as characteristic of our culture and our century as was the divinity of Greek gods in the sixth century B.C. or the chivalry of knights and courtly lovers in the Middle Ages. It has not yet driven heroism, sainthood, or martyrdom completely out of our consciousness. But with every decade it overshadows them more. All older forms of greatness now survive only in the shadow of this new form. This new kind of eminence is "celebrity."

The word "celebrity" (from the Latin *celebritas* for "multitude" or "fame" and *celeber* meaning "frequented," "populous," or "famous") originally meant not a person but a condition—as the *Oxford English Dictionary* says, "the condition of being much talked about; famousness, notoriety." In this sense its use dates from at least the early seventeenth century. Even then it had a weaker meaning than "fame" or "renown." Matthew Arnold, for example, remarked in the nineteenth century that while the philosopher Spinoza's followers had "celebrity," Spinoza himself had "fame."

For us, however, "celebrity" means primarily a person—"a person of celebrity." This usage of the word significantly dates from the early years of the Graphic Revolution, the first example being about 1850. Emerson spoke of "the celebrities of wealth and fashion"

(1848). Now American dictionaries define a celebrity as "a famous or well-publicized person."

The celebrity in the distinctive modern sense could not have existed in any earlier age, or in America before the Graphic Revolution. *The celebrity is a person who is known for his well-knownness.*

His qualities—or rather his lack of qualities—illustrate our peculiar problems. He is neither good nor bad, great nor petty. He is the human pseudo-event. He has been fabricated on purpose to satisfy our exaggerated expectations of human greatness. He is morally neutral. The product of no conspiracy, of no group promoting vice or emptiness, he is made by honest, industrious men of high professional ethics doing their job, "informing" and educating us. He is made by all of us who willingly read about him, who like to see him on television, who buy recordings of his voice, and talk about him to our friends. His relation to morality and even to reality is highly ambiguous. He is like the woman *in* an Elinor Glyn novel who describes another by saying, "She is like a figure in an Elinor Glyn novel."

It is hardly surprising then that magazine and newspaper readers no longer find the lives of their heroes instructive. Popular biographies can offer very little in the way of solid information. For the subjects are themselves mere figments of the media. If their lives are empty of drama or achievement, it is only as we might have expected, for they are not known for drama or achievement. They are celebrities. Their chief claim to fame is their fame itself. They are notorious for their notoriety. If this is puzzling or fantastic, if it is mere tautology, it is no more puzzling or fantastic or tautologous than much of the rest of our experience. Our experience tends more and more to become tautology—needless repetition of the same in different words and images. Perhaps what ails us is not so much a vice as a "nothingness." The vacuum of our experience is actually made emptier by our anxious straining with mechanical devices to fill it artificially. What is remarkable is not only that we manage to fill experience with so much emptiness, but that we manage to give the emptiness such appealing variety.

We can hear ourselves straining. "He's the greatest!" Our descriptions of celebrities overflow with superlatives. In popular magazine biographies we learn that a Dr. Brinkley is the "best-advertised doctor in the United States," an actor is the "luckiest man in the movies today," a Ringling is "not only the greatest, but the first real showman in the Ringling family," a general is "one of the best mathematicians this side of Einstein," a columnist has "one of the strangest of courtships," a statesman has "the world's most exciting job," a sportsman is "the loudest and by all odds the most abusive," a newsman is "one of the most consistently resentful men in the country," a certain ex-King's mistress is "one of the unhappiest women that ever lived." But, despite the "supercolossal" on the label, the contents are very ordinary.

The hero was distinguished by his achievement, the celebrity by his image or trademark. The hero created himself; the celebrity is created by the media. The hero was a big man; the celebrity is a big name.

Formerly, a public man needed a *private* secretary for a barrier between himself and the public. Nowadays he has a *press* secretary, to keep him properly in the public eye. Before the Graphic Revolution, it was a mark of solid distinction in a man or a family to keep out of the news. A lady of aristocratic pretensions was supposed to get her name in the papers only three times: when she was born, when she married, and when she died. Now the families who are Society are by definition those always appearing in the papers. The man of truly heroic stature was once supposed to be marked by his scorn for publicity. He quietly relied on the power of his character or his achievement.

In the South, where the media developed more slowly than elsewhere in the country, where cities appeared later, and where life was dominated by rural ways, the celebrity grew more slowly. The old-fashioned hero was romanticized. In this as in many other ways, the Confederate General Robert E. Lee was one of the last surviving American models of the older type. Among his many admirable qualities, Southern compatriots admired none more than his retirement from public view. He had the reputation for never having given a newspaper interview. He steadfastly refused to write his memoirs. "I should be trading on the blood of my men," he said.

As other pseudo-events in our day tend to overshadow spontaneous events, so celebrities (who are human pseudo-events) tend to overshadow heroes. They are more up-to-date, more nationally advertised, and more apt to have press agents. And there are far more of them. Celebrities die quickly, but they are still more quickly replaced. Every year we experience a larger number than the year before.

Just as real events tend to be cast in the mold of pseudo-events, so in our society heroes survive by acquiring the qualities of celebrities. The best-publicized seems the most authentic experience. If someone does a heroic deed in our time, all the machinery of public information—press, pulpit, radio, and television—soon transform him into a celebrity. If they cannot succeed in this, the would-be hero disappears from public view.

A dramatic, a tragic, example is the career of Charles A. Lindbergh. He performed single-handed one of the heroic deeds of this century. His deed was heroic in the best epic mold. But he became degraded into a celebrity. He then ceased to symbolize the virtues to which his heroic deed gave him a proper claim. He became filled with emptiness; then he disappeared from view. How did this happen?

On May 21, 1927, Charles A. Lindbergh made the first nonstop solo flight from Roosevelt Field, New York, to Le Bourget Air Field, Paris, in a monoplane, *The Spirit of St. Louis.* This was plainly a heroic deed in the classic sense; it was a deed of valor—alone against the elements. In a dreary, unheroic decade Lindbergh's flight was a lightning flash of individual courage. Except for the fact of his flight, Lindbergh was a commonplace person. Twenty-five years old at the time, he had been born in Detroit and raised in Minnesota. He was not a great inventor or a leader of men. Like many another young man in those years, he had a fanatical love of flying. The air was his element. There he showed superlative skill and extraordinary courage—even to foolhardiness.

He was an authentic hero. Yet this was not enough. Or perhaps it was too much. For he was destined to be made into a mere celebrity; and he was to be the American celebrity par excellence. His rise and fall as a hero, his tribulations, his transformation, and his rise and decline as a celebrity are beautifully told in Kenneth S. Davis' biography.

Lindbergh himself had not failed to predict that his exploit would put him in the news. Before leaving New York he had sold to the *New York Times* the exclusive story of his flight. A supposedly naive and diffident boy, on his arrival in Paris he was confronted by a crowd of newspaper reporters at a press conference in Ambassador Myron T. Herrick's residence. But he would not give out any statement until he had clearance from the *Times* representative. He had actually subscribed to a newspaper clipping service, the clippings to be sent to his mother, who was then teaching school in Minnesota. With uncanny foresight, however, he had limited his subscriptions to clippings to the value of $50. (This did not prevent the company, doubtless seeking publicity as well as money, from suing him for not paying them for clippings beyond the specified amount.) Otherwise he might have had to spend the rest of his life earning the money to pay for clippings about himself.

Lindbergh's newspaper success was unprecedented. The morning after his flight the *New York Times,* a model of journalistic sobriety, gave him the whole of its first five pages, except for a few ads on page five. Other papers gave as much or more. Radio commentators talked of him by the hour. But there was not much hard news available. The flight was a relatively simple operation, lasting only thirty-three and a half hours. Lindbergh had told reporters in Paris just about all there was to tell. During his twenty-five years he had led a relatively uneventful life. He had few quirks of face, of figure, or of personality; little was known about his character. Some young women called him "tall and handsome," but his physical averageness was striking. He was the boy next door. To tell about this young man on the day after his flight, the nation's newspapers used 25,000 tons of newsprint more than usual. In many places sales were two to five times normal, and might have been higher if the presses could have turned out more papers.

When Lindbergh returned to New York on June 13, 1927, the *New York Times* gave its first sixteen pages the next morning almost exclusively to news about him. At the testimonial dinner in Lindbergh's honor at the Hotel Commodore (reputed to be the largest for an individual "in modern history") Charles Evans Hughes, former Secretary of State, and about to become Chief Justice of the United States, delivered an extravagant eulogy. With unwitting precision he characterized the American hero-turned-celebrity: "We measure heroes as we do ships, by their displacement. Colonel Lindbergh has displaced everything."

Lindbergh was by now the biggest human pseudo-event of modern times. His achievement, actually because it had been accomplished so neatly and with such spectacular simplicity, offered little spontaneous news. The biggest news about Lindbergh was that he was such big news. Pseudo-events multiplied in more than the usual geometric progression, for Lindbergh's well-knownness was so sudden and so overwhelming. It was easy to make stories about what a big celebrity he was, how this youth, unknown a few days before, was now a household word, how he was received by Presidents and Kings. There was little else one could say about him. Lindbergh's singularly impressive heroic deed was soon far overshadowed by his even more impressive publicity. If well-knownness made a celebrity, here was the greatest. Of course it was remarkable to fly the ocean by oneself, but far more remarkable thus to dominate the news. His stature as hero was nothing compared with his stature as celebrity. All the more because it had happened, literally, overnight.

A large proportion of the news soon consisted of stories of how Lindbergh reacted to the "news" and to the publicity about himself. People focused their admiration on how admirably Lindbergh responded to publicity, how gracefully he accepted his role of celebrity. "Quickie" biographies appeared. These were little more than digests of newspaper accounts of the publicity jags during Lindbergh's ceremonial visits to the capitals of Europe and the United States. This was the celebrity afterlife of the heroic Lindbergh. This was the tautology of celebrity.

During the next few years Lindbergh stayed in the public eye and remained a celebrity primarily because of two events. One was his marriage on May 27, 1929, to the cultivated and pretty Anne Morrow, daughter of Dwight Morrow, a Morgan partner, then ambassador to Mexico. Now it was "the Lone Eagle and His Mate." As a newlywed he was more than ever attractive raw material for news. The maudlin pseudo-events of romance were added to all the rest. His newsworthiness was revived. There was no escape. Undaunted newsmen, thwarted in efforts to secure interviews and lacking solid facts, now made columns of copy from Lindbergh's efforts to keep out of the news! Some newspapermen, lacking other material for speculation, cynically suggested that Lindbergh's attempts to dodge reporters were motivated by a devious plan to increase his newsinterest. When Lindbergh said he would cooperate with sober, respectable papers but not with others, those left out pyramided his rebuffs into more news than his own statements would have made.

The second event which kept Lindbergh alive as a celebrity was the kidnaping of his infant son. This occurred at his new country house at Hopewell, New Jersey, on the night of March 1, 1932. For almost five years "Lindbergh" had been an empty receptacle into which news makers had poured their concoctions—saccharine, maudlin, legendary, slanderous, adulatory, or only fantastic. Now, when all other news-making possibilities seemed exhausted, his family was physically consumed. There was a good story in it. Here was "blood sacrifice," as Kenneth S. Davis calls it, to the gods of publicity. Since the case was never fully solved, despite the execution of the supposed kidnaper, no one can know whether the child would have been returned unharmed if the press and the public had behaved differently. But the press, with the collaboration of the bungling police, had unwittingly destroyed real clues. Then they garnered and publicized innumerable false clues and did nothing solid to help. They exploited Lindbergh's personal catastrophe with more than their usual energy.

In its way the kidnaping of Lindbergh's son was as spectacular as Lindbergh's transatlantic flight. In neither case was there much hard news, but this did not prevent the filling of newspaper columns. City editors now gave orders for no space limit on the kidnaping story. "I can't think of any story that would compare with it," observed the general news manager of the United Press, "unless America should enter a war." Hearst's INS photo service assigned its whole staff. They chartered two ambulances which, with sirens screaming, shuttled between Hopewell and New York City carrying photographic equipment out to the Lindbergh estate, and on the way back to the city served as mobile darkrooms in which pictures were developed and printed for delivery on arrival. For on-the-spot reporting at Hopewell, INS had an additional five men with three automobiles. United Press had six men and three cars; the Associated Press had four men, two women, and four cars. By midnight of March 1 the New York *Daily News* had nine reporters at Hopewell, and three more arrived the next day; the New York *American* had a dozen (including William Randolph Hearst, Jr., the paper's president); the New York *Herald Tribune,* four; the New York *World-Telegram,* the *New York Times,* and the Philadelphia *Ledger,* each about ten. This was only a beginning.

The next day the press agreed to Lindbergh's request to stay off the Hopewell grounds in order to encourage the kidnaper to return the child. The torrent of news did not stop. Within twenty-four hours INS sent over its wires 50,000 words (enough to fill a small volume) about the crime, 30,000 words the following day, and for some time thereafter 10,000 or more words a day. The Associated Press and

United Press served their subscribers just as well. Many papers gave the story the whole of the front page, plus inside carryovers, for a full week. There were virtually no new facts available. Still the news poured forth—pseudo-events by the score—clues, rumors, local color features, and what the trade calls "think" pieces.

Soon there was almost nothing more to be done journalistically with the crime itself. There was little more to be reported, invented, or conjectured. Interest then focused on a number of subdramas created largely by newsmen themselves. These were stories about how the original event was being reported, about the mix-up among the different police that had entered the case, and about who would or should be Lindbergh's spokesman to the press world and his go-between with the kidnaper. Much news interest still centered on what a big story all the news added up to, and on how Mr. and Mrs. Lindbergh reacted to the publicity.

At this point the prohibition era crime celebrities came into the picture. "Salvy" Spitale and Irving Bitz, New York speakeasy owners, briefly held the spotlight. They had been suggested by Morris Rosner, who, because he had underworld connections, soon became a kind of personal secretary to the Lindberghs. Spitale and Bitz earned headlines for their effort to make contact with the kidnapers, then suspected to be either the notorious Purple Gang of Detroit or Al Capone's mob in Chicago. The two go-betweens became big names, until Spitale bowed out, appropriately enough, at a press conference. There he explained: "If it was someone I knew, I'll be God-damned if I wouldn't name him. I been in touch all around, and I come to the conclusion that this one was pulled by an independent." Al Capone himself, more a celebrity than ever, since he was about to begin a Federal prison term for income-tax evasion, increased his own newsworthiness by trying to lend a hand. In an interview with the "serious" columnist Arthur Brisbane of the Hearst papers, Capone offered $10,000 for information leading to the recovery of the child unharmed and to the capture of the kidnapers. It was even hinted that to free Capone might help recover the child.

The case itself produced a spate of new celebrities, whose significance no one quite understood but whose newsworthiness itself made them important. These included Colonel H. Norman Schwarzkopf, commander of the New Jersey State Police, Harry Wolf, chief of police in Hopewell, Betty Gow, the baby's nurse, Colonel Breckenridge, Lindbergh's personal counsel, Dr. J. F. ("Jafsie") Condon, a retired Bronx schoolteacher who was a volunteer go-between (he offered to add to the ransom money his own $1,000 life savings "so a loving mother may again have her child and Colonel Lindbergh may know that the American people are grateful for the honor bestowed on them by his pluck and daring"), John Hughes Curtis, a half-demented Norfolk, Virginia, boatbuilder who pretended to reach the kidnapers, Gaston B. Means (author of *The Strange Death of President Harding*), later convicted of swindling Mrs. Evalyn Walsh McLean out of $104,000 by posing as a negotiator with the kidnapers, Violet Sharpe, a waitress in the Morrow home, who married the Morrow butler and who had had a date with a young man not her husband on the night of the kidnaping (she committed suicide on threat of being questioned by the police), and countless others.

Only a few years later the spotlight was turned off Lindbergh as suddenly as it had been turned on him. The *New York Times Index*—a thick volume published yearly which lists all references to a given subject in the pages of the newspaper during the previous twelve months—records this fact with statistical precision. Each volume of the index for the years 1927 to 1940 contains several columns of fine print merely itemizing the different news stories which referred to Lindbergh. The 1941 volume shows over three columns of such listings. Then suddenly the news stream dries up, first to a mere trickle, then to nothing at all. The total listings for all seventeen years from 1942 through 1958 amount to less than two columns—only about half that found in the single year 1941. In 1951 and 1958 there was not even a single mention of Lindbergh. In 1957 when the movie *The Spirit of St. Louis*, starring James Stewart, was released, it did poorly at the box office. A poll of the preview audiences showed that few viewers under forty years of age knew about Lindbergh.

A *New Yorker* cartoon gave the gist of the matter. A father and his young son are leaving a movie house where they have just seen *The Spirit of St. Louis*. "If everyone thought what he did was so marvelous," the boy asks his father, "how come he never got famous?"

The hero thus died a celebrity's sudden death. In his fourteen years he had already long outlasted the celebrity's usual life span. An incidental explanation of this quick demise of Charles A. Lindbergh was his response to the pressure to be "all-around." Democratic faith was not satisfied that its hero be only a dauntless flier. He had to become a scientist, an outspoken citizen, and a leader of men. His celebrity status unfortunately had persuaded him to become a public spokesman. When Lindbergh gave in to these temptations, he offended. But his offenses (unlike those, for example, of Al Capone and his henchmen, who used to be applauded when they took their seats in a ball park) were not in themselves dramatic or newsworthy enough to create a new notoriety. His pronouncements were dull, petulant, and vicious. He acquired a reputation as a pro-Nazi and a crude racist; he accepted a decoration from Hitler. Very soon the celebrity was being uncelebrated. The Lindbergh Beacon atop a Chicago skyscraper was renamed the Palmolive Beacon, and high in the Colorado Rockies Lindbergh Peak was rechristened the noncommittal Lone Eagle Peak.

The people once felt themselves made by their heroes. "The idol," said James Russell Lowell, "is the measure of the worshiper." Celebrities are made by the people. The hero stood for outside standards. The celebrity is a tautology. We still try to make our celebrities stand in for the heroes we no longer have, or for those who have been pushed out of our view. We forget that celebrities are known primarily for their well-knownness. And we imitate them as if they were cast in the mold of greatness. Yet the celebrity is usually nothing greater than a more-publicized version of us. In imitating him, in trying to dress like him, talk like him, look like him, think like him, we are simply imitating ourselves. In the words of the Psalmist, "They that make them are like unto them; so is everyone that trusteth in them." By imitating a tautology, we ourselves become a tautology: standing for what we stand for, reaching to become more emphatically what we already are. When we praise our famous men we pretend to look out the window of history. We do not like to confess that we are looking into a mirror. We look for models, and we see our own image.

CHAPTER 23

From Traveler to Tourist

SOMETIME PAST the middle of the nineteenth century, as the Graphic Revolution was getting under way, the character of foreign travel—first by Europeans, and then by Americans—began to change. This change has reached a climax in our day. Formerly travel required long planning, large expense, and great investments of time. It involved risks to health or even to life. The traveler was active. Now he became passive. Instead of an athletic exercise, travel became a spectator sport.

This change can be described in a word. It was the decline of the traveler and the rise of the tourist. There is a wonderful, but neglected, precision in these words. The old English noun "travel" (in the sense of a journey) was originally the same word as "travail" (meaning "trouble," "work," or "torment"). And the word "travail," in turn, seems to have been derived, through the French, from a popular Latin or Common Romanic word *tripalium,* which meant a three-staked instrument of torture. To journey—to "travail," or (later) to travel—then was to do something laborious or troublesome. The traveler was an active man at work.

In the early nineteenth century a new word came into the English language which gave a clue to the changed character of world travel, especially from the American point of view. This was the word

---

This chapter is much abridged from my book, *The Image: A Guide to Pseudo-Events in America.* Chapters 21 (page 254) and 22 (page 284) are also adapted from that book. See the Source Note to Chapter 21.

"tourist"—at first hyphenated as "tour-ist." Our American dictionary now defines a tourist as "a person who makes a pleasure trip" or "a person who makes a tour, especially for pleasure." Significantly, too, the word "tour" in "tourist" was derived by back-formation from the Latin *tornus*, which in turn came from the Greek word for a tool describing a circle. The traveler, then, was working at something; the tourist was a pleasure-seeker. The traveler was active; he went strenuously in search of people, of adventure, of experience. The tourist is passive; he expects interesting things to happen to him. He goes "sight-seeing" (a word, by the way, which came in about the same time, with its first use recorded in 1847). He expects everything to be done to him and for him.

Thus foreign travel ceased to be an activity—an experience, an undertaking—and instead became a commodity. The rise of the tourist was possible, and then inevitable, when attractive items of travel were wrapped up and sold in packages (the "package tour"). By buying a tour you could oblige somebody else to make pleasant and interesting things happen to you. You could buy wholesale (by the month or week, or by the country) or retail (by the day or by the individual foreign capital).

The familiar circumstances which had brought this about are worth recalling. First and most obvious was the easing of transportation. In the latter part of the nineteenth century railroads and ocean steamers began to make travel actually pleasurable. Discomfort and risks were suddenly reduced. For the first time in history, long-distance transportation was industrially mass-produced. It could be sold to lots of people, and it could be sold cheap. For a satisfactory return on investment, it *had* to be sold in large quantities. The capital invested in any of the old vehicles—a stagecoach or the passenger quarters in a sailing ship—was minute compared with that in a railroad (even a single sleeping car) or a luxury liner. This enormous capital investment required that equipment be kept in constant use and that passengers be found by the thousands. Now great numbers of people would be induced to travel for pleasure. Vast ocean steamers could not be filled with diplomats, with people traveling on business, or with aristocratic Henry Adamses who were intent on deepening their education. The consuming public had to be enlarged to include the vacationing middle class, or at least the upper middle class. Foreign travel became democratized.

The obvious next step was the "personally conducted tour." Well-planned group excursions could entice even the more timid stay-at-homes. Of course guided tours of one sort or another had been very old: the Crusades had sometimes taken on this character. We can recall, in Chaucer's *Canterbury Tales*, in the late fourteenth century, the knowledgeable, generous host of the Tabard Inn, who offered

> And for to make yow the moore mury,
> I wol myselven goodly with yow ryde,
> Right at myn owene cost, and be youre gyde. . . .

But later guides seldom offered their services free. The guided tour itself actually became a commodity. Adventure would be sold in packages and guaranteed to be consumed without risk. In England, with its short distances, its rising middle classes, and its early-developed railroads, came the first organized tours. According to legend the very first of them was arranged in 1838 to take the people of Wadebridge by special train to the nearby town of Bodmin. There they witnessed the hanging of two murderers. Since the Bodmin gallows were in clear sight of the uncovered station, excursionists had their fun without even leaving the open railway carriages.

The real pioneer in the making and marketing of conducted tours was of course Thomas Cook (1808–1892). He began in the early 1840s by arranging special-rate railroad excursions within England. His first planned tour took nearly 600 people the eleven miles from Leicester to Loughborough for a temperance convention—at a reduced round-trip third-class fare of one shilling a head. Soon Cook was sending hundreds to Scotland (1846) and Ireland (1848), and for thousands was arranging tours of the Crystal Palace Exposition in London in 1851. In 1856 he advertised his first "grand circular tour of the Continent," visiting Antwerp, Brussels, the Field of Waterloo, Cologne, the Rhine and its borders, Mainz, Frankfort, Heidelberg, Baden-Baden, Strasbourg, Paris, Le Havre, and back to London. Then, with the help of his enterprising son, he offered Swiss tours, American tours, and finally, in 1869, the first middle-class Conducted Crusade to the Holy Land. He quickly developed all kinds of conveniences: courteous and knowledgeable guides, hotel coupons, room reservations, and protection and advice against disease and thievery.

Sophisticated Englishmen objected. They said that Cook was depriving travelers of initiative and adventure and cluttering the continental landscape with the Philistine middle classes. "Going by railroad," complained John Ruskin, "I do not consider as travelling at all; it is merely being 'sent' to a place, and very little different from becoming a parcel." An article in *Blackwood's Magazine* in February 1865, by a British consul in Italy, attacked this "new and growing evil . . . of conducting some forty or fifty persons, irrespective of age or sex, from London to Naples and back for a fixed sum." "The Cities of Italy," he lamented, were now "deluged with droves of these creatures, for they never separate, and you see them forty in number pouring along a street with their director—now in front, now at the rear, circling round them like a sheepdog—and really the process is as like herding as may be. I have already met three flocks, and anything so uncouth I never saw before, the men, mostly elderly, dreary, sad-looking; the women, somewhat younger, travel-tossed, but intensely lively, wide-awake, and facetious."

Cook defended his tours, which he called "agencies for the advancement of Human Progress." The attacks on them, he said, were sheer snobbery. The critics belonged in some earlier century. How foolish to "think that places of rare interest should be excluded from the gaze of the common people, and be kept only for the interest of the 'select' of society. But it is too late in this day of progress to talk such exclusive nonsense, God's earth with all its fullness and beauty, is for the people; and railways and steamboats are the result of the common light of science, and are for the people also. . . . The best of men, and the noblest minds, rejoice to see the people follow in their foretrod routes of pleasure."

Still, in the United States, where everything was suddenly available to everybody, it was far more profitable to deal in immigrants than in tourists. Mobile, immigrant-filled, primitive America saw less glamour in travel, whether at home or abroad. Among Americans, even longer than among Englishmen, foreign travel remained close to its aristocratic origins. Until early in the twentieth century, Americans who wanted a planned European excursion still relied on Thomas Cook & Son. President Grant used Cook's. And one of the best testimonials for Cook's new foolproof, carefree travel commodity came from Mark Twain:

> Cook has made travel easy and a pleasure. He will sell you a ticket to any place on the globe, or all the places, and give you all the time you need and much more besides. It provides hotels for you everywhere, if you so desire; and you cannot be overcharged, for the coupons show just how

much you must pay. Cook's servants at the great stations will attend to your baggage, get you a cab, tell you how much to pay cabmen and porters, procure guides for you, and horses, donkeys, camels, bicycles, or anything else you want, and make life a comfort and satisfaction to you. Cook is your banker everywhere, and his establishment your shelter when you get caught out in the rain. His clerks will answer all the questions you ask and do it courteously. I recommend your Grace to travel on Cook's tickets; and I do this without embarrassment, for I get no commission. I do not know Cook.

The principal competitor in the United States was to be the American Express Company. It grew out of the famous Wells, Fargo and other agencies which by the midnineteenth century were forwarding goods and money across the vast American spaces. In the nineteenth century these agencies profited from the immigrant influx, by going into the business of arranging remittances from successful, recently arrived Americans to their needy families back in Europe. In 1891 the first American Express Travelers Cheque was copyrighted, and in the years since it has done much to ease the traveler's cares. In 1895 American Express opened its first European office. At first all it offered traveling Americans was a mail-forwarding service, help in securing railroad tickets and hotel reservations, and help in finding lost baggage. President James C. Fargo, in charge until 1914, insisted there was no money in the tourist business. American Express, he said, should deal exclusively in freight and express. But the consolidation of the different express services as part of the war effort in World War I inevitably changed the business. Even before the end of the war American Express had begun to develop an extensive travel service, and after the war its travel department grew spectacularly.

American Express sent the first postwar escorted tour to Europe in October 1919. Soon afterward the first Mediterranean cruise went out in the Cunard liner *Caronia,* under joint control of American Express and Cook's. In 1922 American Express dispatched the first all-water round-the-world pleasure cruise in the *Laconia.* Afterward a similar cruise was arranged every year. The great backwash had begun. Americans were returning to the Old World in the great tourist invasions of Europe which have fluctuated with our domestic fortunes, but which in recent years have been greater than ever before.

By the middle of the twentieth century, foreign travel had become big business. It was a prominent feature of the American standard of living, an important element in our cultural and financial relations with the rest of the world.

Foreign travel now had, of course, become a commodity. Like any other mass-produced commodity, it could be bought in bargain packages and on the installment plan. It was considered a strange and noteworthy event, a peculiar quirk, when Charles Sumner in early nineteenth-century Boston borrowed money from a couple of old friends who had faith in his future, to finance his tour of Europe. Nowadays more and more travelers take the trip before they can pay for it. "Go Now, Pay Later." Your travel agent will arrange it for you.

When travel is no longer made to order but is an assembly-line, store-boughten commodity, we have less to say about what goes into it. And we know less and less about what we are buying.

A well-packaged tour must include insurance against risks. In this sense the dangers of travel have become obsolete; we buy safety and peace of mind right in the package. Somebody else covers all the risks. The suspense-thriller movie *The High and the Mighty* depicted the troubled flight of a luxury airliner between San Francisco and Honolulu. The assorted vacationers aboard were flying to the mid-Pacific for a week or two of relaxation. As the engines failed, the nerves of the passengers began to fray. Finally, in order to keep the plane in the air, the captain ordered the baggage jettisoned. I saw this movie some years ago in a suburban theater outside Chicago. Beside me sat a mother and her young son. He seemed relatively unperturbed at the mortal risks of the passengers, but when the plane's purser began tossing into the ocean the elegant vacation paraphernalia—fancy suitcases, hatboxes, portable typewriters, golf clubs, tennis rackets—the boy became agitated. "What will they do?" the boy exclaimed. "Don't worry," comforted the mother. "It's all insured."

When the traveler's risks are insurable, he has become a tourist.

Not so many years ago there was no simpler or more intelligible notion than that of going on a journey. Travel—movement through space—provided the universal metaphor for change. When men died, they went on a journey to that land from which no traveler returns. Or, in our cliché, when a man dies, he "passes away." Philosophers observed that we took refuge from the mystery of time in the concreteness of space. Bergson, for example, once argued that measurements of time had to be expressed in metaphors of space. Time was "long" or "short"; another epoch was "remote" or "near."

One of the subtle confusions—perhaps one of the secret terrors—of modern life is that we have lost this refuge. No longer do we move through space as we once did. Moving only through time, measuring our distances in homogeneous ticks of the clock, we are at a loss to explain to ourselves what we are doing, where, or even whether, we are going.

As there comes to be less and less difference between the time it takes to reach one place rather than another, time itself dissolves as a measure of space. It is said that the new supersonic transports will take passengers across our continent in less than two hours, from Europe to America in two hours and a half. We are moving toward Instant Travel. It is then, I suppose, thoroughly appropriate in this age of tautological experience that we should eventually find ourselves measuring time against itself.

We call ours the Space Age, but to us space has less meaning than ever before. Perhaps we should call ours the Spaceless Age. Having lost the art of travel on this earth, having homogenized earthly space, we take refuge in the homogeneity (or in the hope for variety) of outer space. To travel through outer space can hardly give us less landscape experience than we find on our new American super highways. We are already encapsulated, already overcome by the tourist problems of fueling, eating, sleeping, and sight-seeing. Will we enlarge our experience on the moon? Only until tourist attractions have been prepared for us there.

Even our travel literature has shown a noticeable change. Formerly these books brought us information about the conduct of life in foreign courts, about burial rites and marriage customs, about the strange ways of beggars, craftsmen, tavern hosts, and shopkeepers. Most travel literature long remained in the pattern of Marco Polo. Since the midnineteenth century, however, and especially in the twentieth century, travel books have increasingly become a record not of new information but of personal "reactions." From "Life in Italy," they become "the American in Italy." People go to see what they already know is there. The only thing to record, the only possible source of surprise, is their own reaction.

The foreign country, like the celebrity, is the confirmation of a pseudo-event. Much of our interest comes from our curiosity about whether our impression resembles the images found in the newspapers, in movies, and on television. Is the Trevi Fountain in Rome really like its portrayal in the movie *Three Coins in the Fountain?* Is Hong Kong really like *Love Is a Many-Splendored Thing?* Is it full of Suzie Wongs? We go not to test the image by the reality, but to test reality by the image.

Of course travel adventure is still possible. Nowadays, however, it is seldom the by-product of people going places. We must scheme and contrive and plan long in advance (at great expense) to be assured that when we arrive there we will encounter something other than the antiseptic, pleasant, relaxing, comfortable experience of the hundreds of thousands of other tourists. We must fabricate risks and dangers, or hunt them out. To make a glorious adventure out of travel, we can relive ancient adventures. We may rebuild the ships of Columbus and retrace his course. Even Mysterious Tibet—one of the few remaining places which physically challenge the traveler—has had its mystery abolished.

Nowadays it costs more and takes greater ingenuity, imagination and enterprise to fabricate travel risks than it once required to avoid them. We go to great expense to enjoy the rigors of the Antarctic. Almost as much effort goes into designing the adventure as into surviving it. For this the tourist millions have not the time or the money. Only the select few can afford the life-risking perils. Travel adventure today thus inevitably acquires a factitious, make-believe, unreal quality. Both for the few adventuring travelers who still exist and for the larger number of travelers-turned-tourists, voyaging becomes a pseudo-event.

Here again, the pseudo-event overshadows the spontaneous. And for the usual reasons. Planned tours, attractions, fairs, expositions "especially for tourists," and all their prefabricated adventures can be persuasively advertised in advance. They can be made convenient, comfortable, risk-free, trouble-free, as spontaneous travel never was and never is. We go more and more where we expect to go. We get money-back guarantees that we will see what we expect to see. Anyway, we go more and more, not to see at all, but only to take pictures. Like the rest of our experience, travel becomes a tautology. The more strenuously and self-consciously we work at enlarging our experience, the more pervasive the tautology becomes. Whether we seek models of greatness or experience elsewhere on the earth, we look into a mirror instead of out a window, and we see only ourselves.

EPILOGUE:

The Republic of Technology and the Limits of Prophecy

The best qualification of a prophet
is to have a good memory.

THE MARQUESS OF HALIFAX (c. 1690)

AN ATHLETE OF STEEL and iron with not a superfluous ounce of metal on it!" exclaimed William Dean Howells before the centerpiece of Philadelphia's International Exhibition celebrating our nation's hundredth birthday. He was inspired to these words by the gigantic 700-ton Corliss steam engine that towered over Machinery Hall. When President Ulysses S. Grant and Emperor Dom Pedro of Brazil pulled the levers on May 10, 1876, a festive crowd cheered as the engine set in motion a wonderful assortment of machines—pumping water, combing wool, spinning cotton, tearing hemp, printing newspapers, lithographing wallpaper, sewing cloth, folding envelopes, sawing logs, shaping wood, making shoes—8,000 machines spread over thirteen acres.

Others, especially visitors from abroad, were troubled by this American spectacle. "I cannot say that I am in the slightest degree impressed," announced the English biologist Thomas Henry Huxley, "by your bigness or your material resources, as such. Size is not grandeur, and territory does not make a nation. The great issue, about which hangs a true sublimity, and the terror of overhanging fate, is what are you going to do with all these things?"

The monster steam engine was an appropriate symbol of the

305

American future, but not for the reason most of the spectators suspected. The special hopes, opportunities, and achievements, the fears and frustrations that marked the nation's grandeur in its second century were to be even newer than visitors to the 1876 exposition could imagine. These came not from bigness but from a new kind of community. New ties would bind Americans together, would bind Americans to the larger world, and would bind the world to America. I call this community the Republic of Technology.

This community of our future was not created by any assemblage of statesmen. It had no written charter and was not to be governed by any council of ambassadors. Yet it would reach into the daily lives of citizens on all continents. In creating and shaping this community the United States would play the leading role.

The word "Republic" I use as Thomas Paine, propagandist of the American Revolution, used it in his *Rights of Man,* to mean "not any *particular form* of government" but "the matter or object for which government ought to be instituted . . . *res publica,* the public affairs, or the public good; or, literally translated, the public thing." This word describes the shared public concerns of people in different nations, the community of those who share these concerns.

In early modern times, learned men of the Western world considered themselves members of a Republic of Letters, the worldwide community of men who read one another's books and exchanged opinions. Long after Gutenberg's printing press had begun the process of multiplying books and encouraging the growth of literature in the languages of the marketplace, the community remained a limited one. Thomas Jefferson, for example, considered himself a citizen of that worldwide community because of what he shared with literary and scientific colleagues in France, Italy, Germany, Spain, the Netherlands, and elsewhere. When Jefferson offered the young nation his personal library, which was to be the foundation of the Library of Congress, it contained so many foreign-language books, including numerous "atheistical" works of Voltaire and other French revolutionaries, that some members of Congress opposed its purchase. The Republic of Letters was a select community of those who shared *knowledge.*

Our Republic of Technology is not only more democratic but also more in the American mode. Anyone can be a citizen. Largely a creation of American civilization in the last century, this republic offers a foretaste of American life in our next century. It is open to all, because it is a community of shared *experience*.

Behind this new kind of sharing was the Industrial Revolution, which developed in eighteenth-century England and spread over Europe and the New World. Power-driven technology and mass production meant large-scale imports and exports, with goods carried everywhere in steam-driven freighters, in railroad freight cars, on transcontinental railway systems. The ways of daily life, the carriages in which people rode, the foods they ate, the pots and pans in their kitchens, the clothes they wore, the nails that held together their houses, the glass for their windows—all these and thousands of other daily trivia became more alike than they had ever been before. The weapons and tools, the rifles and pistols, the screws and wrenches, the shovels and picks, all had a new uniformity, thanks to the so-called American System of Manufacturing. In fact, this system of interchangeable parts was sometimes called the Uniformity System. The telegraph and the power press and the mass-circulating newspaper brought the same information and the same images to people thousands of miles apart. Human experience for millions became more instantaneously similar than had ever been imagined possible.

This Republic of Technology has transformed our lives, adding a new relation to our fellow Americans, a new relation to the whole world. Two forces of the new era have proved especially potent.

The New Obsolescence. For most of human history, the norm had been continuity. Change was news. Daily lives were governed by tradition. The most valued works were the oldest. The great works of architecture were monuments that survived from the past. Furnishings became increasingly valuable by becoming antique. Great literature never went out of date. "Literature," Ezra Pound observed, "is news that *stays* news." The new enriched the old and was enriched by the old. Shakespeare enriched Chaucer. Shaw enriched Shakespeare. It was a world of the enduring and the durable.

The laws of our Republic of Technology are quite different. The importance of a scientific work, as the German mathematician David Hilbert once observed, can be measured by the number of previous publications it makes superfluous to read. Scientists and technologists dare not wait for their current journals. They must study "preprints" of articles, use the telephone and refer to the latest information "on line" to be sure that their work has not been made obsolete by what somebody else did this morning.

The Republic of Technology is a world of obsolescence. Our characteristic printed matter is not a deathless literary work but today's newspaper that makes yesterday's newspaper worthless. Old objects simply become secondhand, to be ripe for the next season's recycling. An H. H. Richardson or a Louis Sullivan building is torn down to make way for a parking garage. Progress seems to have become quick, sudden, and wholesale.

Most novel of all is our changed attitude toward change. Now nations seem to be distinguished not by their heritage or their stock of monuments, by what was once called their civilization, but by their pace of change. Rapidly "developing" nations are those that are most speedily obsolescing their inheritance. While it once took centuries or even millennia to build a civilization, now the transformation of an "underdeveloped" nation can be accomplished in mere decades.

The New Convergence. The supreme law of the Republic of Technology is convergence, the tendency for everything to become more like everything else. Now the distinction is seldom made between nations that are "civilized" and those that are "uncivilized." Today, when we rely on the distinction between the "developed" and the "underdeveloped" or "developing" countries, we see the experience of all peoples converging. A common standard enables us to measure the rate of convergence statistically, by GNP, by per capita annual income, and by rates of growth. Everyone, we assume, can participate in the newly shared experience.

A person need not be learned, or even literate, to share the fruits of technology. While the enjoyment of printed matter is restricted to those who can read, anybody can get the message from a television screen. The converging forces of everyday experience are both sublingual and translingual. People who never could have been persuaded to read *Faust* or *The Tale of Genji* will eagerly drive a Mercedes or a Nissan.

The great literature that brought some people together also built barriers. Literary classics may nourish chauvinism and create ideologies. Wars tend to reinforce national stereotypes and to harden ideologies. When the United States entered World War I, its schools ceased teaching German. Beethoven and Wagner were taboo. Still, at that very moment, American military research teams were studying German technology. Even while Indira Gandhi restricted American newsmen and American publications, she desperately tried to make the Indian technology more like the American. Technology dilutes and dissolves ideology.

In each successive world war, the competition in technology has become more fierce—and more effective. The splitting of the atom and the exploring of space bear witness to the stimulus of competition, the convergence of efforts, the involuntary collaboration of wartime enemies. Technology is the natural foe of nationalism.

With crushing inevitability, the advance of technology brings nations together and narrows the differences between the experiences of their people. The destruction by modern warfare tends to reduce the balance of advantage between victor and vanquished. The spectacular industrial progress of Japan and West Germany after World War II was actually facilitated by the wholesale destruction of their industrial plants.

Each forward step in modern technology tends to reduce the difference between the older categories of experience. Take, for example, the once elementary distinction between transportation and communication: between moving the person and moving the message. While communication once was an inferior substitute for transportation (you had to read the account because you couldn't get there), it is now often the preferred alternative. The television screen, by traditional categories a mode of communication, brings together people who still remain in their separate living rooms. With the increasing congestion of city traffic, with the parking problem, and with the lengthened holding patterns over airports, our television screen becomes a superior way of getting there. So, when it comes to public events, now you are often more there when you are here than when you are there!

Broadcasting is perhaps the most potent everyday witness to the converging powers of technology. The most democratic of all forms of public communication, broadcasting converges people, drawing them into the same experience in ways never before possible.

The democratizing impact of television has been strikingly similar to the historic impact of printing. Even in this, television's first half-century, we have seen it reenact Thomas Carlyle's prophecy for the effects of movable type. We have already seen its power to disband armies, to cashier presidents, to create a world democratic in ways never before imagined, even in America. We cannot ignore the fact that the era when television became a universal engrossing

American experience, the first era when Americans everywhere could witness in living color the sit-ins, the civil rights marches, was also the era of a civil rights revolution, of the popularization of protests on an unprecedented scale, of a new era for minority power, of a newly potent public intervention in foreign policy, of a new, more publicized meaning to the constitutional rights of petition, of the removal of an American President. The Vietnam War was the first American war which was a television experience. Watergate was the first national political scandal which was a television experience. The college-student protests of the sixties were the first nonsporting college events to become television experiences.

The great levelers, broadcast messages and images, go without discrimination into the homes of rich and poor, white and black, young and old. It is a rare American household that does not have at least one television set. If you own a set, no admission fee is required to enter TV land and to have a front seat at its marvels. No questions are asked, no skill is needed. You need not even sit still or keep quiet. To enjoy what TV brings, the illiterate are just as well qualified as the educated—some would say even better qualified. Our Age of Broadcasting is a fitting climax, then, to the history of a nation whose birth certificate proclaimed that "all men are created equal" and which has aimed to bring everything to everybody.

We have reaped myriad benefits as citizens of the new Republic of Technology. Our American standard of living is a familiar name for these daily blessings. Our increased longevity, the decline of epidemics, the reduced hours of labor, the widening of political participation, our household conveniences, the reduction of the discomforts of winter and of summer, the growth of schools and colleges and universities, the flourishing of libraries and museums, the unprecedented opportunities to explore the world—all are by-products of the New Obsolescence and the New Convergence. They have become so familiar that they are undervalued. But some strange fruit is apt to grow in the fertile orchards of our technological progress. If we remain aware of the special risks in the community of our future, we will run less risk of losing these unprecedented benefits that we have come to take for granted.

Here are a few of the forces at work in the Republic of Technology that will shape our American lives in the next century:

Technology Invents Needs and Exports Problems. We will be misled if we think that technology will be directed primarily to satisfying "demands" or "needs" or to solving recognized "problems." There was no "demand" for the telephone, the automobile, radio or television. It is no accident that our nation, the most advanced in technology, is also the most advanced in advertising. Technology is a way of multiplying the unnecessary. And advertising is a way of persuading us that we didn't know what we needed. Working together, technology and advertising create progress by developing the need for the unnecessary. The Republic of Technology where we will be living is a feedback world. There wants will be created not by "human nature" or by century-old yearnings, but by technology itself.

Technology Creates Momentum and Is Irreversible. Nothing can be uninvented. This tragicomic fact will dominate our lives as citizens of the Republic of Technology. While any device can be made obsolete, no device can be forgotten, or erased from the arsenal of technology. While the currents of politics and of culture can be stopped, deflected, or even reversed, technology is irreversible. In recent years, Germany, Greece, and some other countries have gone from democracy to dictatorship and back to democracy. But we cannot go back and forth between the kerosene lamp and the electric light. Our inability to uninvent will prove ever more troublesome as our technology proliferates and refines more and more unimagined, seemingly irrelevant wants. Driven by "needs" for the unnecessary, we remain impotent to conjure the needs away. Our Aladdin's lamp of technology makes myriad new genii appear, but cannot make them disappear. The automobile—despite all we have learned of its diabolism—cannot be magicked away. The most we seem able to do is to make futile efforts to appease the automobile —by building parking temples on choice urban real estate and by deferring to the automobile with pedestrian overpasses and tunnels. We drive miles—and when we are at the airport we walk miles—all for the convenience of the airplane. Our national politics is shaped more and more by the imperious demands of television. Our negotiations with the Genie of Television all seem to end in our unconditional surrender. We live, and will live, in a world of increasingly involuntary commitments.

Technology Assimilates. The Republic of Technology, ruthlessly egalitarian, will accomplish what the prophets, political philosophers and revolutionaries could not. Already it assimilates times and places and peoples and things—a faithful color reproduction of the *Mona Lisa*, the voice and image of Franklin D. Roosevelt, of Winston

Churchill, or of Gandhi. You too can have a ringside seat at the World Series, at the Superbowl, at Wimbledon, or anywhere else. Without a constitutional amendment or a decision of the Supreme Court, technology forces us to equalize our experience. More than ever before, the daily experience of Americans will be created equal—or at least ever more similar.

Technology Insulates and Isolates. While technology seems to bring us together, it does so only by making new ways of separating us from one another. The "One World" of Americans in the future will be a world of millions of private compartments. The progression from the intimately jostling horse-drawn carriage to the railroad car to the encapsulated lone automobile rider and then to the seat-belted airplane passenger who cannot converse with his seatmate because they are both wearing earphones for the recorded music. The progression from the parent reading aloud to the children to the living theater with living audiences to the darkened motion-picture house to the home of private television sets, each twinkling in a different room for a different member of the family—these are the natural progressions of technology. The cellular car phone isolates us from the traffic, the Walkman carries our private world as we jog. The multiplying cable stations make even television an increasingly personalized experience. All of us are in danger of being suffocated by our own tastes. Moreover, these devices that enlarge our sight and vision in space seem somehow to imprison us in the present. The electronic technology that reaches out instantaneously over the continents does very little to help us cross the centuries.

Technology Uproots. In this Republic of Technology the experience of the present actually uproots us and separates us from our own special time and place. For technology aims to insulate and immunize us against the peculiar chances, perils, and opportunities of our natural climate, our raw landscape. The snowmobile makes a steep mountain slope or the tongue of a glacier just another highway. Our America has been blessed by a myriad variety of landscapes. But whether we are on the mountaintop, in the desert, on shipboard, in our automobile, or on an airplane, we are protected from the climate, the soil, the sand, the snow, the water. Our roots, such as they are, grow in an antiseptic hydroponic solution. Instead of enjoying the weather given us "by Nature and by Nature's God" in Jefferson's phrase, we worry about the humidifier or the air-conditioner.

Many of these currents of change carry us further along the grand and peculiarly American course of our history. More than any other modern people we have been free of the curse of ideology, free to combine the nations, free to rise above chauvinism, free to take our clues from the delightful, unexplored, uncongested world around us. We have, for the most part, avoided the brutal homogeneities of the concentration camp and the instant orthodoxies that are revisable at the death of a Mao. During our first two centuries, a raw continent made us flexible and responsive. Our New World remains more raw and more unexplored than we will admit.

The Republic of Technology offers us the opportunity to make our nation's third century American in some novel ways. We remain the world's laboratory. We like to try the new as do few other peoples in the world. Our experiment of binding together peoples from everywhere by opportunities rather than by ideologies will continue. The Republic of Technology offers fantastic new opportunities for opportunity.

A world where experience will be created equal tempts us in new ways and offers new dilemmas. These are the New World dilemmas of our next century. Will we be able to continue to enrich our lives with the ancient and durable treasures, to enjoy our inheritance from our nation's founders, to exploit the benefits of our countless "fertile verges," while the winds of obsolescence blow about us and while we taste the delights of ever-wider sharing? Will we be able to share the exploring spirit, reach for the unknown, enjoy multiplying our wants, live in a world whose rhetoric is advertising, whose standard of living has become its morality—yet avoid the delusions of utopia and live a life within satisfying limits? Can we be exhilarated by the momentum that carries us willy-nilly beyond our imaginings and yet have some sense of control over our own destiny?

ACKNOWLEDGMENTS

This book brings together my forty years' reflections on Hidden History. None of these selections is taken from my trilogy *The Americans* or from *The Discoverers*. For all of them, my wife, Ruth F. Boorstin, has been my editor, and she conceived this book. I would like also to thank the editors at the publishing houses and periodicals named below for their advice and assistance, Gina Heiserman of Bessie Books, and especially my fifty years' friend and publisher extraordinary Simon Michael Bessie who helped shape this book. The chapters from my earlier books have been revised.

PROLOGUE. "The Fertile Verge": Keynote lecture at the first meeting of the Council of Scholars of the Library of Congress, Washington, D.C., on November 19, 1980. Copyright © 1980 by Daniel J. Boorstin.

CHAPTER 1. "A Wrestler with the Angel": Never before published. Copyright © 1985 under the title, "The Quest for History: A Personal View" by Daniel J. Boorstin.

CHAPTER 2. "The Transforming of Paul Revere": First published by Book-of-the-Month Club in *Paul Revere and the World He Lived in* by Esther Forbes, Foreword © 1983 by Daniel J. Boorstin.

CHAPTER 3. "The Adamses: A Family in the Public Service": From *The Adams Chronicles: Four Generations of Greatness* by Jack Shepherd. Introduction Copyright © 1975 by Daniel J. Boorstin. By permission of Little, Brown and Company.

CHAPTER 5. "Timetables of History": From *The Timetables of History* by Bernard Grun, copyright © 1975, 1979 by Simon & Schuster; English language foreword copyright © 1975 by Daniel J. Boorstin. Reprinted by permission of Simon & Schuster, Inc.

CHAPTER 6. "The Therapy of Distance": From *The Exploring Spirit* by Daniel J. Boorstin. Copyright © 1975, 1976 by Daniel J. Boorstin. Reprinted by permission of Random House, Inc.

CHAPTERS 7 & 8. "Why a Theory Seems Needless" and "Revolution Without Dogma": Reprinted from *The Genius of American Politics* by Daniel J. Boorstin, by permission of The University of Chicago Press. Copyright © 1953 by the University of Chicago. All rights reserved.

CHAPTER 9. "The Equality of the Human Species": Reprinted from *The Lost World of Thomas Jefferson* by Daniel J. Boorstin, by permission of The University of Chicago Press. Copyright © 1948, 1981 by Daniel J. Boorstin. All rights reserved.

CHAPTER 10. "The Rhetoric of Democracy": First published in *Democracy and Its Discontents*, Random House, 1974. Copyright © 1974 by Daniel J. Boorstin.

CHAPTERS 11 & 12. "A Nationally Advertised President" and "An American Style in Historical Monuments": Adapted from *America and the Image of Europe* by Daniel J. Boorstin. Copyright © 1960 by Meridian Books, Inc. Reprinted by arrangement with NAL Penguin Inc., New York, NY.

CHAPTER 13. "The Perils of Unwritten Law": Copyright © 1969 by Daniel J. Boorstin. Reprinted from *The Decline of Radicalism* by Daniel J. Boorstin, by permission of Random House, Inc.

CHAPTER 14. "The Courage to Doubt": First appeared in *Free Inquiry*, Summer, 1983.

CHAPTERS 15, 17, 19, 20, & Epilogue. "Political Technology," "A Laboratory of the Arts," "Two Kinds of Revolution," "From the Land to the Machine," and "The Republic of Technology and the Limits of Prophecy": From *The Republic of*

Technology: Reflections on Our Future Community by Daniel J. Boorstin. Copyright © 1978 by Daniel J. Boorstin. Reprinted by permission of Harper & Row, Publishers, Inc.

CHAPTER 16. "From Charity to Philanthropy": Reprinted from a brochure for the Julius Rosenwald Centennial in 1962 by Daniel J. Boorstin, by permission of The University of Chicago Press. Copyright © 1963 by The University of Chicago. All rights reserved.

CHAPTER 18. "The Amateur Spirit and its Enemies": First appeared as an article in *U.S. News and World Report* entitled "Democracy's Secret Virtues." Dec. 30, 1985.

CHAPTERS 21, 22, & 23. "A Flood of Pseudo-Events," "From Hero to Celebrity," and "From Traveler to Tourist": Daniel J. Boorstin, "A Flood of Pseudo-Events," "From Hero to Celebrity," and "From Traveler to Tourist" from *The Image*. Copyright © 1961 Daniel J. Boorstin. Reprinted with the permission of Atheneum Publishers.

Index

ABOUT THE AUTHOR

Historian, public servant, and author, Daniel J. Boorstin, the Librarian of Congress Emeritus, directed the Library from 1975 to 1987. He had previously been Director of the National Museum of History and Technology, and Senior Historian of the Smithsonian Institution in Washington, D.C. Before that he was the Preston and Sterling Morton Distinguished Service Professor of History at the University of Chicago, where he taught for twenty-five years.

Born in Atlanta, Georgia, and raised in Tulsa, Oklahoma, Boorstin graduated with highest honors from Harvard College and received his doctorate from Yale University. As a Rhodes Scholar at Balliol College, Oxford, England, he won a coveted "double first" in two degrees in law and was admitted as a barrister-at-law of the Inner Temple, London. He is also a member of the Massachusetts Bar. He has been visiting professor at the University of Rome, the University of Geneva, the University of Kyoto in Japan, and the University of Puerto Rico. In Paris he was the first incumbent of a chair in American History at the Sorbonne, and at Cambridge University, England, he was Pitt Professor and Fellow of Trinity College. Boorstin has lectured widely in the United States and all over the world. He has received numerous honorary degrees and has been decorated by the governments of France, Belgium, Portugal, and Japan. He is married to the former Ruth Frankel, the editor of his works, and they have three sons.

Boorstin's many books include *The Americans: The Colonial Experience* (1958), which won the Bancroft Prize; *The Americans: The National Experience* (1965), which won the Parkman Prize; and *The*

Americans: The Democratic Experience (1973), which won the Pulitzer Prize for History and the Dexter Prize and was a Book of the Month Club Main Selection. Among his other books are *The Mysterious Science of the Law* (1941), *The Lost World of Thomas Jefferson* (1948), *The Genius of American Politics* (1953), *The Image* (1962), and *The Republic of Technology* (1978). For young people he has written the *Landmark History of the American People.* His textbook for high schools, *A History of the United States* (1980), written with Brooks M. Kelley, has been widely adopted. He is the editor of *An American Primer* (1966) and the thirty-volume series *The Chicago History of American Civilization,* among other works.

The Discoverers, Boorstin's history of man's search to know the world and himself, was published in 1983. A Book of the Month Club Main Selection, *The Discoverers* was on the *New York Times* bestseller list for half a year and won the Watson Davis Prize of the History of Science Society. This and his other books have been translated into many languages.